Bolivia

LATIN AMERICAN HISTORIES
JAMES R. SCOBIE, THOMAS E. SKIDMORE, EDITORS

James R. Scobie: *Argentina: A City and a Nation,* SECOND EDITION
Ralph Lee Woodward, Jr.: *Central America: A Nation Divided,*
SECOND EDITION
John V. Lombardi: *Venezuela: The Search for Order,*
The Dream of Progress
Brian Loveman: *Chile: The Legacy of Hispanic Capitalism,*
SECOND EDITION
Louis A. Perez, Jr.: *Cuba: Between Reform and Revolution*
Franklin W. Knight: *The Caribbean: The Genesis of a*
Fragmented Nationalism, SECOND EDITION
Herbert S. Klein: *Bolivia: The Evolution of a Multi-Ethnic Society,*
SECOND EDITION

Bolivia

THE EVOLUTION
OF A MULTI-ETHNIC SOCIETY

SECOND EDITION

HERBERT S. KLEIN

New York • Oxford
OXFORD UNIVERSITY PRESS
1992

Oxford University Press

Oxford University Press

Oxford   New York   Toronto
Delhi   Bombay   Calcutta   Madras   Karachi
Petaling Jaya   Singapore   Hong Kong   Tokyo
Nairobi   Dar es Salaam   Cape Town
Melbourne   Auckland

and associated companies in
Berlin   Ibadan

Copyright © 1992 by Oxford University Press, Inc.

Published by Oxford University Press, Inc.,
200 Madison Avenue, New York 10016

Library of Congress Cataloging-in-Publication Data
Klein, Herbert S.
Bolivia : the evolution of a multi-ethnic society / Herbert S.
Klein. —2nd ed.
p.   cm.   (Latin American histories)
Includes bibliographical references (p.   ) and index.
ISBN 0-19-505734-1.
ISBN 0-19-505733-X (pbk)
1. Bolivia—History.   I. Title.   II. Series.
F3321.K54   1991   984—dc20
91-28785

Printing 9 8 7 6 5 4 3 2 1

Printed in the United States of America
on acid-free paper

To Jacob Nathaniel Klein

Preface to the Second Edition

In bringing this survey up to date, I have tried as much as possible to determine the long-range trends which have influenced the evolution of recent Bolivian developments. Given that only ten years have passed since the publication of the first edition, it has not always been easy to understand and interpret the more profound underlying structural changes. The intense political struggles of the last decade have often masked these transformations. The rapid changes in the national economy have caught most analysts by surprise, while the long-term social developments have been less easy for both Bolivians and outsiders to interpret. In a general history of this kind, it is also inevitable, if regrettable, that the closer one comes to the contemporary period, the shorter time frame each chapter encompasses and the more difficult it is to distinguish the ephemeral events from the more profound structural changes that will most influence future developments. For this reason the revisions I have made to this new edition, primarily the substantial revision of Chapter 9, and the inclusion of a new final chapter, should be thought of as only a preliminary assessment. Less problematic has been the revision of the bibliography, which I hope now encompasses the extraordinary outburst of research on Bolivia of the past decade.

In undertaking these revisions I have continued to receive the support and criticism of the friends and scholars whom I mentioned in the first edition, as well as from Ricardo Godoy, Erwin Greishaber, and Eric Langer. I would also like to thank my former students Brooke Larson, Clara Lopez Beltran, and Manuel Contreras for sharing their ideas and research with me; as well as Maria Ligia Coelho Prado for her critical reading of the new materials.

New York H.S.K.
February 1991

Preface to the First Edition

The history of the peoples of Bolivia is one of the more complex and fascinating of historical evolutions. A society created by imperial conquests and native adaptations, it remains today a nation dominated by its peasantry, yet fully participating in the world economy. It is also the most Indian of the American republics: as late as the census of 1976 only a minority of the population were monolingual speakers of Spanish. The Amerindian languages of Quechua and Aymara predominate, and even such pre-Incan languages as Uru and Puquina are still spoken. Thus Bolivia is not simply a colonial replica of its last conqueror, the Spaniards, but a new and complex amalgam of cultures and ethnicities with important elements of non-Western and Western norms co-existing. In the Andean highlands and intra-mountain valleys, an extraordinarily harsh and beautiful climate, the Bolivians have created a new and vital multi-ethnic society.

For the mass of Bolivians, two thirds of whom are rural peasants, their culture is a blending of pre-Columbian and post-Conquest norms and institutions. Spanish systems of government were grafted on to pre-Spanish kinship organizations, ecologically disperse settlements were converted into nucleated villages, and local and state religions were syncretized into a new folk Catholicism highly mixed with the symbols and myths of Mediterranean popular religion. Traditional exchange systems co-exist with a highly developed market, and wheat is grown along with pre-Columbian staples such as potatoes and coca. In the Quechuan and Aymaran languages Spanish loan words form an important part of the vocabulary, while among the acculturated miners and the urban working classes pre-Columbian belief systems can be found mixed with modern Western norms.

But this description of Bolivia as a dual society does not mean to imply that Bolivia is simply a laboratory of peasants developing a new cultural idiom in a difficult environment. For Bolivia is, and has been since the sixteenth-century Spanish conquest, a capitalist Western class-organized society in which the Indians have been and remain an exploited class of workers. The government, which has extracted the surplus from the peasants and workers, has traditionally been a government run for and by the "white" Spanish-speaking and Western-oriented elite. While, phenotypically, the Bolivian "whites" look much like their Indian ancestors, their economic, social, and cultural position has placed them squarely in the classic mold of a western European society. Educated by Europeans to European norms, and even practicing a religion distinct from the folk Catholicism of the peasants, the "whites" have ruled the peasantry and exploited them with the belief that they formed a distinct race. But the elite, which was initially made up of European conquerors, has slowly miscegenated, as in all such multi-racial societies, and over the centuries there has emerged a new biological grouping of mixed background.

Thus Bolivia, like most multi-ethnic societies in the Americas, has come to define race as a social rather than a genetic or even phenotypic term. The upper classes, speaking Spanish, wearing Western dress, and consuming non-indigenous foods, are whites, or, as the peasants call them, *gente decente*. The urban lower classes, the lower middle class, and the rural freehold farmers, who wear European dress and are usually bilingual in Spanish and one of the Amerindian languages, are mestizos or, as they are called in Bolivia, *cholos*. The peasants are the Indians, no matter what their background, and they have served as the workers, miners, farmers, and soldiers of the society. They have been denied access to power except as they abandoned their traditional norms and languages and integrated into the national society as cholos or whites. Thus the more marginal, ambitious, or able of these peasants have constantly fed the white and cholo classes. Even among the traditional monolingual peasantry, there have been internal divisions between rich and poor and hereditary high-status individuals and commoners.

In its political evolution Bolivia has also been typical of such multiethnic societies in the history of the domination of one ethnic group and its fight to maintain its monopoly on power for exploitative purposes. In the nineteenth and twentieth centuries the whites attempted first to organize themselves into a cohesive group capable of denying power to the cholos and Indians and then to work out limited parliamentary republican regimes which were the exclusive preserve of the small elite of Spanish speakers. But like most such systems in the Americas, the impact of modern economic change following the 1880s forced the disintegration of these closed political worlds, so Bolivia went through the troubled times of expanding its political system to include the middle class and workers. But this process of partial inclusion and increasing democratization eventually broke down. At this point in its political evolution, Bolivia sharply diverged from the common American pattern when a massive popular worker and middleclass revolutionary movement swept aside the entire pre-existent political system in the National Revolution of 1952. The resulting social, economic, and political reforms, while they did not destroy the dual society or eliminate the one-sided acculturation of Indians, did radically reduce the level of exploitation. Indians were finally given political power, along with their lands, and most of the basic export sector was nationalized. With its polity, economy, and society so drastically altered, Bolivia's evolution in the last several decades, while sharing the Latin American horrors of military rule and violent class warfare, has nevertheless continued to evolve in a manner distinct from the rest of the hemisphere.

In its economic development as well, Bolivia has also shown itself to be a relatively unusual nation. In a spectrum of economies in the world, Bolivia stands somewhere at the extreme as an almost classic case of an open economy. Concentrating on mineral exports from the sixteenth century until today, the Bolivian economy follows world market conditions to an unusual degree. International changes in supply and demand are immediately felt in a national economy totally dependent on mineral exports to earn foreign currencies. Given the small size and extremely low density of the national population (the lowest in Latin America), a national industrial structure is virtually precluded from developing except under the most extreme conditions of world crisis or international integration. Bolivia thus differs from most of the Third World in its loyalty to the system of comparative advantage despite the nationalization of most of its mining economy. This has meant centuries-long investments in mining and dependency on imports to supply all but the basic necessities. Thus the historical evolution of the post-Conquest Bolivian economy closely follows the patterns of expansion and contraction of the world economy.

Despite this external dependency, Bolivia has also had an unusual degree of national control over its own resources, especially in the national period. Bolivian entrepreneurs made up of whites and cholos have dominated the mining industry and succeeded in passing on their control to the nation without the massive intervention of foreign entrepreneurs and all the travail that that implies for national development. Bolivia has obviously not been immune to the machinations of its neighbors or of more distant powers. Yet the creative spirit of its peoples has enabled it to survive and to condition these external interventions in the context of its own needs and concerns.

For all its fascinating historical evolution and the rapid changes that have occurred in the contemporary period, Bolivia still remains a poor and relatively backward society and, in terms of human survival, one of the harshest in the Americas. Even today its 4.6 million nationals have among the highest death rates, lowest life expectancies, and lowest per capita wealth in the Western Hemisphere. Rather, its social and economic profile is typical of most poor African and Asian nations, which means it shares an unfortunate set of conditions with most of the world's peoples.

Unique as it is in so many ways, Bolivia forms an intimate part of the common history of mankind, from its development as a multi-ethnic conquest society to its contemporary emergence as a nation that has undergone profound social transformations and massive political change. It is this fascinating interaction of Western patterns and pre-Columbian traditions, of class organization and dual social systems, of poverty and exploitation and vigorous independence and social creativity, that I will explore in the pages that follow.

In undertaking this survey of Bolivian history, I have tried to distill some twenty years of reading, research, and participant observation on this subject. Though one not born into a culture will miss many of its nuances, I hope that my distance from the subject will compensate for potential distortions. Equally, as a member of an advanced industrial society, I have tried to remain as objective as possible without suspending my own moral or intellectual judgments or going to the extreme of being patronizing.

    In my long education as a "Bolivianist" I have had the advice, instruction, and constant support of a large number of scholars and friends. Bernardo Blanco-González and Teresa Gisbert introduced me to the subject, and Gunnar Mendoza and Alberto Crespo guided me in my researches. Sylvia Rivera and Antonio Mitre have constantly challenged my assumptions, and kept me abreast of the latest developments among an exciting new group of younger scholars. I am also indebted for guidance, criticism, and support to Xavier Albó, Josep Barnadas, Philip Blair, Thérèse Bouysse-Cassagne, Tristan Platt, Thierry Saignes, Karen Spalding, Enrique Tandeter, and Nathan Wachtel. As intellectual mentors and close friends, Marcello Carmagnani and Nicholás Sánchez-Albornoz have been of inestimable value to me on this project. I would also like to thank Stanley Engerman, Harriet Manelis Klein, and Richard Wortman for critical readings of the manuscript.

Washington, D.C.   H.S.K.
May 1981

Contents

Maps

Tables

Bolivia

Chapter 1 • Geography and Pre-Columbian Civilization

The historical evolution of Bolivian society cannot be understood without a knowledge of the environmental context in which it took place. For in many ways Bolivia represents a paradox within the context of American development. Despite its location close to the Equator, Bolivia shares few features with the tropics. From earliest human settlement to the present day, a good part of its people have lived at an altitude of 5,000 to 13,000 feet above sea level, with the majority of the population and its most advanced cultures being found at 12,000 feet or above. While not a totally prohibitive environment, the highlands have poorer soils and much colder and drier climates, and face constraints that do not hinder the lowlands. This ecology required the domestication of plants and animals unique to the highlands and even had a dramatic impact on human physiology, as highland populations were forced to adapt to the limited supply of oxygen and quite different degrees of air pressure.

Although some two-thirds of Bolivia's territory consists of tropical and semi-tropical lowlands, from the Pacific coast deserts of the Ata-

cama region (until this past century) in the west, to the vast stretches
of eastern lowlands and floodplains forming parts of the Amazonian
and Pilcomayo river basins in the east, humanity has been concentrated in the highlands from remotest times until today. As can be
seen in the distributional map of the ecological zones of Bolivia, the
highlands and their associated intra-mountain valleys formed but a
small part of the total Bolivian landscape.

While the lowlands may have offered better soils and the potential
for a richer life, their inaccessibility until modern times rendered them
useless to all but a small number of semi-nomadic hunters and gatherers isolated from significant contact with the major centers of advanced civilization. On the other hand, the high plateau was well
articulated with the dense populations and advanced culture areas of
coastal and central Peru. Thus, despite its limitations, the broad ex-
panse of its arable lands, its potential as a major grazing zone, and its
deposits of accessible minerals made the Bolivian highlands the logical
center for human settlement.

Known to the Spaniards as the *altiplano,* or high plateau, the Bolivian highlands consisted of an enormous level tableland at an extremely high altitude. Beginning just north of Lake Titicaca, the
altiplano extends some 500 miles to the south at an average altitude
of some 13,000 feet. Created by an opening of the Southern Andes
into two distinct mountain ranges at around 9° south of the Equator,
the altiplano grows from a width of a few miles at its beginning to
some hundred miles in the central areas. A great elliptical sphere with
the enormous lake at its top, the altiplano is the most level and largest
plateau in the Andes, which in its turn is the most extensive mountain
range in the world. Two-thirds of the approximately 50,000 or so
square miles that constitute the altiplano falls within the current
borders of Bolivia.

Each of the mountain ranges which define the altiplano contains
quite different features. The western branch is known as the *Cordillera
Occidental,* and is an extremely narrow and well-defined range averaging some 16,500 feet, rising at its highest point to over 21,000 feet.
It contains few river valleys or habitable plateaus and forms a steep

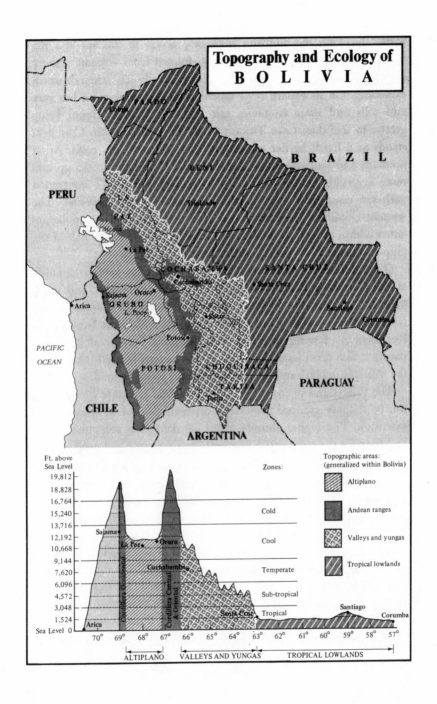

barrier blocking the altiplano from easy access to the sea and the desert of the Atacama coast. Although formed from volcanic activity and highly subject to erosion, it contains relatively few minerals worth exploiting. On its eastern slope touching on the altiplano, it has very arid soils and some enormous salt flats, the flats at Uyuni being greater in size than Lake Titicaca itself. Thus the western Cordillera stands as a harsh barrier preventing easy access to the coast. At its northern and southern edges, however, the Cordillera breaks up into more accessible routes to the sea, encouraging Bolivia's integration with the coast in a more northern or southwestern direction. The western Cordillera itself offers few attractions for human populations either within or near its borders and so defines the western half of the altiplano as the most sparsely settled area of the region.

Quite different is the eastern range of mountains known variously as the *Cordillera Real, Central,* or *Oriental.* Far broader and much more broken than the Western Cordillera, the Royal Cordillera contains numerous fertile plains and river valleys at altitudes from 14,000 feet down to a few hundred feet above sea level. Because of its broken nature it also provides easier access to the eastern foothills (known as the *montaña* region) and the eastern lowland plains beyond.

The valleys and plains of the Cordillera Real are quite complex but can be roughly grouped into major divisions defined by altitude and extension. The higher altitude plains are defined as sub-puna valleys and have for the most part a temperate environment and good ground water though relatively dry climate, and average about 8,200 feet above sea level. They are usually long open plains with relatively easy accessibility from the higher altiplano; the most densely inhabited are the valleys of Cochabamba and Chuquisaca, the western part of Potosí, and the region of Tarija.

The steep river valleys in the central part of the Cordillera, known as the Yungas, are more humid and more tropical. At 8,200 to 3,200 feet in altitude, these valleys are characterized by high humidity owing to Amazonian winds and thus intensive cultivation of tropical and semi-tropical crops. The most important of these Yungas are those located close to the altiplano city of La Paz and called the Nor and Sud Yungas, Larecaja, Muñecas, and Inquisivi. Historically, these valleys were the center of maize and coca production, two fundamental products in high demand on the altiplano and incapable of being cultivated there. They were also the zone of intensive citrus, fruit, and coffee production in the post-Conquest period and thus were complementary to the highland centers. Another series of semi-tropical valleys were the more isolated ones to be found in the provinces of Cochabamba and Santa Cruz. Capable of producing the same crops as the Yungas valleys, they remained largely unsettled and inaccessible until the twentieth century.

The other major zone of pre- and post-Conquest production and settlement in the Cordillera Real was the more temperate and open sub-puna valleys. Best exemplified by the Cochabamba Valley system, these broad valleys were the primary producers of maize in the pre-Columbian period and of wheat after the Spanish Conquest. They were also the major manufacturers of *chica,* the alcoholic beverage made from maize. Given the importance of all these crops, the sub-puna valleys were in constant contact with the core highland populations. These valleys would also become the first centers of Bolivian cattle production, just as the altiplano became the center of the Spanish-introduced sheep.

Before reaching the flat plains of the Amazonian and Chaco lowlands, the eastern Cordillera turns into a series of small hills and mountains called the montaña area. Passing these one enters the open sea-level plains. These are divided into two quite distinct zones. In the north are the *Llanos* (or plains) *de Mojos,* sometimes called the Northern Humid Llanos or those of the Beni. These tropical savannas are usually heavily flooded in the December–April summer rainy season. In their center is the Rio Mamore, which forms part of the Amazonian basin system. To the south of the Mojos plains are the highlands of the Macizo Chuquitano, named after the old province of Chuquitos. At slightly higher elevation, this area shares much of the Mojos environment but is also a center of mineral deposits. Then to the south are the dry plains or *Llanos del Chaco.* Stretching from Santa Cruz south to the Brazilian, Argentine, and Paraguayan borders and beyond, these sandy dry chaco plains, which form the Pilcomayo river basin, are covered with scattered scrub forest and form a large part of the territory of the nation, yet contain only one-fifth of its population.

Because of inaccessibility and harsh seasonal variations, these low-lands were unexplored and unexploited until recent times. While some coca production and cattle raising were developed in the colonial period along the eastern montaña edge of the lowlands in those areas close to the cities of Santa Cruz and La Paz, it was only with the de-velopment of commercial production of wild rubber in the late nine-teenth century that systematic exploitation and commerce became important. Since then commercial agricultural production in sugar and cotton has developed into major industries, and cattle raising has become centered in the northeastern Mojos and Beni regions. These developments did not get under way on a major scale until the middle decades of the twentieth century, and even now only a third of the national population is found in this region.

Throughout the history of human settlement in Bolivia the altiplano and its associated eastern valleys remained the primary zone of human activity, with the altiplano the core of the system. But, despite its centrality and the density of its population, the altiplano was not uniformly hospitable for human settlement over its entire area. The western half of the altiplano contained few minerals, largely infertile soils, and extraordinarily dry climate; the eastern half, however, had reasonably fertile soils, enormous mineral deposits, and a relatively more humid and warm climate resulting from the presence of Lake Titicaca. With its 3,500 square miles, Lake Titicaca exerts an enor-mous influence over the local climate and provides humidity and relative warmth unavailable on the rest of the altiplano. As a result, intensive agriculture and herding became essential occupations of the peoples surrounding the lake and provided the ecological support for the creation of an important food surplus. This in turn provided the incentive for the creation of more complex cultural systems. The set-tlement around the lake took place in a series of open plains defined by foothills, known as *cuencas,* which stretch south to the great river valley that would become the city of La Paz, some fifty-six miles south of the lake. The cuenca on the shores of the lake and the one of Jesús de Machaca are the most valuable in terms of soils and humidity and are linked by the Desaguadero River. This in turn binds together the two lakes, Titicaca to the north and Poopó to the south, and also passes through the two southern cuencas of Oruro and Uyuni. The Oruro cuenca is moderately populated, while Uyuni—the driest zone in all Bolivia—is the center of salt flats and largely uninhabited.

It was the altiplano where the domestication of the staple products of Andean civilization from the distant pre-Columbian past to the present day took place. In the Lake Titicaca region the potato was domesticated—a development which was to have a profound impact on the populations of Europe—as well as quinoa and a host of nutritional root crops. Frozen and dehydrated, these numerous roots have been fundamental staples in the Bolivian diet.

The altiplano was also the scene of the domestication of the American cameloids: the llama, alpaca, and vicuña. Beasts of burden, producers of wool, and sources of meat, fertilizer, and heat, these cameloids were to play a fundamental role in the Andean ecology and economy. From the remotest times these animals were found in close contact with human populations on the altiplano, though it was during the epoch of the historic Aymara kingdoms that the domestication and use of these animals reached its fullest development. So important were their herds that in all their fortified settlements the pre-Incan Aymaras provided space for their animals as well as their people.

An excellent grazing zone of natural and artificial pastures, the altiplano also became the home of the European domesticated sheep after the Spanish Conquest. While usually incompatible with other grazing stock, sheep successfully integrated with the American cameloids, and the two today remain integral parts of the Amerindian herding economy. Thus, between the great herds and the intensive root crop agriculture, the altiplano Indian populations were able to produce both sufficient foodstuffs and woolens for their own survival and replacement, as well as surpluses to exchange for fish, fruits, condiments, maize, and coca which could not be produced in the highlands.

The altiplano also contained a wealth of mineral deposits which has been exploited from pre-Columbian times to the present and which marks this region as one of the great mineral zones of the world. The distribution of these minerals closely parallels the primary agricultural areas of the altiplano. Just as the best soils were in the eastern side of the altiplano, some 80 percent of Bolivia's vast mineral deposits is to be found in the same area. Concentrated in a zone that has been given the general name of the "faja estañifera," or tin belt, most of Bolivia's minerals are found in the Cordillera Real and its associated plains and upper valleys, running from just northeast of Lake Titicaca, through the eastern Cordillera range, to the Argentine frontier in southern Bolivia. Going from north to south, the minerals belt is divided into several roughly defined areas. From southern Peru to about the level of Mururata is the oldest geological section, which contains all the gold deposits, taken mostly through placer mining since pre-Columbian times, as well as wolfram and other metals. From Mururata south to Oruro are more deposits of wolfram and the first important deposits of tin. But the major tin districts appear in the third zone heading south, in the region from Oruro through Potosí to the southern frontier. Known as the "poli-metal province" because of its unique association of tin with silver, this region is the heartland of Bolivia's mineral deposits and contains not only tin and silver in extraordinary abundance but a host of rare metals, many of them unique to Bolivia, and such minerals as lead, bismuth, zinc, and antimony. The only major metal deposits located outside this zone are copper in the eastern altiplano, and the large nitrate and copper concentrations on the other side of the western Cordillera in the Atacama desert. The Cochabamba Valley contained a host of nonferrous metals. In the eastern foothills were large deposits of natural gas and petroleum and the only iron ore in the whole region. Thus, the only minerals or hydrocarbons Bolivia lacked were coal, bauxite, chrome, platinum, and precious stones.

This extraordinary mineral heritage, while only modestly exploited in pre-Columbian times, would become the basis for Bolivia's importance in the world economy once the region was discovered by Europe. Moreover, even during its more modest pre-sixteenth-century beginnings, the metallurgy of the highland populations was an important trade item between themselves and the high civilizations of the Peruvian coast, and it was in metallurgy and in their creation of a unique highland ecology adaptive to man's needs that the early Bolivian populations showed their greatest originality.

Given the extraordinary importance of minerals, root crops, and cameloid products in the Andean economy, the highlands remained the primary zone of exploitation for the peoples of pre-Conquest Bolivia, and thus set the pattern which would predominate down to the present day. But the utility of the altiplano environment, for all the creativity of its human populations, was limited. For this reason, the highland populations have constantly interacted with the valley and lowlands peoples to obtain basic complementary food products which they could not produce. This so-called "vertical ecological integration," involving exchanges of products from sharply different ecological zones, has been a common feature of human life in this region from the beginning. From earliest known times colonists from the altiplano were to be found in all the valleys to the east and also as far away as the Pacific coast on the west. Intense inter-regional trade became the hallmark for all the advanced cultures on the altiplano. Trading root crops, meat, and wools from their vast cameloid herds of llama, alpaca, and vicuña, the highland peoples obtained coca, maize, fish, fruits, and beans from the lowland areas and maintained a varied subsistence base. Through centuries of expansion, change, and finally European conquest, the highland peoples kept this vertical ecological integration intact, and fought all attempts to isolate the altiplano from its regional sources of trade. To this very day, in fact, vertical ecological integration is a dominant theme of social and economic organization in rural Bolivia.

In this, as in so much else, the area that would eventually make up the Bolivian nation shared much in common with the entire Andean region, of which it formed only the southern sector. In the central and southern highlands of what is today Peru, similar geographic settings created similar patterns of integration, especially in the region north of Lake Titicaca. Moreover, the entire Andean area would also share a common cultural history.

The arrival of early man in the Andean area dates back at least 21,000 years, though the remnants of their presence in the highlands have been less well preserved than along the Andean Pacific coast-line. But both highland and coastal cultural areas in the period prior to 2500 B.C. shared a largely hunting and gathering subsistence with semi-nomadic settlements. Whereas in the coastal zone, human popu-lation concentrated on the resources of the sea, the highland peoples engaged in wild-animal hunting for subsistence. From the end of the last glacial period *ca.* 8000 B.C. there began the slow development of domestication of plants and animals. Agriculture and herding finally became the predominant forms of subsistence only after some 6,000 years of experimentation.

By 2500 B.C. the highlands of Peru were the scene of a major transformation to settled village agriculture. Permanent settlement, increased population density, and more complex social organization in terms of multi-community governments became the norm. For the next thousand years both the coast and highlands experienced this increasing tempo of settled agricultural life. More truly urban centers were formed, and the establishment of religious ceremonial centers marked the beginnings of non-food-producing specialists who pro-vided services to the full-time agriculturists.

Although the process that moved village horticulturists to sacrifice some of their surplus to non-food-producing groups is not fully under-stood, the record from the Andes suggests that it was primarily tech-nical and/or religious motivations that led to the formation of complex inter-community governments. The existence of ceremonial centers isolated from agricultural settlements and the creation of complex irrigation systems seem to re-enforce this interpretation.

The next major phase of Andean development, the widespread use of pottery, arrived late to the Peruvian area, coming only *ca.* 1800 B.C.

Ceramics, along with the development of metal technology, were important indications of the creation of increasingly larger states and more dense populations. In the highlands, copper pieces of the Wankarani culture from the region near Oruro date from 1200 to 1000 B.C., while pottery was found on all major coastal and highland sites dating from this period.

Around 800 B.C. the development of the "Chavín" culture brought changes throughout the Andean area. This culture, whose core was in the central highlands and associated coastal valleys, saw the first massive spread of influence of one major culture over a very large area. It was a period marked by extensive use of textiles and gold, as well as the development of advanced pottery techniques and urbanization. Major ceremonial centers were built along the coast and highlands, and almost all of the valleys and plateaus were now fully and permanently settled. In all of these developments, the southern highlands of Bolivia, though sharing many of the traits found elsewhere, seemed to concentrate on metallurgy, of pure metals such as gold and silver, but refined alloys as well. Though Chavín culture did not reach as far south as Lake Titicaca, a coterminous and later culture known as Paracas did influence the southern coastal and highland areas, but the extent is still not fully known.

At about 100 B.C. the Chavín style disappeared from the Andean area and was replaced by vigorous local styles confined to a given valley or drainage area. On the coast there developed the Moche and Nazca cultures. In the highlands, Waru culture developed near Cuzco, and a major center appeared at the small town of Tiahuanaco just south of Lake Titicaca. These cultures saw the final introduction and domestication of all the known plants and animals and the full development of Peruvian technology. In the Bolivian highlands, the copper and tin alloy, bronze, was discovered. Though fully developed by the southern highlands, bronze was not universally adopted in the Andean area for use in war or agriculture and, unlike Eurasia, had little technological impact.

The growth of a viable and important center of culture at Tiahuanaco represented a major development in Bolivian history. Situated some 30 miles south of Lake Titicaca on the altiplano at an elevation of 13,120 feet, Tiahuanaco was an advanced agricultural settlement with pottery and metal objects from *ca.* A.D. 100 onward. It was only after A.D. 600, however, that its influence began to spread beyond its local site. Its importance in Andean history was due to both its unusual location and its dominance within the entire region from approximately the seventh century until the thirteenth century A.D. The most southern of the great pre-Columbian Andean empires, it was also one of the few highland ones. Because its distinctive art styles and designs influenced pottery throughout the highlands and most of the coastal areas, it was initially thought that the Tiahuanaco empire was established through conquest. But all the major Tiahuanaco cities so far discovered have been unfortified settlements with a religious style of architecture. Thus some scholars have assumed that Tiahuanaco influence was purely religious, and that such secular kingdoms as that of the Waru (A.D. 700-1100) in the region of Ayacucho were more important in spreading its influence. The continued discovery of new Tiahuanaco "religious" centers with their characteristic square, or rectangular platform surrounded by sandstone and basalt blocks (called a *Kalasasayas*), has suggested a possible third interpretation: that of Tiahuanaco religions and/or commercial colonies distributed among the highlands, valley, and coastal regions which spread the influence of Tiahuanaco culture through direct contact.

In the highlands, this period is associated with an intensification of agriculture and a major new expansion of terraced farming. It can thus be assumed that Tiahuanaco civilization was associated with a major increase in the tempo of highland economic and social changes. But lack of systematic archaeological evidence makes it impossible to determine what caused this new empire to expand so rapidly after A.D. 1000, and why it collapsed so suddenly after A.D. 1200.

With the collapse of Tiahuanaco and the parallel breakdown of the Waru empire, there emerged in the Andean area over the next three centuries a plethora of regional states and empires. Among the most distinctive of these new states was that of the Chimu on the northern Peruvian coast, with their large urban center at Chan-Chan. In the highlands around Lake Titicaca, the most important groups were the Chanka federation just north of Cuzco, and the kingdoms of the Aymara speakers on the shores of Lake Titicaca and in the southern altiplano.

The development of the Aymara kingdoms marks the beginning of the historic period of Bolivian history. It is the Aymara who dominated the central highlands of Bolivia from the end of the twelfth century until the arrival of the Spaniards in the sixteenth century. From the oral traditions recorded in the Spanish and mestizo chronicles and from the archaeological record, it is clear that the Aymara kingdoms represent an important departure from the previous Tiahuanaco period. The concentration of towns along the lakeshore in open communities, the commonality of pottery styles and decoration, and the concentration on terraced agriculture were now replaced by fortified towns (or *pucara*) on hilltops well back from the lake, a much more intensive development of a cameloid herding culture, and a more localized religion as represented by the *chulpas,* or local burial and ceremonial houses, in all the communities.

The rather warlike and aggressive Aymara-speaking peoples seem to have carried the Peruvian penchant for moiety organization to an extreme. While it is currently assumed that there were at least seven major "nations" of Aymara speakers, it appears as if each nation was divided into two separate kingdoms. Thus the Lupaca and the Colla, to mention just the largest of these nations, both had an *Urcusuyu* and *Umasuyu* government, each with its own separate "king" and each controlling different territories. Linguistic and geographic evidence suggests that the Urcusuyu division of any nation was primarily concentrated in the mountaintop fortified centers to the west and southwest of Lake Titicaca, with their colonies grouped along the Pacific coast, while the Umasuyu of any nation were in the eastern highlands and had most of their colonies in the eastern associated valleys and montaña region.

Looking at the distribution of these "kingdoms" the observer can see that the Aymara extended from just south of Cuzco into the northern highlands of present-day Bolivia. The core of the region was the

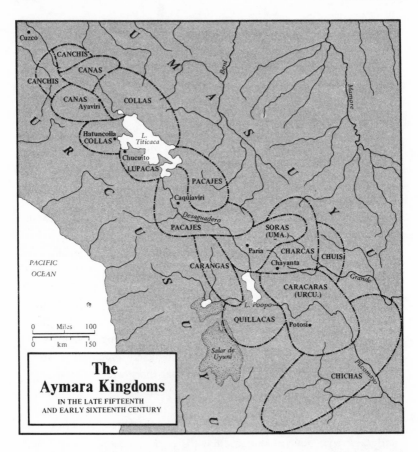

The Aymara Kingdoms
IN THE LATE FIFTEENTH
AND EARLY SIXTEENTH CENTURY

highland settlements of the altiplano, and the moiety division of the "nations" ran more or less uniformly along a northwestern-southeastern axis intersecting Lake Titicaca. The most powerful states were those centered on the lake, and this can be considered the heartland of the Aymara peoples. Between them the Collas and the Lupaca controlled most of the Titicaca shore, and, with the Canas to the north, were considered the most important of the Aymara kingdoms.

Just as with the better-known Incan society, the pre-Hispanic Aymara kingdoms were also organized in a complex amalgam of corporate and class structures. There existed the *ayllus,* or kin groupings, with each ayllu divided into an upper (*hanansaya*) half and a lower (*urinsaya*) half, to which everyone belonged. But the nobility in any particular kingdom were associated with the hanansaya ayllus, and the commoners with the urinsaya part. Although ayllu membership was vital to all Indians, and its common rights to land suggest a communal corporate style structure, the Aymara also had regional chiefs, or *kurakas,* who held land independently of the ayllus and extracted free labor from the ayllu members they governed. In turn these kurakas were served by assistants at the local ayllu level who were known as *jilakatas,* who seem to have been the moiety leaders.

Thus between the kings, the regional nobles, and the local elders, there existed a group of individuals with access to private property and with inheritable rights to land and labor independent of the basic ayllu structure. It is not known if these rights were ultimately dependent on royal favor or were truly personal, thus suggesting an incipient class structure. Also there existed some groups of artisans and special workers who may not have pertained to any ayllu but depended directly on the nobility. These were called in Incan times the *yanaconas,* and they appear to be either serfs or slaves.

Besides the complex socio-political and economic structures which existed in the core highland regions, both kurakas and ayllus also had colonists working for them in different ecological zones. Called *mitimaq,* these highland colonists were the vital link binding the inter-regional and multi-ecological economy that was so crucial in maintaining the core highland populations. Each ayllu and each nation and its nobility had colonists farming the temperate and semi-tropical valleys. In exchange for highland meats, potatoes, quinoa, and woolen products, these colonists paid with everything from fish and salt from the Pacific coast villages to corn, coca, and fruits from the Yungas and sub-puna valleys. In these distant regions, many colonists co-existed with the local non-Aymara populations. Thus many of the eastern escarpment valleys held a complex of institutions, communities, and properties, ranging from private estates of kurakas and colony communities of altiplano ayllus to native ayllus of local groups. Thus slave and free labor, dependent villages, and even independent nations co-existed in these valleys and lowlands.

This whole system of vertical integration of micro-ecological systems (which has been likened to an archipelago), based on the production of different crops and bound into a non-market economy through elaborate systems of kinship, exchange, and labor obligations, was fundamental in maintaining a powerful and economically vital society on the altiplano. So extensive were these colony-core arrangements that even full-fledged gold- and silver-mining colonies were maintained by highland peoples in Carabaya and other eastern valleys, making the Aymara the premier gold producers of the Andes as well as the leading herdsmen. Such was the wealth of these kingdoms that, despite Inca and Spanish conquests, they were still considered to be unusually wealthy provinces in the sixteenth and seventeenth centuries.

But the Aymara were not alone on the altiplano. Along with these peoples there co-existed a large number of Uru- and Puquina-speaking peoples known generically as Uru. Grouped like the Aymara into dual ayllus, the Uru were nevertheless denied access to lands and herds, although they lived among the Aymara. They had no broad-based political organizations and worked primarily as fishermen or as laborers for the Aymara. Whether they were a subjected and conquered peoples held in control by the Aymara is difficult to judge. The Puquina speech of the Uru represented one of the three major altiplano languages in pre-Conquest Peru, along with Quechua and Aymara. By the time of the Spanish Conquest the Uru were a poor people living in small groupings among all the highland kingdoms, though they still retained scattered colonies along the Pacific coast and in the eastern valleys. Moreover the cultural, if not political and economic, deference paid by the Aymara to the Urus seems to imply that the Uru may have preceded the Aymara and have been remnants of an earlier and more advanced civilization. Some have even argued that they were the people of Tiahuanaco. Whatever the situation may have been, by the time of the Spaniards the Uru, though still quite numerous, were all so poor that most of them escaped Spanish taxation.

Warlike, economically potent, and covering most of the altiplano and the regions to the east and west of it, the Aymara by the late fourteenth century were the dominant peoples within Bolivia and in an important section of southern Peru. But given the growth of population and wealth throughout the Andes by this time, it was inevitable that a new imperial organization would again be attempted for the region. While many powerful states flourished on the Peruvian coast, the highland cultures had become the vital centers of expansionist states since the epoch of Tiahuanaco. By the late fifteenth century the numerous Aymara kingdoms found themselves in direct competition with the emerging imperial state of a Quechua-speaking nation in the region of Cuzco north of the lake. By the early decades of the fifteenth century the various competing states in the central highlands had sorted themselves out into major groupings, and the Cuzco-Quechua speakers emerged as the most powerful of the new nations. By the middle decades of the century, the expansionist Quechuans, who came to be known as Incas from the name of their rulers, had spread into the northern highlands and were slowly penetrating south toward the Lake Titicaca district. In the 1460s they were able to extend their influence over the Aymara kingdoms, which were incapable of uniting against the Inca threat because of traditional animosities among themselves. That weakness, despite the relative military power of the Aymara—who undoubtedly were the strongest possible contenders to Inca hegemony in the entire highland region—led to the gradual loss of independence for the Aymara kingdoms by the end of that decade.

The arrival of the Incas in the second half of the fifteenth century, surprisingly, changed little of the social, economic, and political organization of the Aymara kingdoms. Retaining the traditional rulers and contenting themselves with extracting surpluses through tribute payments, the Incas did little to disturb the fabric of Aymara life. This wealthy region was organized into its own province known as *Kollasuyo* (one of the four of the empire). Nevertheless, integration was not peaceful, and in 1470 there was a major revolt against the Incas in the lake kingdoms area. The result was that the remaining independent kingdoms were conquered and Quechua-speaking mitimaqs established in colonies in all of their areas, especially so in the valley of Cochabamba. In fact, this revolt and associated wars would determine the linguistic composition of Bolivia from the fifteenth century until today.

The Lupaqa and Collas among the Aymara retained the most autonomy; but even they were now integrated ever more tightly into the Inca empire, as roads, warehouses, fortresses, new urban centers, and military colonists spread throughout the Bolivian highlands and valleys. Like the three other sectors of the Inca empire, Kollasuyo was required to pay tribute, to send its sacred objects to Cuzco, and to allow its youthful nobles to be educated by the rulers of that city. That the Aymara of Kollasuyo retained their languages and autonomous social, economic, and even political structures to such an extent is a tribute to their wealth and power in the pre-Incaic times as well as their sense of powerful ethnic identity. Even the Spanish Conquest, with its deliberate support for increased "Quechuanization," could not wipe out the Aymara culture.

By the time that the Incas had completely dominated the Aymara kingdoms, their allies, and the smaller sub-puna valleys and Yungas groups within the highland cultural zone, they had already fully elaborated the basic outlines of their imperial organization. Yet the principles of a coherent economic, social, and political system were still only being slowly implanted when some eighty years later the Spaniards ended the experiment in Inca organization. The early demise of the Inca state just as it was beginning to mature has made it extremely difficult to analyze the exact nature of Inca society in the late fifteenth and early sixteenth centuries.

As officially recounted to the Spaniards, the Inca state was an authoritarian and benevolent organization based on rational principles of equality and justice. Prohibiting private property, the state distributed goods and services by taxing up to two-thirds of the produce of the Andean peasantry. The peasants in turn were organized hierarchically into decennial groups of 10s, 100s, and so on, and finally the empire itself was administered in four basically homogeneous regions by a state bureaucracy dependent totally upon the Inca and associated by clan groupings with the rulers of the state. A state religion which stressed the civic virtues and was totally syncretic to all previous religions was the instrument which guaranteed the consensus of the popular masses.

But while the rulers of the empire may have perceived their society in quite coherent and rational terms, in fact the rapid and recent conquest of all types of peoples made for a relatively heterogeneous society. True, the road network was fully constructed and the incredibly large warehouse system was in place so that in fact the Incas could store surplus from any area for use throughout the empire during times of emergency as well as maintaining non-agricultural artisans and a professional army. But there did exist important elements of private property within this broader non-market system. Thus, nobles who had surrendered peacefully to the Incas retained their lands and their workers, just as distinguished Inca nobles were able to obtain private lands and the use of yanaconas, or landlessa servants of the state. Moreover, though pre-existent states might be organized into broader provinces in the Inca structure, they retained many pre-Inca forms of government. Finally, despite the removal of religious objects to Cuzco and the forceful Quechuanization of the local elites, the masses tended to retain local religions unchanged and to continue to speak local languages. Moreover, as in the case of the Aymara, pre-Conquest arrangements of highland colonists and dependent peoples were left largely intact by the Incas, who did not seriously challenge the viability of the old social and political structures so long as they were not a threat to their own control.

Thus the Inca empire retained a mosaic of political structures, religions, and languages and even had an important element of private property within its borders. Though not completely congruent with its perception of itself, the Inca empire was nevertheless a powerful and cohesive force and probably the most sophisticated state and economic structure elaborated by the peoples of pre-sixteenth-century America. It also performed some of the most amazing engineering and agricultural projects in America. From Ecuador to the southern

Bolivian borders, a maze of roads was built which facilitated the easy access of all parts of the empire to Cuzco for man and animals. Thousands of acres of new agricultural lands were created through complex terracing of the steep Andean mountainsides, and vast compounds of warehouses were built to store enormous quantities of non-perishable foodstuffs for the entire population. The empire, thus, functioned as a major distributor of goods and services in a non-market manner and probably created a well-being and wealth among all the population unmatched from those times to the present. Finally, its extremely coherent economic and social organization provided an unusual measure of social and economic justice, as even the Spaniards recognized, for the Incas went to great lengths to alleviate onerous working conditions through carefully selected labor drafts, which were of a short terms and fully insured by the state in terms of providing maintenance and compensation for the workers' families. Thus, the peasantry were called upon for *mitas,* or forced draft labor in the mines, on engineering projects, in the armies, or on personal service for quite limited periods and were fully and effectively compensated for this work.

So efficient was this Inca organization that it proved to be a military power that none could oppose. It could mobilize large numbers of troops, feed and supply them over long periods of time, and thus remained impervious to agricultural cycles. The Incas were able to wear out their opponents by their numbers, equipment, and persistence. In the period of less than a hundred years that the empire existed, it swept all before it, easily taking both coastal and highland societies— in fact, any state where a settled peasantry was the primary base. By the end, few states could resist the *Pax Incaica,* and many societies voluntarily joined the powerful new empire. It was, by the time the Spaniards arrived, one of the greatest experiments in human organization that the world had seen.

But there were limits to the Inca expansion, and these were defined more by social and economic organization than by military activity. Despite all their use of colonists and armies, the Incas proved incapable of subduing cultures that were not primarily based on peasant agriculture. This was especially evident in the region of Kollasuyo, the zone encompassing Bolivia. Here the Incas had been successful in the conquest of the Aymaras, their Uru dependents, and the smaller populations living in association with the highlanders—that is, the cultures of the sub-puna valleys and Yungas. Though evidently speaking languages distinct from Puquina, Aymara, and Quechua, these valley peoples were easily subsumed in the Inca state, and both during Inca times and in the post-Conquest Quechuanization programs, their languages were destroyed and converted into Quechua. Clearly the dominance of Quechua over Aymara as the major language in the entire Bolivian region has as much to do with the conversion of these local language groups to Quechua as with the placement of Quechua colonists in these formerly Aymara-dominated territories.

Outside this highland system stood an important human frontier in the montaña region and the lowland plains. Here a complex combination of hunters and gatherers, village agriculturalists, and even multivillage states existed, which prevented the highland peoples from expanding eastward. Though the Incas attempted the conquest of this region, they were unsuccessful, and the peoples of these areas blocked highland cultural penetration and domination. Generically called the Chiriguanos by the Spaniards in the post-Conquest era, the lowlands peoples consisted of a large number of different groups that ranged from the Siriono-type hunters and gatherers at a primary level of development to the sophisticated dwellers of the Mojos floodlands. The later, probably the most advanced group in the region, would disappear by the time of the Spanish Conquest. Nevertheless, it was evident from their remains that they were major causeway builders who maintained a year-round settled agriculture in the lowland floodplains of northeastern Bolivia. Constructing wide causeways, which stretched for hundreds of miles in some cases, the Indians living in the Mojos region successfully resolved the crisis of annual flooding and maintained fairly dense populations and complex governmental structures on this artificially constructed high ground.

So powerful was this frontier which blocked access to both the Amazonian and Pilcomayo river basins to the northeast and southwest that even the Spaniards were unable definitively to conquer and settle this region. In fact, some of the lowland tribes remained isolated until the twentieth century, and overall the lowland tribes until recently have preserved a surprisingly large part of their languages and cultures.

To the southwest, another frontier of resistant Indians successfully opposed Inca access to the Chilean coastal plains. These so-called Araucanians, though fairly advanced materially, were governed by loose inter-community confederations. Nevertheless, they proved to be an extremely effective military group. Despite repeated attempts by the Incas, they successfully prevented highland penetration to the southwestern coasts. In this case, however, the frontier seems to have been slightly more porous than the eastern lowlands, for trade and contact were farily frequent between the two regions.

Only to the direct south, in the Andean foothills where the two Cordilleras again merged, in what today is northwestern Argentina, was there strong highland conquest and penetration. Quechua military colonists successfully entered this territory and clearly would have fully settled the northern Argentine plains region, had it not been for the early destruction of the Inca state by the Spanish Conquest.

While the potential for expansion was not totally blocked, the Inca empire had found its natural limits by the time of the Spanish Conquest, and these limits, interestingly enough, were to prove to be the limits of Spanish expansion for most of the colonial period; for advanced and complex state organizations in the Andean area ultimately depended upon the existence of a stable and taxable peasantry. Where that peasantry existed and survived, the Incas and their successors could construct powerful state organizations based on the surplus of the peasant class. With land resources abundant, it was the labor input that was always the expensive element in American society, for the stability and productivity of that factor was essential for the existence of non-food-producing classes.

Thus at the base of the Andean culture stood the peasants organized into tightly knit fictive kin organizations known generically by the term "ayllu," which organized work and distributed land among its members. While some classes existed outside the ayllu structure, the overwhelming majority of all commoners, nobles, and rulers were members of an ayllu. Unlike the contemporary Indian peasant *comunidades,* or the free communities organized by the Spaniards and called ayllus after the Conquest, the pre-Columbian ayllu was essentially a kin group that was not defined by a single residential community. Ayllus had members in all the various ecological zones and, while retaining a central residential area, were not confined to one space. Although land rights ultimately resided in the ayllu, to be granted to its members on an individual basis, members could hold land in a widely spaced and dispersed regional setting, from the coast to the highlands and the eastern valleys. This relatively unstructured geographical setting was an inevitable response to the harshly different ecological zones inhabited by the Andean peoples. It was in sharp contrast to the clustered village pattern of the Mediterranean peasants which was the distinguishing feature of Spanish culture. It was also quite different from the closed corporate-style community described by anthropologists which would emerge as the dominant form of peasant organization in the post-Conquest period.

By the first decades of the sixteenth century there had emerged within the southern Andean highlands a highly developed society and state organization firmly anchored in a dense and complex village agricultural system. Something like 3 million Indians were to be found under Inca control (compared with some 7 million Spaniards in Spain at the time), with close to a third of them within the southern province of Kollasuyo. Here a multiplicity of societies speaking numerous languages were grouped together into a vast non-market exchange system which involved a continuous transfer of products among starkly different ecological systems. It was also one of the world's richest mineral zones and one of the more densely populated peasant societies at this time. Given this potential, it was inevitable that the southern Andean region would become one of the most important centers of Spanish colonization in the Americas. In turn, the Bolivian highlands, once integrated into Western Europe's expanding overseas empire, would become a source of new foodstuffs and minerals that would have a profound impact on the entire world economy.

Chapter 2 • The Creation of a Colonial Society

The Iberian Peninsula in the fifteenth and sixteenth centuries was the leader of European expansion on a global scale. The Portuguese initiated European world domination through the conquest of the oceanic trade routes of Africa and Asia. And Spain, and more specifically the Castillian kingdom within the Spanish state, undertook the conquest and settlement of vast territories of the Western Hemisphere. America, unlike Africa and Asia, was unknown and unintegrated into the world system prior to the fifteenth century. By its American conquest Spain provided a whole new arena for exclusive European settlement and development which in turn gave Europe a decided advantage in its race for world influence. Thus the Castillian conquest of the lands of America, along with the Portuguese conquest of the international sea lanes, finally tipped the balance of world economic power to Europe and helped prepare the way for its ultimate industrial domination as well. The conquest of America in the late fifteenth and early sixteenth century was thus crucial in changing the relative role of Europe in the world and beginning a new world historical era.

Whereas the Europeans may have initially viewed America as an empty land filled with simple peoples to be exploited for European benefit, in fact America would also change what contemporary social scientists call the "cognitive map" of the Europeans themselves. America did not fit the world view of early modern Christian Europe, since it was totally outside the Mediterranean cultural tradition and its Christian sub-cultural perceptions. The Bible did not mention America, and its Indians had never heard of either Christ or the older religions of the Eurasian land mass. At first the Europeans ignored these totally new factual data in their conceptions of historical reality, but in the following three centuries the role of America would begin to help erode some of the traditional beliefs and verities of European cultural norms. Thus the impact of America slowly began to under- mine, along with the changing nature of the economic structure, long- held European belief systems.

Finally, the possession of American empires defined the relative power within Europe itself of the various contending nation states. New World territories provided a European state with an important new market and required a powerful navy to make itself felt in the intra-European struggles. That Castille first entered the race for an American empire and possessed most of its lands, resources, and peoples gave the new Spanish state a power over its European contenders that remained unbroken until well into the seventeenth century. For close to a century and a half Spain was the dominant power in Europe, just when Europe itself was establishing its economic hegemony over the rest of the world, and it was America that made this difference.

The Spanish state, which unleashed the resources of Europe upon America, was then the most modern and one of the most recently formed within the European continent. As a result, it was able to combine a broad range of private initiative in the conquest and settle- ment of America with a very rapid integration of these newly won territories into a centrally controlled and coherent empire run from Europe. Just as their Inca predecessors were known for their administrative and organizational ability, so the genius of the Spaniards would ultimately reside in their ability to integrate the powerful European drive of private enterprise into the context of formal government structures. They were also the first people in world history to create and maintain an inter-continental empire for four centuries.

Thus the conquest of America meant both its integration into the world market and its organization within the world's largest imperial structure. Until the eighteenth century, no European power could rival the Spanish empire. And this empire stretched from Tierra del Fuego to the Puget Sound and from Sicily in the east to the Philippines in the west. But despite the vital importance of the American colonial empire to Spain in providing the resources to dominate European politics, it was not the only resource of the Spanish state. Even without America, Spain entered the sixteenth century as one of the wealthiest nations in Europe with a thriving international trade in wool and a complex set of exports of the classic Mediterranean crops. It also had an important mining sector and a very dense and commercially active population. Thus it was able to mobilize enormous internal resources which, with those coming from America, were used to create Europe's most powerful army and navy. With this invincible force, Spain not only fought the Turkish power to a standstill in the eastern Mediterranean but conquered large parts of southern Italy and Sicily and maintained an important colonial area in the Low Countries. It actively intervened in the politics of the German states and in the French regions, and even was involved in the dynastic struggles of England.

Thus both within Spain and within the rest of Europe there were enormous areas for personal opportunity for the upwardly mobile members of Spanish society. Spain itself expanded tremendously: its bureaucracy was growing into the largest in Europe, and its army and its commercial sectors were developing apace. The distant and relatively dangerous Americas therefore attracted only the most daring and the most marginal of the non-peasant groups within Spain. It was the poor journeymen and not the master craftsmen who went to America, the bastard sons of poor gentry and not the eldest or even second sons of the very well-to-do latifundistas. The junior nephews of the leading merchant families in Seville left for America as did the poorest of lawyers and notaries who had not the funds to purchase a position after obtaining their degrees. It was, in short, the lowest groups within the potentially upwardly mobile classes who left for America. As for the upper and middle nobility, they were all doing well enough on the Continent and in Spain not to need to risk the long Atlantic crossing; while the vast peasantry were too poor to undertake the voyage.

This background helps explain the surprising nature of the social structure that would be created by the Spaniards in their American empire. To begin with, there was the total absence of the Spanish peasant class, which was replaced in the New World by the American Indian peasants. Moreover, with no pre-existent institutions or classes to compete with, and with human resources scarce, all those going to America experienced an extremely rapid elevation of status in relation to their former positions within Spanish society. For many of these individuals, their success in America would in fact make it impossible for them to return to Spain. Though it became the classic myth both in Spain and the rest of Europe that one could go to make one's fortune in America and return, in fact successful Americans could find no place in the more rigid Spanish society. Thus, while the rare conquistadores like Pizarro and Cortés would obtain wealth equal to the greatest of Spanish grandees, they found that the Spanish nobility refused to incorporate them within their ranks, and their wealth could not buy them a place in Spain equivalent to their status in America. Many of these famous conquistadores, after a brief visit to Europe, returned to America. The same occurred at all ranks of society, with the journeyman who never finished his apprenticeship in Europe quickly becoming a powerful and wealthy artisan in America and being unable to transfer his new status back to Europe. Only those who had gained their titles or had their connections established prior to migration could use the wealth they obtained in the New World to achieve position in Spain. The previously poor lawyer or notary could now buy a wealthy practice in Spain, and quickly did so.

Moreover, the poor nephew quickly became the rich American merchant and in turn left his poor relatives behind when he returned to Europe. But these were the few exceptions to the general rule that it was difficult to go home again for those who migrated to America.

These factors therefore made for an establishment of a permanent Spanish or Creole society in America virtually from the first days. It was also a society which in many ways proved to be far more mobile than the home society. While the first generation of conquistadores would attempt to maintain their station, even when their wealth and status changed, their children knew no such restraints. By the second generation the honorific titles of Don and Doña were no longer carefully restricted to the elite, but were becoming general to all whites. Moreover, the rigid guild structure of Spain could not be established in America, where the skilled trades became relatively open to all persons who wished to participate in them.

This open quality does not mean that Creole Spanish America became a classless society. In fact, the Creoles worked very rapidly to establish class lines and quickly absorbed the best resources in an unequal distribution. Thus a class structure quickly took form and even existed at the very moment of conquest, the spoils of the wars being strictly divided according to the economic investment and relative rank of the members of the conquering army. The new elite also used such extra-market mechanisms as free land grants and kinship and marriage alliances to cement land, resource, and capital acquisitions, to close entrance into their ranks as much as possible. But the jealous Spanish Crown never permitted them to create as rigid a class structure as existed in Spain. Entail and primogeniture were rarely used in America until the very end of the colonial period, so the upper class had to maintain itself in the context of a wide-open system of partible inheritance in which all children of both sexes participated equally. That they succeeded in maintaining class lines is obvious when one examines the class structure anywhere in America. Nevertheless, these societies had far more mobility built into them than was apparent in metropolitan Spanish society.

Just as the Spanish-American elite was more mobile than its metropolitan counterpart, it was also less politically powerful. It was denied control over the local governmental structure and had to share its power with a royal bureaucracy alien to local influences to an extent unknown in Europe. That the elite influenced that bureaucracy was obvious, but even with all their wealth they could not control or dominate the government as was the case in Europe. In one area, however, they exceeded their counterparts in Europe. In relation to the Indians, all Spaniards exercised more power and control than the equivalent groups did in relationship to the peasants of Spain. The excuse of conquest and cultural-racial differences gave the arriving Spaniards, of whatever class and background, a dominant position unknown in Europe.

The establishment of American society was as much influenced by the nature of the conquest process itself as by the social background and political structure of the metropolitan society. For the Spanish-American empire, especially as it was established in the Andean world, was fundamentally and primarily a Conquest creation. A minority made up of whites and their black slaves would dominate an initially separate and wholly distinct mass of American Indians. However differentiated internally, the Indians were still considered as an isolated and repressed mass, lower in status than even the poorest and most illiterate conquistador.

At first, the Spaniards appeared to the Andean populations merely as a more powerful foreign conquering group that did not differ significantly from the Inca conquering host. For this reason, and because of the relatively recent Inca subjugation and the existence of antagonistic non-Quechua groups still not fully assimilated within its borders, the Spanish Conquest was initially an easy process. As the Spaniards seemed to promise a continuation of internal class structures, recognition of traditional Indian nobilities, and all other types of special privilege accorded to a supportive group in the midst of a war of conquest, many Indians joined the Spaniards as allies. The future pattern of racial discrimination and class oppression was not apparent in the first phase of the Spanish Conquest in the 1530s.

Thus the Spanish Conquest of Peru, as the area that is now divided into Bolivia and Peru was called, proceeded much as had the conquest of Mexico. Overwhelmingly superior military technology permitted several hundred Spaniards to overcome Indian armies of thousands. At the same time the Spaniards effectively used the recent nature of both the Inca conquest along the frontiers and the results of the internal civil war between the Inca brothers Huascar and Atahualpa to further their own ends. Initially they convinced the Inca leadership that they were a simple mercenary force that would leave once their appetites for gold and silver were satiated. To the former independent states and tribes conquered by the Incas they proclaimed themselves liberators, while to the losing Huascar side of the famous Inca civil war they claimed to bring justice and recompense for all their losses.

Astutely using all of these appeals, the Spaniards effectively isolated the recently victorious Atahualpa and his professional Quito armies from the rest of the population south of Ecuador and obtained much needed intelligence, supplies, and auxiliary Indian military allies. Once the Quito troops were dispersed and Atahualpa was killed, they created their own puppet Incas from the previously defeated Huascar faction. When these leaders in turn rebelled, they got the support of their own Indian yanacona servants and anti-Inca forces, which helped them overcome the great last Inca rebellions. Such Indian assistance, combined with their unqualified military superiority, meant that only in rare and special instances were many Spaniards killed in all the fierce and bloody fighting. Spaniards suffered more deaths from battles among themselves than they suffered from the Indians. Finally, whatever hope local Indian victories may have engendered, the onslaught of new Spanish troops and immigrants arriving daily clearly meant that the loss of a few hundred soldiers in no way crippled the Spanish ability to mount a century-long war of conquest and colonization.

It was only the progressive hardening of Spanish rule, with its increasingly odious extraction of surplus resources from the Indian elite and peasantry, that finally drove the various Indian forces into even a moderately unified anti-white front. This alienation was inevitable given the constant flood of hungry colonists intent on extracting whatever they could from a population that had already been totally despoiled. But by then the Spaniards were too powerful and the Indian rebels too weak to throw the conquerors back into the sea. The great Inca-led rebellions from the late 1530s onward were thus doomed to total defeat.

It was in the context of this intricate web of alliances and rebellions that altiplano groups south of Lake Titicaca finally entered into the history of the Spanish Conquest of Peru. The great rebellion of the supposedly puppet Manco Inca in April 1537 brought about the need for the various Aymara groups finally to choose sides. While they had initially supported the Spaniards because of their own earlier alliance with the losing Huascar faction in the pre-Conquest civil war, the desertion of the leader of that faction from the Spanish cause forced them to decide loyalties. In the great siege of Cuzco by the rebel Incas, levies of militia were sent from many of the highland areas, with the Lupaqa being particularly strong supporters of the rebellion. The Colla, however, remained stubbornly pro-Spanish, a fact which finally led to a combined Inca-Lupaqa attack on the Colla.

In coming to the defense of the embattled Colla in 1538, Francisco Pizarro led a major expeditionary force to Chuquito and the Rio Desaguardero to destroy the Inca rebel armies and those of the Lupaqa. The end result was the usual one of total victory for the Spaniards, given their consistent superiority in armor, steel weapons, and horses. Caught in the open plains, the rebels were no match for massed cavalry charges and were destroyed. At this juncture Pizarro decided to leave his brothers in the area to undertake the full-scale colonization of the Bolivian highlands and valleys while he returned to Cuzco. It was thus some six years after the beginning of the Conquest that the Andean region from Lake Titicaca to the south was finally pacified by the Spaniards.

The arrival of the Spaniards in 1532 for their definitive conquest of Peru initially had not been felt in the altiplano and valleys south of Lake Titicaca. A region rich in peasants, herds, wools, and traditional Indian food crops, it contained neither the armies nor the gold and silver so sought after by the Spaniards. The urban centers of the Aymara kingdoms and Quechua colonies were small and relatively less developed by the standards of Cuzco. Also, the region had been intensely loyal to the Huascar faction in the Inca civil war and as a result initially welcomed the Spanish intervention as a victory over their enemies. Because of this loyalty, none of the Quito armies which so concerned the Spaniards in the early years remained in the area, and thus they did not attract Spanish military concern.

It was not until the full-scale conquest of Cuzco by Pizarro and his followers in 1533 and the subsequent royal division of Peru that formal expeditions were even sent into the altiplano. The first of these was led by Diego de Almargo, the contender against Pizarro for title to the southern territories, who first passed through the region in 1535 with a large contingent of loyal Huascar-related Inca troops under the command of Manco Inca's brother, Pullapa Inca, who had close ties to the Aymara kingdoms. The expedition quickly and peacefully passed through the western edge of the altiplano along the Desaguadero River and then south to Lake Poopó, across the Andes, and down into Chile.

But Almargo and his followers concentrated their attention first on Chile and then on a long and bitter civil war with the Pizarro family for control of Cuzco. It was thus left to Francisco Pizarro, who beheaded Almargo in early 1538, to undertake the definitive settlement of the region south of Lake Titicaca which the Spaniards would call by the name of Charcas or Upper Peru. In late 1538 Pizarro's two brothers Hernando and Gonzalo entered the southern altiplano and established two important centers. The first and most crucial was the town of Chuquisaca (today Sucre) in a densely settled sub-puna valley at the southern edge of the altiplano, and the second was a small mining camp at Porco to the east of the city on the highlands.

With the establishment of these two Spanish communities, the settlement of the Charcas region finally began, some five years after the capture of the Inca at Cajamarca. While Charcas was a desirable area in terms of its Indians and mines, the Spaniards were initially too busy establishing effective control over Lower Peru and fighting among themselves to pay much attention to the southern region. This relative indifference, however, would dramatically change when some of the Porco miners discovered the continent's richest veins of silver in the nearby zone which would become known as Potosí in 1545. Thus at the height of the last major Peruvian Spanish civil war, in which Gonzalo Pizarro was attempting to defy the royally appointed viceroy, the *Cerro Rico* (or rich mountain) was first discovered at Potosí, and the mining rush was on. As soon as Gonzalo Pizarro was defeated in Lower Peru, the Lima authorities sent a new expedition into the Charcas region which in 1548 secured the Chuquisaca-Potosí-Cuzco road with the creation of the crucial city of La Paz in the heart of the Aymara region. La Paz quickly became both an important commercial and trans-shipment center and a major agricultural market town.

But it was Chuquisaca which was to prove the dynamic frontier town of the new Charcas region. Whereas both Potosí and La Paz turned inward to develop their local regions, Chuquisaca became the staging area for a series of major expeditions into the northeastern Argentine regions around Tucuman. In fact, during the next few decades Chuquisaca attempted to make Tucuman and the northern Argentine towns into a satellite region. While eventually losing administrative control to Santiago de Chile, Upper Peru nevertheless made the northern Argentine region an economic dependency through the latter's close involvement in the highland mining economy.

Meanwhile the Pizarro-sponsored thrust from north to south had been met by a counter-thrust of another Spanish group coming from the distant eastern regions of the Rio de la Plata area. In the mid-1530s the Spaniards finally settled the riverine port of Asunción on the Paraguay River, and the local entrepreneurs, deciding that their future wealth could be obtained in the western interior heartlands, proceeded to explore the entire Chaco region. In 1537 a Paraguayan group had successfully crossed the Chaco. By the early 1540s they were establishing permanent outposts in the Chuquitos and Mojos region at the foothills of the Andes. Quickly running into opposition from the Lima and Cuzco entrepreneurs, the Paraguayan conquistadores were finally forced to accept the lowlands as their frontier and after several expeditions settled the region of Santa Cruz in the late

1550s, finally establishing the settlement of Santa Cruz de la Sierra in 1561 with Paraguayan troops.

By the 1560s the outer limits of the frontier of Charcas were thus fully established. The Paraguayans had opened up a route to the lowlands and secured a few strategic towns guarding a thin communications link to the east. But this frontier region, filled with hostile and semi-nomadic Indians, with no metals and few settled peasant agriculturalists, proved uninviting to Spanish settlement. Moreover, the Chiriguano, Toba, and other Chaco and lowland Indian groups quickly adapted their warfare to that of the Spaniards and succeeded in killing many Spanish troops. This same hostile eastern and southeastern Indian frontier sometimes extended westward, where semi-nomadic Indians often disrupted the vital southern communications links to the Tucuman region and thence on to the Atlantic ports of the Rio de la Plata. The *Gran Chaco* lowland plains region was such a violent frontier that it would take missionaries and permanent fortifications to hold it against the tribes, and even by the end of the colonial period it still remained fully independent of direct Spanish control.

Within the settled Charcas territory the primary orientation was thus north and south. With the mining center at Potosí becoming one of the primary reasons for the Spanish presence in the Charcas region, the supplying of those mines with animals and equipment became the reason for existence of the northeastern Argentine towns. At the same time Chuquisaca became Potosí's administrative headquarters and its nearest agricultural supply center. La Paz both served Potosí as its major linkup city on the road to Arequipa, Cuzco, and Lima—and thence by sea to Spain—and itself became a major provisioning center of laborers and goods for the mines.

Though the mines were the primary concern of the Spaniards, the Charcas area was rich in that other extraordinary resource that was so limited in America: Indian labor. The Cuzco and the La Paz regions were the most densely settled Indian peasant areas in Peru, and the Spaniards were aware of the wealth potential of this scarce resource. Leaving the lands in the hands of the Indian peasants, they attempted to continue the Inca patterns of domination through indirect rule. Thus the ayllus were maintained, and the local nobility—the *kurakas,* or *caciques* as the Spanish sometimes called them—were confirmed in their rights. In return, the goods and services which formerly went to the Inca government and the State religion now went to the Spaniards alone. The Indian peasant communities were divided up into districts and these in turn into *encomiendas,* or grants. A grantee of these labor taxes, the so-called *encomendero,* was a Spaniard who was required to pay for religious instruction and otherwise acculturate the Indians into Spanish norms, in return for which he was granted the rights to the labor and the locally produced goods of these Indians. Such grants, which were the single largest source of wealth to be had in sixteenth-century Peru, were given to a very small percentage of the Spanish conquistadores. The granting of encomiendas thus created a local Spanish nobility in everything but name. The encomenderos in fact became the governing authority in their regions and had at their disposal vast labor power. Though a highly exploitative system, the encomienda was fundamentally postulated on the idea of the preservation of the pre-existent Indian society and government.

Within the Charcas region by the 1650s, there were some 82 such encomiendas, 21 of which contained over 1,000 Indians each. While the total of Upper Peruvian encomenderos was small compared with the 292 encomenderos found in the Arequipa-Cuzco region alone in the same period, the latter region had only 14 encomiendas that held over 1,000 Indians. Thus the Charcas encomenderos, though far fewer in number, tended to be wealthier and more powerful on average than their southern Peruvian compatriots. The average Cuzco-Arequipa encomienda contained something like 400 Indians, whereas the average Upper Peruvian encomienda encompassed double that number, or over 800 Indians. Also this group of elite Upper Peruvian encomenderos was relatively new, or at least had sided with the anti-Pizarro factions in the various civil wars, for by the 1560s the overwhelming majority of them had received their grants from the Lima viceroys. But this was probably the high point of the encomenderos; already by this date over half of the encomenderos were second-generation grantees, and the Crown had succeeded in taking over some 20 encomiendas in its own name.

Although the reorganization of Charcas rural life had followed fairly well-established Spanish principles which went back to Cortés and the conquest of Mexico, the creation of an effective mine labor force was something new, and in Peru a whole new set of institutions was developed to extract Indian labor for the mines. Here the Spaniards tried everything from slavery to wage labor and finally settled upon a system of corvée labor which was rotated among a large number of Indian towns. But to standardize this system and solve the problems of governance in the rural area, it was necessary to reorganize totally local law and custom. And this, in effect, was the task laid out for the great Lima Viceroy Francisco Toledo, who visited Upper Peru in the period 1572-76, in the midst of his viceregal regime.

The Toledo reforms marked a major turning point in the social and economic organization of the Spanish empire in the region of Upper Peru. Faced with several major problems, Toledo decided to reorganize the Spanish effort in the light of royal needs and colonial demands. He also tried to legitimize Spanish exploitation more effectively by tying it into the pre-existent Inca system of organization. To begin with, Toledo faced two crucial problems in the area of rural social and economic organization. On the one hand, the Spaniards had attempted to preserve as much of the existing population and government as possible so as to obtain the greatest benefits at the cheapest costs. But the European diseases they brought with them decimated the lowlands Indians and severely affected the highland population as well. By the 1570s it was clear that all regions of Peru had experienced severe population declines since the arrival of the Spaniards, and this decimation was continuing. Thus the encomienda was no longer as financially remunerative an institution as it had been before.

Secondly, the Crown had informed Toledo of its hostility to the idea of creating a local colonial Spanish nobility based on encomiendas and sought to pressure the elite into giving up this institution altogether and allowing the Indian towns to revert to royal control as regular royally "owned" villages. But even here, Toledo faced the problem of maintaining the village populations in the face of their constant overexploitation and their demographic decline. For him, the only solution was a reorganization of the social and economic bases of Andean life. To this end he decided to "reduce" the Indians into permanent fixed villages and attempted to convert the remaining ayllus into nucleated communities. The model he used was evidently the Mediterranean agricultural community, but in the highlands the communities were made up of many ayllus, all of which had colonists in various ecological regions. It was the aim of Toledo to force these highland ayllus to separate themselves from their colonies and also to regroup themselves into more permanent larger settlements with fixed and contiguous lands so as to be managed and taxed more easily. Thus the model of the *communidad indígena* (or rural Indian community) comes from the time of Toledo, and, despite his rapid creation of numerous *reducciónes,* or new towns, his reforms took at least a century or more to be consolidated. Just how massive an operation this reducciónes campaign was can be seen in the numbers involved. In some five sampled districts of the many which made up Upper Peru at this time, 900 communities involving over 129,000 Indians were reduced to just 44 pueblos. Whereas prior to this "congregation" of the Indians their villages averaged 142 persons, the Toledo reduction policy created towns containing some 2,900 persons each. Large numbers of these "reduced" towns created by Toledo were abandoned, and many of the lowland and valley communities were never successfully separated from their highland core ayllus, as the Indians fought to preserve their ecologically diverse inter-regional system from destruction. But by and large the system he created eventually became dominant in the Andes.

In other areas Toledo was more immediately successful. He broke the power of the encomenderos and limited most of the encomienda grants to three generations, thus recapturing direct control over the Indian populations for the Crown. Moreover, he systematized the tribute that the now royally controlled Indians would have to contribute to the Crown. The free Indian communities were henceforth to pay the majority of their taxes in specie, rather than in goods. This action standardized the Indian tax structure by making the unit of taxation common to all, with variations then being based not on the changing market value of the goods taken by the tax collectors but on some agreed-upon principle of the relative ability of the Indians to pay. The amount of tribute was made to correspond to the amount and quality of the land which the Indians possessed.

This apparent rationalization of the tax structure ultimately proved to be a major weapon forcing the Indians to integrate into the Spanish economy. Since currency could be obtained only by selling goods on the Spanish markets where money was exchanged for goods and services, Indians had to supply either goods demanded by the Spanish or their labor for wages on that market. In the end, they did both things. Wheat and specially produced cloth fit for the urban market were produced and/or traditional products were brought to the new Spanish urban centers for sale. Equally, the demands of the Spanish farmers, merchants, and artisans for harvest and seasonal or even temporary labor were met by free community Indians who sold that labor on the Spanish markets for cash. Although traditional markets for the exchange of Indian goods continued to thrive in Peru, especially as the ecological imperative for mixed cropping remained, a large part of the Indian peasant population was forced to enter the monetary market created by the Spaniards. Thus the need for specie to pay royal taxes proved a major factor in integrating the dual markets developing in the Charcas region.

Just as Toledo was to reorganize the rural structure of Upper Peruvian society, he was also able to reorder dramatically its mining economy. From 1545 until the early 1560s Potosí had produced an ever larger quantity of silver, quickly becoming the single richest source of this mineral in the world. But this growth was based on extraction of surface deposits which had extremely high ore contents and were easily refined through traditional pre-Columbian smelting processes. But as the surface deposits gave out and shaft mining developed, the purity of the ore declined, the costs of smelting rose, and productivity fell. Thus when Toledo arrived on the altiplano in the 1570s, the industry was in full crisis, with production declining and the Crown desperately concerned to preserve this enormous resource.

Toledo attacked the Potosí problem on several fronts. First of all in 1572 he introduced the amalgam process, whereby the silver ore was extracted from the other metals by amalgamation with mercury. In one stroke, the Indian control over refining was broken, and the more than 6,000 Indian open-hearth smelters were replaced by a few hundred large refining workshops controlled by Spaniards and driven by water power. To guarantee the mercury supply needed by the Potosí miners, Toledo also organized the royal mercury mine at Huancavelica in Lower Peru, which thenceforth became the exclusive supplier of mercury to the highland mines.

To deal with the problem of government control over the industry and the classic problem of smuggling and evasion, Toledo also created a royal mint at Potosí and demanded that all silver mined and refined in the city had to be turned into bars and bullion in the royal mint. It was at the mint that the Crown extracted its royal fifth of production, as well as minting taxes. Moreover, now that mercury was a fundamental necessity in the extraction of silver, the Crown established a mercury monopoly. This monopoly not only gave it a profit on a basic necessity but, equally, allowed it to determine actual production and guarantee itself against tax evasion. With all mercury purchases registered by the Crown, the smelter owners, or so-called *azogueros,* had difficulty in shipping out unminted and untaxed silver, since the combination of mercury with ores was a fairly fixed ratio. Thus the potential silver output of all the smelters was known.

Toledo also established the basic mining code. He reiterated standard royal claims to the monopoly of sub-soil rights, requiring miners to pay one-fifth of their output for the use of the royal properties. Moreover, the registration of claims and the rights of use of shafts and other technical matters were all codified by Toledo. The establishment of legal rules was especially important in Potosí because of the extremely complex nature of mine ownership. Unlike other mining areas in the New World, the concentrated nature of the silver veins in one huge mountain of ore at Potosí resulted in a multitude of mines constructed virtually on top of each other. No one miner owned anything greater than a few mineheads leading into one of the countless veins of silver, with numerous owners using different shafts often working a common vein. By 1585 there were about 612 separately owned mines in the Cerro Rico mountain, each representing a different shaft. Elaborate rules of determining ownership of veins were essential to prevent constant armed conflict.

Finally, and most important of all, Toledo resolved the labor question for the miners. Shaft mining was an extremely expensive enterprise, with labor being the highest cost item in the entire process. To construct and maintain a proper shaft cost as much as it did to build a cathedral. Moreover, the enormous quantities of water needed to drive the grindstones in the smelting processes eventually required the construction of a complex series of dams and some twenty artificial lakes, the total cost of which was estimated at the extraordinary sum of over 2 million pesos. At the wages paid for free labor in the mines in the 1570s, it was evident that there was simply not enough capital available to continue the massive mining output that the Crown wished to maintain. Since he was already reorganizing the rural communities and standardizing their tax structure, Toledo went one step further and decided to use a pre-Columbian corvée labor system, the so-called *mita*, to extract forced labor for the mines at Potosí.

Some sixteen districts stretching from Potosí to Cuzco in the highland area were designated as mita supply areas. Here one-seventh of the adult males were to be subjected to a year's service at the mines, serving no more than once in six years. This provided an annual labor force of some 13,500 men, which was in turn divided into three groups of over 4,000 each. These latter groups worked on a rotating basis of three weeks on and three weeks off, thus maintaining a continuous labor supply and yet providing rest periods for the workers. While the miners were obliged to pay the *mitayos* (as they were called) a small wage, this was not even a subsistence amount. In fact, the mitayo communities were required to provide the food for their workers as well as maintain the families of their absent mitayos and to pay for their transportation to the mines. Most of the food and coca consumed at the mines were in turn paid for by the workers themselves. Thus at one stroke, a good half to two-thirds of the mine labor force was now provided to the mine owners by the Crown at extremely low prices, which greatly stimulated production.

The introduction of the mercury amalgamation process, the regulation of the mining legal structure, the provisioning of mercury, and the supplying of the labor needs of the miners at very low cost all had their impact on the lagging industry. With the Toledo reforms production soared by the late 1570s, and the famous Potosí boom was on, with silver production reaching extraordinary levels between the 1570s and the 1650s.

Having resolved the issues of rural organization and mine industry reorganization, Toledo then turned toward problems of Spanish settlement in the region. While the frontiers of Upper Peru were now well defined, there were many interior regions which as yet had not been fully exploited by the Spaniards. Thus Toledo sponsored a whole new wave of Spanish settlements. The single most important of these new towns promoted by Toledo was the city of Cochabamba, which was established in 1571. Situated in the heart of a broad series of sub-puna valleys, Cochabamba also became the central city for controlling the valley Quechua Indians. It also quickly became Upper Peru's major wheat- and maize-producing region and would be intimately tied to the Potosí market in the next century of economic growth. Toledo also better integrated the southern Andean region with the establishment of the city of Tarija in 1574. Like Cochabamba, it was situated in broad sub-puna valleys well populated with Indian peasants. Finally, to secure the eastern frontier against the Chiriguanos, Toledo encouraged the settlement of the town of Tomina in 1575.

Between the final settlement of the frontiers and the interior towns, the growth of the new mine industry, and the integration of the older Indian agricultural base with a new Spanish one, Upper Peru became one of the wealthiest centers of the new Spanish empire in America. Its dense populations of settled Indians provided a seemingly inexhaustible labor force, while its mines were quickly recognized as the principal source of silver in the Americas, if not in the entire world at this time. Thus the Crown was not slow in establishing a viable and semi-autonomous government to control the destiny of this region and guarantee its adherence to the empire.

While Lima and Cuzco had always wanted to dominate the southern highlands, in fact, all the rebellions during the famous epoch of the civil wars showed that Upper Peru could easily operate as an independent and quite dangerous element. Reluctantly the Lima authorities therefore agreed that a separate and powerful government under ultimate viceregal authority would have to be established in the area south of Lake Titicaca. This decision led in 1558 to the creation of an independent *Audiencia,* or royal court, which was placed in the city of Chuquisaca. The Audiencia of Charcas would prove to be one of the few such audiencias constructed in the New World which had both judicial authority and executive power at the same time. The president of the Audiencia, himself a judge, thus became the chief administrative and executive officer in the region.

To control the largely urbanized and western minority of the population, the Audiencia constructed a system of government much like that which existed in Spain prior to the Conquest. Municipal governments were created based on the free suffrage of its citizens (or *vecinos*), and these governments had quite extensive power. With their borders spreading well into the rural hinterlands, they were the primary granters of land titles in the earlier days, controlled local markets, and provided for local justice and police powers. In every principal town there were also royal officials, going from an executive officer known as a *corregidor* (there were some four Spanish *corregimientos* by the early seventeenth century) through a series of royal finance officials whose job it was to tax trade and production. By the standards of Spain at the time, these local governments were rather responsive and representative of the interests and needs of the local elite.

The rural areas contained over 90 percent of the population, all but 10 percent of whom were monolingual-speaking Indian peasants. For these, the Spaniards devised a complex system of indirect rule. Toledo in his reforms had guaranteed local autonomy to the new "congregated" or "reduced" towns, and a complex government of elders of the community began to develop on the local level. Formally elected by the *originarios,* or original members of the community, these local administrations consisted of representatives from all the local ayllus which went to make up the community and had charge of local land divisions and distribution, local justice, and the collection of all taxes. This same government also maintained the local community church and sponsored local community patron saint festivals. The community governments, though supposedly elected in the Spanish style, most probably continued pre-Conquest practices by selecting the most experienced and the most successful older men to represent them. Such men tended to be extremely conservative, being the eldest and most responsible members of the community, and the royal officials made them responsible for everything from the maintenance of local peace to the vital role of providing taxes and mita labor. So long as the exactions on the community were considered reasonable by the members of the community, such a government of elders (or *jilakata*) proved to be a bulwark of conservative stability. But once such leaders were convinced that the exactions of their surplus were beyond acceptable limits, these same elders proved the most dangerous of enemies, since they were able to call out the entire community in their support. The innumerable Indian rebellions in the period after Toledo, which lasted well into the middle of the twentieth century, were never disorganized individual affairs but were always united community efforts exclusively led by the elders of the community. This explains the often strange phenomenon of rebellions confined to a few clearly defined local communities, without affecting their neighbors.

Moreover these community governments over time began to serve not only as an institution of governance and leadership but also as a means of internal redistribution of resources within the community. Faced by a hostile and threatening environment, in terms of both ecology and economic exploitation, the communities could not afford serious internal differentiation among their original participant members. Therefore an elaborate "ritual impoverization" system came into play in many of these communities whereby wealth distinctions were considerably reduced through the forceful dispersion of savings of its more successful or lucky members. Only successful farmers were selected for offices in the civil and religious hierarchy that made up the local community government, and they were required to spend considerable sums of money and a great deal of their time in their offices during the year. Especially in the religious part of their duties, *cargos,* or obligations, were established to sponsor local religious festivals which required the expenditure of savings. In return for the expenditure of time, food, drink, and money, successful elders were rewarded with honor and local power. But such expenditures usually reduced their lifetime savings and thus tended, through the whole ritual process, to reduce their income to the general level of the community. The system guaranteed that no original member of the community with access to land would dominate the others and accumulate an advantage that might threaten the communal nature of property and the integrity of the community. Civil-religious office holding and ritual impoverishment were a general model of a complete system and were not totally operative in all places and at all times. Nor did it prevent, as we shall see, the emergence of groups of non-landholding Indians living in the communities. But for the landholding members, when it functioned effectively, it helped prevent the operation of normal market mechanisms from destroying communal unity.

For most of the colonial period, there also existed in the rural area a group of local Indian nobility known as the *kurakas* who played much the same role as they had under the Incas. The kurakas were usually in charge of several villages and, as local nobles, had recourse to their own private estates within the various communities as well as the rights to community labor and a host of other local resources. In return, the kurakas were to protect the local religion and customs of the community members, to represent them formally to the Spanish authorities, and to act as a buffer between the local peasant and their jilaqatas and the Spanish authorities. Theirs was a brutally difficult position, because not only was the kuraka a landowner and labor exploiter but he himself was heavily taxed by the Spanish authorities and required to guarantee all the local taxes and mita obligations. He of course relied on the jilaqatas to carry out these demands in the local communities, but he, his lands, and his goods were made ultimately liable for the non-collection of taxes or the non-delivery of labor. Thus over the three centuries of Spanish colonial rule the local Indian nobles would slowly be ground down by Spanish exactions and would eventually be reduced to peasant status if they remained in the countryside, or absorbed into the middle or upper classes if they escaped into the cities. Moreover, the whole institution finally would be wiped out as a really effective force in the great rebellion of Túpac Amaru in 1780, in which the kurakas played such a key organizational role.

However indirect their principles of governance, the Spaniards did ultimately control the system. For this reason, they divided up all the rural zones, much like the urban areas, into rural corregimientos under the control of royal officials known as *corregidores de indios*. These under-paid officials were in charge of the extraction of taxes and labor at the district level, and to pay for their offices could force their Indian subjects to purchase goods which they imported into the rural areas. The forced sales of Spanish products to Indian communities proved an enormous source of wealth and corruption for these officials and made them an object of continual hatred by the local Indian populations.

Finally, to guarantee loyalty to the state both from Spaniards and the recently pagan Indians, the Crown forcefully sponsored the establishment of the Catholic religion in the region of Upper Peru. With the arrival of the first Spanish settlers in 1538 had come the secular clergy to minister to the needs of the conquerors and begin the conversion of the Indians. These seculars were quickly joined by the regular missionary clergy from all the major orders in America: the Dominicans, Franciscans, Augustinians, Mercedarians, and, after mid-century, by the Jesuits. The direction for all such activity came from Cuzco and ultimately from Lima. But this system changed in 1552 with the naming of the first bishopric in the region. Called the bishopric of La Plata, it was placed in the city of Chuquisaca, where a decade later the royal Audiencia was also situated. The establishment of a dominant ecclesiastical authority was crucial in the formation of an independent center for Upper Peru.

Meanwhile, the entire Peruvian Church was concerned with evangelization and in 1561 began a series of all-Peruvian Church Councils, the results of which were to provide direction for the regular and secular clergy in the evangelization process. The first council of 1561 ordered that the catechism texts be translated into Quechua, while the third Council in 1582-83 finally ordered a full set of materials in Aymara as well. The result of this was the publication of the first work in Aymara in Lima in 1584. By the first decades of the seventeenth century, the Jesuits Ludovico Bertonio and Diego de Torres Rubio published full-scale Aymara grammars and dictionaries. This was almost a generation behind the publication of Quechua catechisms, grammars, and dictionaries, also undertaken by the various missionary priests. Given the predominance of Quechua, even in Charcas, this late start for Aymara is understandable. But this meant that Quechua became far more of a lingua franca, pushed as it was by the missionaries, even in the traditional highland areas and surrounding valleys. This earlier concern of Lower Peru with Quechua evangelization helps explain the disappearance of all non-Aymara or non-Quechua languages in the sub-puna valleys after the Conquest, to be replaced most often by the dominant Quechua brought by the missionaries.

In other aspects the Church was not slow in striking out into the Aymara populations. Already by 1582 the Bishop of La Plata had granted the kurakas of Copacabana the right to establish a brotherhood in honor of the Virgin in this traditional Lake Titicaca Aymara religious center. The sanctuary built here to the Virgin of Copacabana, along with the sanctuary to the Cross built around the same time at Carabuco, became vital syncretic symbols of the evangelization process. In fact the image of the Virgin at Copacabana became the region's unquestioned central religious symbol. This creation of the outward forms of Christianity does not mean that pre-contact re-

ligion disappeared, or that the clergy had universal success in its evangelization among the Indians. The existence of private encomiendas
in most areas until late in the sixteenth century prevented direct access to Indians, and even with the division of Charcas into effective
provinces of the missionary orders there were far fewer clergy to go
around than were needed. Every reduced town and older settlement
now had a church, but most Indians saw a priest only rarely. Thus
traditional beliefs, especially as related to family and work, were preserved to a large extent, and also systematically protected by the local
jilaqatas and kurakas. It was at the higher spheres of State religion
and the broader cosmological order that Christianity made itself most
effectively felt. The best evidence for this change is to be found in
the progressive decline of anti-Christian revolts throughout the century, and their replacement by the end of the sixteenth century with
revolts, steeped in messianic Christian symbolism, that at the same
time were both heavily Catholic and totally anti-Spanish. No longer
were the local *huacas,* or community religious objects (usually stones),
called upon for support in battle against the hated Spaniards, but now
the dark Copacabana Virgin was called upon to lead the Aymara and
Quechua against the white oppressors.

That local belief changed little is also evident in the late six-
teenth- and early seventeenth-century bishopric pastoral *visitas* and
inquisitorial investigations, which show that in curing, in activities associated with planting and harvesting, and with all those events associated with re-enforcing family, kin, and local ayllu ties, pre-contact
religious belief and practice predominated, often practiced by the sac-
ristans of the local Catholic Church. While the more zealous and
consistent high Church clergy attempted to destroy these beliefs, the
weakness of their numbers and the concerns with the preservation of
indirect rule essentially guaranteed the continuance of local belief so
long as it did not challenge the state-wide and societal legitimacy of
Christianity.

As for the Church itself, the period of internal organization continued, following somewhat the changing economic and social importance of Charcas as a mining center in the post-Toledo period. In rec-

ognition of the growth of the La Paz district as the center of Aymara
highland civilization, the Crown and Papacy created a new bishopric
in La Paz in 1605, while the entire frontier area of the lowlands was
recognized as a separate zone with the establishment of a bishopric in
Santa Cruz in the same year. For the missionaries, work with the
Aymara and Quechua peasants quickly lost some of its romantic appeal, and so the various missions in the Mojos zone, near Santa Cruz
and south in the Chaco, all drew vigorous missionary activity, especially in the seventeenth century. The elevation of Santa Cruz to a
bishopric gave impetus to this work. To complete the colonial organization, the Chuquisaca bishopric was raised to an archbishopric four
years later and the Chuquisaca archbishop made into the primate of
the Charcas Church. The preponderance of the Chuquisaca administrative and religious center was finally crowned with the establishment
of a university in the city in 1624. Thus Charcas now could graduate
its own clergy in all the advanced degrees, and by 1681 this essentially theological center was also offering legal degrees as well, becoming the premier legal institution for the entire Rio de la Plata and
southern cone area until the end of the colonial period.

Thus with its state bureaucracies and state Church, the Spaniards
quickly consolidated effective rule in the settled peasant areas of Upper Peru. Some six major towns of Spaniards (La Paz, Chuquisaca,
Potosí, Cochabamba, Santa Cruz, and Tarija) were strategically located to control vast hinterlands and different ecological and economic
zones. Secure frontier towns were established, along with an effective
mission frontier in the eastern lowlands to prevent the semi-nomadic
Indians from entering into the settled areas, and finally a complex system of indirect rule was introduced to control the Indian peasant populations. But all of these plans conceived of Charcas, or Upper Peru,
as essentially a dual social, economic, and political system. There was
to be a Western-oriented Spanish-speaking white elite, more or less
divided along peninsular class lines based on birth and money, and
alongside them a vast self-governed but fully exploitable Indian peasant mass, also differentiated into a class of peasants and nobles but
otherwise interacting little with their conqueror's world. In fact, the

conquest process and the nature of the conquerors themselves would slowly erode this relatively simple model and create a complex amalgam of new classes, castes, and groups both within the rural Indian world and in the Spanish-dominated urban centers as well.

To begin with, the conquerors brought with them a new set of European diseases unknown to the highland Indians. A system of exploitation based on a population of something like one million peasants would soon find itself oppressing just half that number with the same taxes by the end of the century. Each generation of post-Conquest Indians seemed to develop immunities to the new diseases only to suffer repeated epidemics in roughly twenty-year cycles, epidemics which did not end until well into the seventeenth century. Moreover, the 10,000 or so Spaniards who reached the Charcas region were predominantly male and thus uninhibited by the tight European family restrictions which they had left behind them in Spain. They also brought with them almost an equal number of black African slaves. The result was the creation of a whole new mulatto and mestizo (known as *cholos* in Bolivia) racial grouping. Thus the Indian population loss would be replaced somewhat by an intermediate racially amalgamated group mixing the parentage of Indians and whites, and, to a lesser extent, of Africans.

Nor was the rigid and unchanging social order projected by the Crown the one which was to be, in fact, created by the Conquest. Just as the racial composition of the population was slowly changing, so too was its social structure. The base of the entire economic and social order was the Indian male head of household aged 18 to 50 who was an original member (or *originario*) of his ayllu with direct access to land rights. This so-called originario Indian was the primary producer in the Charcas economy. He paid the basic tribute tax—which was the royal equivalent of the encomienda tribute obligation now directly collected by the Crown—and was the only one subject to the mita labor tax. Moreover, the originarios were also the primary producers for their own kurakas, who continued to collect their own tribute obligations and for the local Church taxes. Given the land base and the labor supply that the Spaniards initially inherited from the Incas, the levies on the originarios were not excessive and could easily be borne by the large numbers of such originarios available in each community.

But the demographic collapse of the Indian population caused a shrinking of the originario class without any consequent relief from the extractions of their surplus product. The pressures on the originario continued to mount throughout the two centuries of demographic decline. The result of this was both the wholesale abandoning of communities and the massive withdrawal of Indians from the originario status. Given the large amount of community abandonment and the policy of new community foundations under Toledo and his successors, there quickly developed a floating Indian peasant population. Arriving as migrants to the old communities or latecomers to the new ones, these *forasteros* (foreigners)—sometimes also called *agregados*— were given lesser land rights or no land at all, and simply took up residence as landless laborers on the plots of the originarios. In changing status, they may have lost their lands, but they removed themselves from all their tax obligations as well. Until the eighteenth century, forasteros did not have to pay the tribute tax, nor were they subject to the mita.

The same demographic and economic pressures which created the forasteros also created an entirely new group of Indians who pertained to no free communities but were living on the estates of the Spaniards. As the value of the encomiendas declined and the Crown forced their revocation, wealthy Spaniards found alternative sources of income in direct agricultural production. With the decline of Indian populations and the constant reorganization of communities, much land in traditional areas became available for private exploitation. These lands were quickly absorbed by the wealthier Spaniards and a new class, the *hacendados* (or large landowners), was created. Initially obtaining their labor from the floating population of Indian servants known as *yanaconas*, the Spaniards soon found that ex-originarios were more than willing to work the Spanish estates in exchange for usufruct land use. Moreover, the Spaniards made no attempt to destroy the ayllu structure, which functioned in the communities and on the haciendas as well. Although the term "yanaconas" came from the Inca period and initially meant those workers without ayllu connections or land who were assigned to leading nobles and other officials by the Inca as their servants or almost slaves, by the end of the sixteenth century the term came to mean simply landless worker. The early conquistadores may have used some pre-Incan yanaconas, but this new yanacona class came primarily from the labor force released by the breakdown of the more traditional communities.

Though the haciendas quickly developed, starting in the second half of the sixteenth century, they soon reached a limit in growth once the free communities stabilized themselves in the second half of the seventeenth century. This resulted in an end to the first epoch of hacienda expansion. By that time, the haciendas were to be found throughout the highlands and major sub-puna valleys, but they absorbed only about a third of the Indian labor force in the entire region of Charcas. The free communities remained the dominant form of social organization and landownership in the rural areas, absorbing two-thirds of the Indian peasantry. But unlike the homogeneous communities and ayllus of the pre-Conquest period, the seventeenth-century free Indian communities contained two distinct classes, the original landed members and their families and the later-arriving forasteros who had far fewer land rights and were obligated to perform free labor service to the originarios. While the communities were still corporate entities controlled by their members and in turn held ultimate land title for all, they now contained second-class citizens who in fact made up the majority of the membership of most of the free communities. But these various categories were not fixed and immutable. Many originarios gave up their rights in their lifetimes, and became either yanaconas on the estates of the Spaniards or forasteros in other communities. Equally, yanaconas moved relatively easily into forastero status. Only entrance into the originario status proved to be difficult, and marriage into that status seemed to be the sole possibility for those not born to that right.

This change and movement within the rural areas was also accompanied by much inter-regional and rural-to-urban migration. Indian originarios who did mita service in Potosí often found it difficult or unattractive to return to their original communities, and many became free wage laborers, or *minganos,* in the mine region. Many originario Indians also decided to give up rural life altogether and moved to the Spanish towns. These towns of several thousand quickly began to fill up with Indians who took on all the urban laboring work tasks and became the dominant element among the urban working class. Speaking both their native languages and Spanish, these new urban Indians often gave up their traditional costumes and began to dress in an adaptation of the Spanish manner and consume Spanish-style foods, such as bread. They became urban cholos, even though they were of a pure Indian stock. The designation of Indian, cholo, and white thus quickly lost its biological significance and became cultural or "social caste" terms determined by such externalities as speech, dress, and food consumption. Nor were the miscegenational Spanish elite immune to these changes, as concubinage and illegitimacy became the norm, and bastard offspring of multi-racial backgrounds were brought into the elite class itself, along with the Hispanicized kurakas who became members of the local landed classes.

The pace of social change in Bolivia was influenced by such negative factors as the demographic decline and the exploitation of the mita. But the tremendous economic growth which affected the entire region after the reforms of Toledo was also influential. The first mining boom of the 1540s and 1550s had been spectacular, but it was as nothing compared to the massive growth of silver exports in the great boom of the 1570-1650 period. During this period, Potosí alone produced over half of the silver of the New World and was unquestionably the world's single most important source of the mineral. The impact of Potosí on Europe and on its trade with Asia was staggering. For Europe, Potosí silver was influential in causing the long-term trend toward rising prices. Equally in its trade with Asia, Europe was finally able greatly to increase its importations of Asian goods owing to its ability to make up for the ongoing negative trade balance with the payment of Potosí silver.

For Charcas the growth of Potosí in the late sixteenth century was even more traumatic than it was for Europe. The location of Potosí in the center of the Upper Peruvian region in an arid and poor agricultural and grazing zone meant that everything used in mining, from the food and tools to the animals and labor, had to be imported. With its mines so far from the sea, it was also necessary to develop a complex communication system to supply both the European imports and export the finished silver. Thus the backward linkages between this export sector and the local regional and international markets were extensive. The growth of the town of Potosí and its silver industry was to be felt from northern Argentina to southern Peru, as one vast economic supply area was integrated into the Potosí market. Equally, the merchants, traders, and shippers from Lima, Arequipa, Cuzco, and La Paz came to play a vital role in linking the mines of Potosí and its satellite elite of Chuquisaca to the outside world.

Potosí's growth from a settlement of a few hundred Spaniards and their Indian laborers to a population estimated at between 100,000 and 150,000 by the early seventeenth century had a profound impact on the growth and settlement of other highland regions. Cochabamba and its associated valleys became major producers of maize and wheat for the Potosí markets, and the growth of the haciendas in the areas was so rapid and powerful that the free communities were pushed early into a minority position within the region. In addition, the demands for labor and the very early breakdown of the ayllus and communities meant that the Cochabamba Valley would become the most "choloized" and bilingual Indian zone in all of Upper Peru. While Quechua remained the predominant language of the valley, Spanish language and culture spread quickly. Many of the agricultural peasants became bilingual and gave up most of their traditional Indian culture to adopt a new mestizo cultural norm which emerged unplanned between the two old groups of conquerors and conquered.

At the other extreme, the growth of mining at Potosí led to the expansion of Aymara culture in the eastern valleys known as the Yungas through the development of the new areas of coca production. Whereas coca leaf mastication had been an important source of stimulants in the diet of the pre-Conquest Indian nobility, and thus a native domesticated plant from well before the arrival of the Spaniards, its use would now undergo a major transformation. With the state apparatus of the Incas destroyed, coca chewing after the Conquest spread to all classes, and the Spaniards quickly found that its consumption was an absolute necessity for the miners working the high-altitude silver mines. Thus the demand for and production of coca increased enormously after the Conquest, and the traditional centers around Cuzco were no longer sufficient to meet demand, especially in Upper Peru. While coca had been grown in the Yungas near La Paz and even in the Chapare region near Cochabamba from pre-Conquest times, its production was quite limited compared to Cuzco. Now, however, demand outpaced supply, and the Yungas, above all, became the prime center for the growth of Upper Peruvian coca which soon displaced the Cuzco variety from the mine center markets. The increase in Yungas production, which would grow steadily throughout the colonial period, meant that the nomadic Indians of these valleys would be replaced by Aymara peasant settlers from the highlands; and this process of settlement, once begun in the sixteenth century, continued uninterrupted into the nineteenth century. The Yungas colonization involved African slaves, who quickly adapted to the dominant culture and became monolingual speakers of Aymara by the end of the period. Thus from zones with only a sprinkling of Aymara colonists, the Yungas became a totally Aymara culture stronghold, even to the extent of having a black Aymara sub-culture.

Potosí was also vital for the development of the Tucuman region, with the ranches of the northeast of Argentina becoming the vital suppliers of mules, wine, and sugar to the Potosí market. In between Tucuman and Potosí, the region of Tarija became a major grain supply area, while the sub-region of the Cinti Valley saw the development of irrigation agriculture, largely owned by Potosí miners, which became the source of local wines. To the north of Potosí the altiplano became the prime supplier of labor, traditional foodstuffs for miner consumption, and the vast llama herds needed for shipping out the silver to the coast. Beyond Lake Titicaca, the mines of Huancavelica became the exclusive providers of the vital mercury for Potosí, and the mita labor demands were also to be met from this region as well. Moreover, tropical fruits, wines, and other food consumption items came to Potosí from both the highland valleys and the coastal plains. This enormous trade and movement of goods and services was financed by both the Potosí and Lima merchant classes. The latter, in fact, appear to have been the primary source of capital, financing the movement of most goods from the north to Potosí and exclusively controlling all Potosí's international trade until well into the eighteenth century.

The late sixteenth-century boom and expansion of Potosí also had an impact on further settlement and development of the interior spaces of Charcas. At the end of the century, the search for mineral deposits was intense, and even the poorest altiplano communities had some mining activity. Gold was being panned in the Sorata region in the northeastern Cordillera valleys, and such communities as Berenguela just south of Lake Titicaca continued to develop as a small but important mine center. It was from among these highland small-time miners that the initiative came to settle the Uru Indian region just north of Lake Poopó. The whole region of the corregimiento of Paria, as it was then called, was filled with small mines, but in 1695 the very biggest mine of the area was discovered near the site of what would become the city of Oruro. The mine took the name of San Miguel and was soon producing vast quantities of fine silver ore.

The result of this discovery was to create a new silver rush among the highland miners from all the nearby small mine centers. It was the Pacajes region miners who supplied the capital and expertise to get these new mines in operation, and by the first decade of the new century the mining camp counted some 3,000 Indian workers and 400 resident Spaniards (or *vecinos*).

Without royal provisions for mita labor, the Oruro miners, like those elsewhere in these northern regions, had to rely on free wage labor. They began by offering wages of five *reales* per working period (*jornal*) for basic miners, and much higher wages of over one *peso* per day for skilled workers. Such wages were effective in quickly drawing a large free Indian labor force to the mines, but at the same time kept Oruro mine costs so high that production developed only slowly. In 1605 the local miners felt that the settlement had become important enough to obtain official status, and after much negotiation the town of Oruro was formally established in late 1606. From then until the 1680s the town grew at a rapid pace. By 1607 there were 30,000 inhabitants, of which 6,000 were Indian miners, and by the 1670s the town reached its maximum size of some 80,000 persons.

Despite this rapid growth, however, Oruro never rivaled the power of Potosí, as its production at best was no more than a fourth of the latter's output. Nevertheless the town and its mines quickly took on great significance. It became a crucial transit stop on the Lima-Arequipa-La Paz-Potosí route on the one hand and the chief highland port of entry for the vital mercury shipments on the other. Since the cheapest route for the Huancavelica-produced mercury to Potosí was that by sea from Lima to the Pacific coast port of Arica and then by mule to the highlands, Oruro turned out to be the closest highland city to the Arica port. Oruro was thus able to secure its mercury at more favorable terms than Potosí, and to obtain an important income from provisioning and financing the mercury shipments.

Just as important as its central location was Oruro's crucial development as the largest free mine labor center in all of Charcas. As long as its richest veins of minerals lasted, which was until late in the seventeenth century, the Oruro mines became a lodestone for free Indian laborers throughout the region and kept wages high elsewhere, to the bitter complaint of even the Potosí miners. Although the higher wages made shaft mining, when it came, an extremely expensive undertaking, it nevertheless provided the Indians with a welcome alternative to the harsher Potosí conditions. This combination of factors led to the establishment of a more permanent settlement, so the city quickly developed a lively and thriving cholo population. It also proved to be one of the more open and violent cities in the Charcas area, with mestizos reaching even the upper levels of power. Oruro became known as a relatively unruly place and one with a taste for political independence, which in the eighteenth century would lead to several important anti-royalist revolts.

In terms of its regional impact, Oruro tended to re-enforce the market patterns developed by Potosí. It too was forced to rely on lower Peruvian mercury production, and it generated the bulk of its labor force from among the Aymara highland Indians. Like Potosí, the majority of its foodstuffs came from eastern valley sources, though in this respect Oruro was even more heavily dependent on the nearby Cochabamba Valley system, which became the city's single most 'important producer of temperate and semi-tropical foodstuffs. Oruro replicated much of Potosí's market impact because it too was situated within an essentially poor and infertile agricultural zone, and thus forced to import virtually all of its basic necessities.

With the permanent establishment of Oruro, the basic period of Spanish settlement in the highlands and principal eastern valleys came to a close. Though the next century would see the growth and expansion of the eastern lowlands mission frontier, the core area of Charcas by the beginning of the seventeenth century was now fully defined. From then until the end of the seventeenth century there was a constant growth of the Spanish and cholo populations, accompanied by a slowing but still evident decline among the Indian populations.

This initial period of extraordinary urban expansion and unusual wealth, which lasted until the end of the seventeenth century, created with it a major cultural and artistic boom. For the riches pouring into such cities of the realm as Chuquisaca, Potosí, Oruro, and La Paz led to a massive construction of churches and cathedrals with the consequent growth of the plastic arts.

In the first century of the Conquest, the Spaniards brought their artists and artistic ideas with them. Spanish, Italian, and Flemish artisans, artists, and architects predominated in the sixteenth century, and many of them were priests. It was in the churches that the most advanced artistic ideas of colonial life were expressed, since the Europeans most conspicuously expended the great wealth they extracted from the mines and the Indians in the construction and adornment of their temples. An average-sized church took decades to construct and adorn and was often the most costly item of construction in the entire region. A large urban church or monastery could absorb hundreds of thousands of pesos and be equivalent to the total royal revenues of a given city.

Before 1600 major church construction and artistic activity were concentrated in the city of Chuquisaca, the administrative and religious capital of the region. In this first period the predominant influences were European, as mature artists were brought in directly from Europe to undertake the construction, painting, and sculpture desired by the colonials. The clerics—migrating for the needs of their various orders—were the most accessible and inexpensive artists at hand, though by the end of the first century non-clerics began arriving in large numbers. While Indians were taught the rudiments of all the plastic arts, since they formed the working class everywhere, it was the Europeans who provided all the initial models, ideas, and techniques. Given the fact that Spain itself was a major world artistic center for most of the sixteenth century, and a good part of the seventeenth as well, it was evident that the latest of European styles—filtered through Spanish concerns—would predominate in the colonies.

In the earlier part of the sixteenth century the architectural norms were determined by traditional Renaissance themes and ideas, while in the last two decades of the century there was a rise of Iberian Mudejar influences. In the plastic arts, influences were more varied, with Italian and Flemish styles of the period having a profound impact on the migrating artists. Given the wealth of Upper Peru, the altiplano cities were able to draw upon the most advanced artists coming to America, and soon the churches of Chuquisaca were being adorned by the same artists who were carrying out the artistic development of Lima and even of Sevilla. The most outstanding of these early artists working in Upper Peru was the Italian Jesuit Bernardo Bitti, one of the most original painters working in America in the sixteenth century. As was typical of such men, Bitti had developed his formative ideas in Europe, being much influenced by Michelangelo, and was to pass through all the major centers of population of both Perus from his arrival in the 1570s until his death in the first decade of the new century.

By the last two decades of the sixteenth century the dominance of

European and white artisans was being challenged by the appearance of the first Indian and cholo artisans. Sculpture was their first field of effort. Since wood and stone craftsmen were prevalent among the Indians from the beginning, and it was Indian workers and artisans who did all the basic church constructions under European direction, it was natural that they made their first impact in sculpture. The most important of these early Indian artists was the sculptor Tito Yupanqui of Copacabana. Trained by Europeans in the cities of Upper Peru, Yupanqui was famous for his rather original style and for the important sculpture he did of a Virgin for his native city of Copacabana, which became a cult figure for the entire region. Beginning with European forms, Yupanqui quickly developed his own style and created several important and innovative pieces for local churches.

As the seventeenth century arrived, there was a subtle but important shift of influences and origins among the artists and artisans of the region. With the incredible amount of religious and civil construction which had taken place, there had developed of necessity important workshops of Europeans who had needed to train Indian artisans to help them in their work. Once developed, these skills were readily salable in the Upper Peruvian market. Since the time needed for the full construction and adornment of a given church could take decades, either master artisans began projects and moved on to others, leaving their Indian assistants to complete their designs, or they died and could be replaced only by their assistants. Thus by the seventeenth century a new *"criollo"* (or native American) style developed by Indian and cholo artists and artisans would begin to emerge in the region.

While architecture and the plastic arts were undergoing a vital growth in the sixteenth and the early seventeenth century, the first century of Spanish rule was not a particularly fertile period for non-artistic intellectual endeavors. Charcas was still in many respects a rough mining frontier dominated by a nouveau-riche mentality. Thus its expressions of an intellectual "high culture" were left to priests and government officials, who in turn were primarily concerned with conversion and governance of the Indian population. Given the limited intellectual marketplace, Upper Peru did not obtain a printing press until the end of the colonial period, and its few authors were forced to send their works to Lima or Europe to be published.

Aside from the grammars and dictionaries of the Aymara and Quechua languages, the most important single work produced by a Charcas writer in the sixteenth century was undoubtedly the treatise on "Government in Peru" written by the *oidor* (or royal judge) of the Audiencia of Charcas, Juan de Matienzo, in 1567. A profound analysis of local Indian conditions and patterns of government, the Matienzo work was of fundamental importance in determining the shape of the Toledon reforms. Aside from Matienzo, however, there were few if any Charcas writers to compare with the contemporaneous group of Cuzco and Lima ethnographers and chroniclers. Upper Peruvians produced few works of any significance on pre-Columbian developments, in contrast with the extraordinary productivity of the Lower Peruvian writers of both Spanish and Indian background.

Rather, the Spanish writers of Upper Peru concentrated in the late sixteenth and the early seventeenth century on the writing of their own post-Conquest history. Missionaries wrote the histories of their respective provinces, or the histories of local shrines, the several written about Copacabana being the most important. Finally, the first of a famous series of chronicles was begun about the history of Potosí itself, with the most important of these early historians being Luis Capoche, who wrote in 1585.

It was this intense concern with the present and the future development of the region that most marked the writers of Upper Peru in the first century and a half of Spanish rule. This was also a period in which intensive colonization had occurred in response to the rising level of silver production. But the eventual crisis in silver production, which began to be felt in the middle decades of the seventeenth century, had an adverse effect on the economic, social, and political opportunities of the more recently arriving immigrants. This background of declining opportunities and increasing stratification helps explain the series of urban conflicts among the Spaniards which came to be known as the "civil wars" of the seventeenth century.

The most important of the new urban conflicts occurred in the heart of the export sector itself, the city of Potosí. The early seventeenth century was to prove a period of particularly intense conflicts among Spanish miners and merchants over the control of the mining industry, disputes which finally led to open warfare among the various factions. The most notorious of these conflicts involved a long and protracted series of violent confrontations between the Basques and all other Spaniards—known generically as *vicuñas* because of the type of clothing they wore—over control of the urban government of Potosí. This so-called civil war between *vascongados* and vicuñas occurred between 1622 and 1625 and essentially involved an attempt by the non-Basques to remove the entrenched group from their control over both the mines and the *cabildo,* or town government. Despite a fair amount of rioting, the total number of deaths was relatively small, and the end result was the retention of power by the traditional Basque miners.

But the increasing tension among the urban Spaniards, which involved similar power struggles in many of the other urban centers, was another indication of the seriousness of the long economic decline which was beginning to be felt by the middle decades of the century. Already the available resources were becoming exhausted, with the result that the stranglehold of key groups over those resources meant the elimination of opportunities for newly arriving but unconnected Europeans who wished to make their wealth. Having failed to dislodge the entrenched elites from their control over mines and Indians, newly arrived or poorer Spaniards would migrate from Upper Peru during the next century, and a long-term decline would begin in all the major urban centers. Thus the end of the first century of economic expansion was to be followed by a century-long period of depression which would have profound and long-term effects on both the urban and rural sectors of the Bolivian society and economy.

Chapter 3 • Late Colonial Society: Crisis and Growth

With the peaking of silver production by the middle decades of the seventeenth century, both at Oruro and more importantly at Potosí, a fundamental shift in the economic space and social organization began to occur within the overheated boom-like society that was Upper Peru. The most immediate impact of the precipitous decline in silver output, which would last for almost a century, was a steady fall in the population of the urban centers. This in turn would profoundly affect the regional supply networks and thus change the relative importance both of regions in the Upper Peruvian economy and of social and economic institutions such as the hacienda and the free community. Also the decline of Upper Peru was matched by the rise of Mexico as the new center of New World silver production, which accordingly changed the relative importance of the altiplano within the empire.

The dramatic decline in the cities was the first response to the silver mining depression. Both the number of miners and the number of townsmen fell sharply in the century from 1650 to 1750. The annual number of mitayos going to the mines fell from 13,500 or so Indians that were serving each year in Potosí in the 1570s to some 2,000 Indians by the 1690s. The decrease in mitayos was both a consequence of the diminishing pool of originarios in the sixteen "obligated" provinces—either through death or escape into forastero or yanacona status —and a shrinking in demand at the mines. The reduction in the labor market also seriously affected free Indian miners, most of whom returned to the countryside.

Among the whites, the depression had an equally profound impact. About 100,000 Spanish-speaking whites migrated out of the mine centers and away from the region seeking their fortune in more economically dynamic areas of the empire. In this century-long depression both Oruro and Potosí lost over half of their respective populations, with Potosí falling to just 30,000 persons and Oruro to some 20,000 by the middle of the eighteenth century. In fact every city, save La Paz, either lost population or stagnated in the depression period.

The contraction of population and of silver production led to a constriction of the extensive hinterland markets serving the mining centers. This was well illustrated in the fate of the important food-supplying region of Cochabamba. With the grain demands from Potosí lessened, it was found that the region around Chuquisaca was productive enough to supply most mining needs, so the more costly Cochabamba products were eliminated. Cochabamba thus exported less and less from its valleys and turned more toward a subsistence economy, exporting its surplus wheat and maize to the highlands only when the latter suffered severe local harvest crises. In turn, the end of significant exports meant the decline in the power of the Cochabamba hacendado class and the conversion of their large estates into smaller rented parcels. Since most of the free communities of Indians already had been replaced by landless laborers on the estates of the Spaniards, these parcelings led to the rise of a whole new group of largely cholo small farmers producing on rented properties. Cochabamba thus became the major center for small-scale, non-community, freehold-style farming and the most important region of minifundia agriculture in Upper Peru.

While the pattern of change was rather unique in the Cochabamba Valley, changes in land ownership were occurring throughout the

Charcas region. As production declined in response to declining urban and mining markets, haciendas went bankrupt and progressively lost their yanacona populations. In these cases, most landowners turned to either parcelization, outright sale, or abandonment of their estates. Thus the trend was for the total number of haciendas to decline, for all estates to lose workers, and for a consequent increase in the population of the free communities.

Whatever the local pattern, it was common to all regions that hacienda growth stopped completely. There was in fact a long-term trend toward retrenchment of haciendas until well into the late eighteenth century. This meant that challenges to the control of land by the free communities declined, and these in turn tended to expand at the expense of the private estates. This community expansion was re-enforced by population expansion, since the period of the great colonial silver depression in Upper Peru corresponded to the period of renewed growth in Indian population. It was only in the late seventeenth century, a good half-century after such a change in the lowland areas of South and Middle America, that the native Indian populations of the region finally showed themselves immune to the endemic European diseases and capable of surviving with a level of mortality little different from that of their European conquerors. This change did not occur until the last decades of the seventeenth century, but, once begun, there developed a long-term trend toward growth throughout the eighteenth and well into the nineteenth century, when epidemics would again become an important check on population expansion. But by then, there were new diseases such as cholera, which affected all classes. Until then, however, population growth in the rural areas was impressive, and this increase prompted a strengthening of the free community system.

Thus a combination of declining pressure on their lands and increasing population created a major period of growth for the free communities at the time of the urban and mining decline. This seemingly paradoxical situation is explained by the fact that the peasant populations always suffered greatly in the period of greatest prosperity for the mining centers. Mita labor obligations forced the Indian communi-

ties to subsidize the mine labor force and extracted even greater surpluses from the community, in addition to the already onerous taxation system. Equally the Crown controlled all the money incomes
going into the communities and forced these communities to grant
mortgage funds to the Spanish hacendados. These mortgages at 5 percent interest per annum proved difficult to collect and the Indian communities often found that they could neither obtain the interest due
them nor even recuperate their capital. With the temporary halt of
hacienda expansion, the need for such funds disappeared, and the
pressure on the *cajas* (or treasuries) of the communities declined, allowing them to retain more of their income.

Thus the high level of exploitation in the relationship between
Spaniards and Indians meant that the decline of the Spanish urban
populations and their market demands for labor and products ultimately benefited the peasants who now were able to keep a larger
share of their surplus production as well as retain more of their own
labor time. This in turn encouraged increasing production for interior
and regional markets and promoted traditional inter-ecological trading
and the growth of the non-Spanish market system. This growth was,
of course, relative, since the need to pay the tribute tax forced the
Indians to have constant recourse to the Spanish markets to obtain
money income. The dual market arrangements continued to function,
but with the emphasis shifting somewhat in favor of the local exchange
markets as opposed to the largely urban free markets where money was
the prime form of exchange.

Along with the comparative growth and decline of different populations and regional economies, there was also a relative shift in the importance of given districts within Upper Peru as a result of the silver
depression. With the contraction at Potosí had come a corresponding,
though less severe, decline of Chuquisaca. Retrenchment of Cochabamba Valley production led to a loss in its urban population, and
Oruro as well was considerably reduced. The city of La Paz, on the
other hand, seemed to have continued its steady if unspectacular
growth, so that by the end of the period of secular decline, that is,
sometime in the middle of the eighteenth century, La Paz emerged

with its 40,000 inhabitants as the most populous city in the entire region. The growth of La Paz at the time of the relative decline elsewhere can largely be attributed to the growth of the local Indian markets and production. With its hinterland of some 150,000 to 200,000 Indian peasants, La Paz thrived as a major administrative and market center both for the area's most densely populated highland zone as well as the thriving eastern Yungas valleys.

The mining crisis of the late seventeenth and early eighteenth century was thus far more than a temporary economic depression. It brought about long-term structural changes which were not reversed until late in the nineteenth century. Under Spanish rule, Upper Peru never recaptured the glory of its early colonial mining industry. Though silver production and exports would begin a long-term rise in the 1750s, and a prosperous industry would develop, peak production during this period reached no higher than 50 percent of late sixteenth-century output. For this reason, the late colonial silver boom was incapable of renovating the work force or the urban populations. The Upper Peruvian populations of Europeans and their supportive urban Indian and mestizo work force never revived. Production increased, but it did so on the basis of relatively stagnant urban populations, at least in the major mine centers. This would mean that the development of the late eighteenth-century mining industry, while important in reviving the regional economic ties of local producers, was unable to recapture fully the enormous pan-Andean market which had existed before the crisis. Cochabamba, for example, would never again be integrated as a producer for the Potosí market, as local production of Chuquisaca was sufficient to supply the grain needs of the mining population. Cochabamba therefore turned toward specialization in cloth production and, despite the dominance of agriculture in its economic life, primarily exported crude popular textiles (*tocuyo* cloth) from its central valley. Thus everywhere the linkages between local markets and the mining centers were now greatly reduced in importance or had disappeared altogether.

While the eighteenth century was to prove a relatively productive period for colonial Charcas, and one in which artistic and intellectual life was well developed, growth in the urban sectors and regional economies was very modest compared to the glories of the fifteenth and early sixteenth century. Moreover, in the total American production, Potosí was now a distinctly secondary source of silver output. Mexico early in the crisis of the seventeenth century had bypassed total Peruvian silver output, and that trend continued despite the modest renewal of Upper Peruvian mines after 1750. Though Potosí and Oruro, even in their reduced production, were still major sources of silver for the world market, they were no longer the dominant center even for America. In contrast to the Mexican mines, where the Crown was able to expatriate large quantities of bullion every year, the Peruvian mines generated enough taxes to pay only for the royal bureaucracy of the southern region of South America. After 1700 little bullion passed from Upper Peru to Spain.

The eighteenth century boom for Upper Peru was thus a relatively fragile and limited affair which would not survive a series of structural, market, and political problems that arose early in the nineteenth century. Limited as it was, however, Upper Peruvian mining still represented the region's single most important industry. Thus a major power struggle developed in the second half of the eighteenth century for control over the Audiencia of Charcas, which pitted the older merchant wealth of Lima and Cuzco against the rising power of the new merchant groups of Buenos Aires.

Beginning in the late sixteenth century, the port city of Buenos Aires had been finally settled, and a small but prosperous regional economy had begun to develop on the basis of local trade and a grazing industry. But this growth was quite limited, as Buenos Aires and its hinterland were unable to use its primary asset—its seaport and fast European connections—to promote its growth until the second half of the eighteenth century. While contraband certainly thrived in Buenos Aires, it was not until the Crown of Spain officially changed its policy toward open imperial trade that the real growth set in. With trade officially permitted between Buenos Aires and Europe on the one hand and Buenos Aires and the interior on the other, the growth of the region was phenomenal. Already by the end of the seventeenth century the Crown was showing interest in this growth potential by forcing Potosí to send an annual subsidy (*subsidio*) to Buenos Aires to help defray local administrative costs and to sustain its long-term conflicts against Portuguese incursions into the Rio de la Plata estuary.

Then in 1776 the Crown decided the growing conflict between Buenos Aires and Lima for control over trade to Potosí in favor of the former. Upper Peru and the Audiencia government were placed under the direct control of Buenos Aires, which now became a new and independent viceroyalty. In 1778 this control was re-enforced when most of the trade restrictions for the Buenos Aires Viceroyalty were removed. These political decisions were crucial in shifting the preponderance of Potosí trade from the northerly direction toward a southerly one. Whereas previously the southern route had involved only imports, from the northern Argentine towns, of mules and food-stuffs, and from Paraguay of yerba mate, Potosí now slowly turned its whole export system southward and opened up a major new exporting route all the way through its traditional northern Argentine satellite towns in the Tucuman district toward the sea at Buenos Aires.

The reorganization of the economic space of Upper Peru and its connections to the outer world meant a consequent decline of Lima. No longer did Lima merchants hold a monopoly over Charcas's trade with Europe, nor was it any longer its single major source of capital. This decline in trade dominance to their mining hinterland brought in a long-term decay of Lima's economic power. This decay, in turn, allowed the growth of alternative regional centers of economic power. The most powerful of the new centers was, of course, Buenos Aires. But the relatively marginal captaincy of Chile would also find the potential for growth developing rapidly at the expense of the former Lima monopoly. Thus the reorganization of Upper Peru's trade links to Europe, would in fact both reflect long-term changes in the relative economic and political power of different South American regions and help foster these trends to such an extent that the power of Peru itself, and to a lesser extent, Upper Peru, would now be much reduced, to be replaced by new and now more dynamic areas such as Chile and, above all, the Rio de la Plata.

All of these trends would, of course, continue well beyond the eighteenth century and have important consequences for the relative position and power of the post-colonial regimes. But in the early decades of the eighteenth century such long-term changes were only beginning. Moreover, the Crown in creating the new viceroyalty, hoped in fact to stimulate further the export economy of Upper Peru. Thus the Audiencia of Charcas was soon staffed by a group of extremely able administrators with unusually broad backgrounds, whose efforts were primarily directed toward reviving the silver-mining industry of Oruro and Potosí by whatever means possible. As would be evident from later developments, it was quite clear that the silver veins were still plentiful in the Upper Peruvian minefields. But they were now to be found at much deeper levels, most often below the local water tables, and were more often found in mixtures with other metals and at lower quality per unit of crude ore than they had been in the early period. The collapse of silver production had more to do with the exhaustion of richer and more easily accessible surface and near-surface deposits than it did with the exhaustion of mineral deposits themselves.

To get at this next level of silver ore large capital expenditures would have to be made, and the local mining industry of Upper Peru was incapable of generating that amount of capital. Therefore it was essential that the Crown provide the financial support necessary to open up deeper shaft mining. The Crown finally recognized this need in the eighteenth century. In 1736 it agreed to lower its tax share from 20 percent to 10 percent of total output, a decision made much earlier in Mexico. Next, it assisted in the creation of a minerals purchasing bank, the Banco de San Carlos, which was established by the smelters in 1751. The bank's direct purchase of refined silver eliminated private silver merchants (*rescatadores*), thus guaranteeing high prices to smelters (*azogueros*) and miners and, even more importantly, providing credit for purchasing mine supplies. In short, it brought order into the chaos of the local capital market. When the bank went into a severe crisis in the 1770s, it had become such an important institution that the Crown was forced to take it over and directly support its functions. Finally, the Crown not only reorganized the mercury trade after the collapse of the Huancavelica production in the 1770s, and brought in major shipments from Almaden in Spain via the port of Buenos Aires, but it subsidized the price as well. In 1784 the price of mercury to the local miners was reduced by almost a fifth.

While the population of Potosí continued its decline, going from an estimated 70,000 persons in the 1750s to some 35,000 in the 1780s, production slowly began to revive after 1730, especially after the systematic assistance granted by the Crown. After some debate, the mita, now much reduced to some 2,500 mitayos per annum, was nevertheless maintained and strengthened, and still provided a crucial labor base for the miners. For, despite their severe decline in numbers, by the end of the eighteenth century the mitayos still represented close to one-half of the underground shaft miners and thus still made the crucial difference between profit and loss in the Potosí mines.

Supported by royal grants and forced labor, the Upper Peruvian miners were able to foster steady growth in mine output in the late eighteenth century. However, despite the tax structure and the increasing exaction of labor and savings from the free communities, the agricultural sector of the economy was booming from the late seventeenth century to the end of the colonial period. Thus, just as Potosí was no longer the dominant American mining center, even within its local economic environment its role was somewhat reduced by the growth of an active and powerful agricultural sector which was based on an increasingly expanding peasant population. While this agricultural sector was limited to the regional and Andean markets, its activity was lively enough to provide the Crown with a growing income in the form of commercial taxes and above all the Indian head tax. This tribute tax by the end of the eighteenth century was the second leading source of royal income in the Audiencia of Charcas district.

The increased role of tribute income was due to essentially three separate phenomena which occurred in the eighteenth century. The first and obviously most important factor was the long-term positive growth trend in the rural population which began after 1700. Secondly, the reduction of exploitation of the rural population as a result of the mining crisis had enabled the free communities to recoup their resources and to develop further their local production. Finally, the tribute tax was extended to all Indian males regardless of their land access status, and this in turn profoundly altered the burdens and the extension of the entire tribute taxation system.

Since much of the agricultural produce Indians traded among themselves or produced for local regional markets was exempted from taxation, the Crown was forced to rely on its tribute tax as the primary mechanism both to force the Indians into the Spanish markets and to provide the Crown with direct income. But given the tax laws, the Crown was exclusively taxing the originario members of the communities, and despite the general growth of Indian rural populations, the number of originarios either remained unchanged or declined. This failure of the originarios to grow along with all other Indian groups was obviously related to the fact that mita and tax obligations rendered the originario status less than profitable for all but the very few wealthiest peasants. Even the Crown recognized that it was destroying the legal class of originarios to its own detriment, and in 1734 finally accepted the advice of local royal officials and extended the head tax to include all Indians.

Maintaining its recognition of local distinctions, the Crown now provided a fixed tax of five pesos per annum for all forasteros living in the communities and yanaconas living on the estates of the Spaniards. While the former were required to pay their own tax, the latter had their tribute tax paid for them by the Spanish landowner, which was another inducement for encouraging rural labor to migrate to the haciendas. In both cases, however, the new extension of the tribute tax to all rural Indians increased royal tribute income by some one-half to two-thirds in the years that followed and also stabilized the originario class, as the advantages of changing status were no longer so great as they had been in the period prior to 1734.

With the tax burden more evenly spread and with taxes remaining relatively fixed, the increasing population in the rural area was better able to handle the state and private extraction of its surplus and to survive and prosper to some extent. Equally, while the Crown maintained the mita as an institution vital to the prosperity of the silver-mining region, it did not increase the number of mitayos by making the forasteros or yanaconas subject to this obligation; thus the regional weight of mita obligation remained much reduced from its sixteenth and seventeenth century burden.

With mita obligations less oppressive, the Indians also were less bothered by the haciendas. Though the mining revival had increased demand on the local urban markets, that demand was met by bringing in marginally productive haciendas or reviving production on the better estates. It brought little major expansion in the hacienda system, which appeared to remain relatively stable throughout the eighteenth century. Thus, the growing Indian population did not find themselves dealing with the problems of massive hacienda encroachment.

But despite the relative relaxation of exploitation of the expanding rural Indian peasant population, that population remained bitterly opposed to its overlords. The unending exactions of local corregidores and hacendados, the demands of local corvée labor obligations which often went for private Spanish interests rather than state concerns, and the steady taxation which constantly forced all Indians into the marketplace were thoroughly resented. Moreover, the local kurakas found themselves being constantly attacked in their own privileges and exploited by the Spaniards and were forced to the wall to defend their increasingly eroding leadership position. Finally, the more literate and cultured Church of the eighteenth century was equally as opposed to non-Christian activity as the Church ideologues of the previous centuries had been, and there was a never-ending attack on local religious belief systems that forced the Indians to defend themselves constantly.

It was this complex of factors which helps to explain the massive Indian rebellion which occurred in Upper Peru and the Cuzco area in 1780, at the height of the eighteenth-century expansion and economic and social revival. Such Indian uprisings in the rural area, or urban mestizo and criollo uprisings in the cities, as represented by the Great Rebellion of 1780-82, were not new to Upper Peru or to the Spanish empire. Local community or even provincial uprisings occurred periodically in Upper Peru throughout the colonial period. Usually responses to immediate local causes, these rebellions most often took place among the free communities because of the abusive taxing of a local corregidor who went beyond the usual norms of exploitation, because of conflicts over land with non-Indians, or, most importantly of all, because of local interference in the appointment of local kurakas by the Spaniards. In the urban areas such rebellions were also common, ranging from local subsistence riots in times of crisis and food hoardings, to protests against local taxes or royal officials. Such movements or conspiracies had occurred in Oruro and in Cochabamba in the 1730s.

But all of these endemic revolts were usually short-lived and quite local affairs which wanted nothing so much as temporary relief of taxes or elimination of corrupt officials. "Long Live the King and Death to Bad Governors" was the traditional appeal of these revolts. Such movements were an essential part of local government and were recognized by all as a more or less normal outlet for local protest. This did not mean that suppression could not be quite violent and lead to extensive killings. It was evident that, unlike comparable situations in Europe, such riots in the face of the general oppression of Indian masses provoked more violent responses from the authorities than might have otherwise been the case. But the pattern of such movements was well known, so the government never felt itself severely threatened in its ultimate power by such typical local protests.

In this respect, the great Túpac Amaru rebellion of 1780-82 was in fact a profound and fundamental departure from the norm. It was massive in its participation and its extension. Probably encompassing over 100,000 rebel troops in all its activities, the rebellion involved relatively well-coordinated activity from the highlands of southern Peru in the Cuzco area, through all of Upper Peru, into the highlands of northern Argentina. It was a multi-class, multi-caste, and extremely well-led revolt which ultimately had as its aim the establishment of an autonomous region under control of the local classes to the exclusion of all Spaniards. It was, in short, an independence movement.

The rebellion had its preparations well before November 1780, its official opening, in the contact which its able leader, Túpac Amaru, had with all the leading kurakas of Charcas and southern Peru. A direct descendant of the Incas and a leading kuraka in the Bishopric of Cuzco, Túpac Amaru was a well-educated and literate member of the Indian noble class. Given the legitimacy of his background and his own undoubted intellect, he was able to convince the overwhelming majority of the Quechua and Aymara kurakas that Spanish rule had to be destroyed.

As the rebellion developed, there were essentially two major phases. The first was the actual rebellion led by Túpac Amaru himself, who seized most of the province of Cuzco and besieged its capital city from November 1780 to March 1781. Involving large numbers of troops on both sides, the siege of Cuzco was eventually broken by the local Spaniards, and Túpac Amaru and his immediate entourage were captured by the latter date.

But the execution of its leader did not stop the massive revolt from spreading, nor dissident local leaders from joining the rebellion. The second phase of the rebellion began just as the Cuzco activity was being crushed and took place largely in Upper Peru. In January 1781 Tomás Catari, a powerful kuraka who had been denied his office by the local corregidor, rose up in rebellion in the southern mining province of Chayanta near Potosí. Then in March the nephew of Túpac Amaru, Andres, conquered the entire province of Larecaja along the eastern shore of Lake Titicaca in the region of La Paz and after a three-month siege took the provincial capital of Sorata in August 1781, killing all the Spaniards. He then marched on the regional capital of La Paz and began a formal siege. Here he was joined by the local leader Julian Apaza, one of the very few non-kuraka leaders of the rebellion, who had decided to adopt the combined names of the two leading rebels and called himself Túpac Catari. The two carried out together a siege of the city of La Paz, which lasted until late in the year when troops from Buenos Aires finally succeeded in breaking it and capturing Túpac Catari.

In the meantime, in February 1781, a criollo urban revolt had begun in Oruro, led by Jacinto Rodriguez. The rebels, who were closely allied with Túpac Amaru, succeeded in seizing the city from the peninsular Spaniards. This was the most powerful mestizo and criollo support that the Indian kurakas received, and Oruro was the largest Spanish city ever taken by the rebels. Though Rodriguez worked closely with the local kurakas, the alliance between Indians, mestizos, and American-born whites or criollos was not an easy one as class differences quickly made themselves felt. Here, as elsewhere, the royal forces eventually seized the town, and the rebels were executed.

The final group that joined the rebellion were mestizo artisans in the southern town of Tupiza who killed the local corregidor in March 1781. But this was the movement most easily suppressed. It had only a quite local impact and short existence.

By the end of 1781 the rebellion had been crushed in most rural areas, and all captured cities were again in the hands of the Spaniards. The rebel leaders were executed in the usual brutal manner, and there was a massive confiscation of property. All rebel kurakas were removed from office, and thenceforth most of the free communities in the central zones of the rebellion were controlled by Spaniards, who now took the title of kurakas. This was the effective deathblow for the kuraka class in Upper Peru. Following the rebellion of 1780-82, the Indian noble class ceased to be a major factor in the social, economic, and political life of the region.

The destruction of human life and property during the rebellion had been massive, especially around La Paz and the Lake Titicaca region. But general economic and demographic growth—quite pronounced in this decade—enabled most of the haciendas to be rebuilt by the end of the 1780s. Thus, in the immediate years after the revolt, local documents described the massive loss of farm implements, animals, and workers on abandoned haciendas, but by the end of the decade almost all of these haciendas were again operating at normal capacity and attained the same level of wealth that they had had prior to the revolt. The population losses were also soon made up, and by the 1790s most of the former rebel territory contained population densities equal to the pre-rebellion period.

Despite its massive and far-reaching impact and its extraordinarily broad mobilization, the Túpac Amaru rebellion was soon a distant memory in the minds of the population of Upper Peru. It was also the last attempt to bring both social justice and independence to the region prior to the nineteenth century. Later rebellions and the ultimate winning of independence would finally come from the criollos and would be distinctly upper-class and largely non-Indian affairs. Thus the Túpac Amaru rebellion, despite its actual and symbolic importance, had little lasting impact on Upper Peru and represented the last great effort of the Indian nobility to give their people freedom and justice.

The rapid recovery of Upper Peru from the effects of the Túpac Amaru rebellion had a great deal to do with the successful impact of the Bourbon reforms of the economy which originated in Spain in the middle decades of the eighteenth century. The reforms of the mining economy soon brought a renewed prosperity to Oruro and Potosí production, and a general reform of the commercial structure led to a healthy rivalry between Lima and Buenos Aires for the trade of the Audiencia of Charcas. This in turn opened up a second set of economic networks and trading systems which increased the general tempo of commercial and market activity on the altiplano and the associated eastern valleys. Finally, to bring some order to its political structure, and thus to bring the administration in line with the more advanced policies of freer trade and open competition, the Crown carried out a major administrative reorganization.

The symbol of this new governmental structure was the creation of a new local administrator known as the intendant. Modeled upon the institution which had such success in France, the colonial American intendants effectively superseded the old corregidores and created jurisdictions which now encompassed both Spanish and Indian territories under one regional administration. In 1784 four such intendancy districts were established in Upper Peru (or Charcas), covering the regions of La Paz, Cochabamba, Potosí, and Chuquisaca. These new officials were very highly paid and thus independent of the need to engage in local commerce as had the old corregidores in order to obtain funding. They were also carefully selected from among experienced administrators throughout the empire, and their primary function was seen as being promoters of regional economic and social growth.

This careful process of selection and the well-endowed salaries given to the new officials resulted in the creation of an extraordinary corps of literate and sophisticated administrators who governed Upper Peru in the last two decades of the eighteenth century. Such figures as Francisco Viedma in Cochabamba and Juan del Pino Manrique in Potosí were outstanding among these new officials. Concerned with reviving trade, experimenting with agriculture, promoting general well-being, and increasing royal revenues, these men have left behind wonderfully detailed memorials on the life and times of the peoples whom they governed. They also appear to have examined all the major issues related to the problems of a social and economic nature in their areas and provided detailed debates on alternative strategies. To these intendants should be added the rather unusual roving *oidor extraordinario* of the Audiencia of Charcas, Pedro Cañete. Jurist, historian, and administrative investigator, Cañete examined and legislated on the mining industry, the government's tax structure, the issue of the mita, and even the relationship between the Crown and the Church. Often he engaged in bitter disputes with the intendants, the results of which provided even more detailed memorials on the state of society. Viedma, Pino Manrique, Cañete, and the other intendants represented well eighteenth-century enlightenment thought and brought to Upper Peru both a new administrative structure and a new sense of leadership and development potential.

This new government concern with the colonial economy did lead to increased trade and commerce. Francisco Viedma of Cochabamba, for example, spent a great deal of energy promoting regional growth and seemed to have played an important role in breaking the pattern of stagnation which Cochabamba had suffered since the seventeenth-century crisis. By the end of the century Cochabamba became a major Peruvian manufacturer of rough textiles (*tocuyo*) and was again being integrated into larger regional markets. As for the mining industry, the Crown's constant intervention in local affairs produced an ever-increasing subsidy of private miners with everything from guaranteed mercury supplies to support of the minerals' purchasing bank, which became a formal royal institution in the 1770s. All this activity, along with booming trade throughout the Spanish-American empire, produced a major growth in regional trade and population, if not a complete revival of the silver mining glory of the previous epoch.

Thus the Túpac Amaru disaster was relatively easily absorbed by the Upper Peruvian economy, and within three or four years of the rebellion treasury income was equal to pre-conflict levels, and most of the rural hacienda system which had been destroyed was completely restructured and recapitalized. But whatever the long-term effects of governmental subsidization, freer trade, and general economic growth may have been, not all classes or groups benefited equally. Thus, despite all reforms, and the change of their names, the Crown still retained the oppressive system of local corregidores de indios (now called sub-intendants) in the Indian areas, and these men still actively exploited their Indian subjects through the usual processes of forced sales, intervention in the election of officials and selection of kurakas, and periodic shakedowns of community officials. Moreover, the increasing accuracy of the government census, established on a modern basis in 1786, meant an increasing impact of the more effectively collected tribute tax on all Indian male heads of household, and a more efficient registration of mita laborers. Although general growth softened somewhat the impact of the old tax structure, the more efficient government administration canceled out these gains by collecting the revenues more systematically, while at the same time leaving untouched the old exploitative mechanisms.

The patterns of decline and renewed growth which were evident in seventeenth- and eighteenth-century Upper Peru were to have their influence on the patterns of artistic activity as well. Whereas the first major urban construction and massive artistic adornment had occurred in the city of Chuquisaca from its foundation until about 1650, in the second half of the century, the city of La Paz and its hinterland became the new area of church construction, with Potosí following closely behind. The late start of this latter city was due to the initial commitment of the local elite to more prosaic construction in Potosí and to more refined architectural investments in the nearby city of Chuquisaca. By the second half of the century, however, just as its production was going into long-term decline, Potosí finally got around to developing an urban center of some distinction.

This new period of artistic expression not only occurred in a new geographic setting, but also reflects certain fundamental changes in style and organization. Stylistically, the period from approximately 1650 to 1700 is dominated in Upper Peru by baroque themes, then much in vogue in Spain itself. But the artists who developed this style were more likely to have been born locally, even if they were white. The great age of the immigration of artists from European centers was drawing to a close, and there existed enough local workshops and experts to supply local needs, with only the occasional European priest to give the latest news of styles and changes. Moreover, among the American-born artists, there appeared Indians and cholos even as painters, a field, like architectural design, that had been an exclusively European-controlled occupation until that time.

In the field of painting, there was so much intense activity in the seventeenth and eighteenth centuries that one can distinguish several different "schools" at work. There was first the abundant "popular" school of Indian and mestizo artists whose paintings were usually unsigned and lacked perspective. This anonymous group of popular artists were often sculptors and masons as well as part-time painters, and they left works everywhere in Upper Peru, even in the best cathedrals. By the eighteenth century these popular painters were beginning to merge with one of the formal "schools"—that of the Colla—or artists of the La Paz and Lake Titicaca region. The other two formal schools, whose artists signed their works and used standard perspectives, were those of Chuquisaca—where mannerist styles coming from the works of Bitti were the norm—and Potosí, which tended to stress the current Spanish interests. While the fifty or so artists who signed their paintings seemed initially to be defined as a different class and group, the increasing sophistication of popular artists and the increasing influence of mestizo styles on the more professional elite led in the late eighteenth century to a virtual blending of popular, Colla, and the important Cuzco styles into a quite distinctive Upper Peruvian criollo or mestizo style.

Whereas the Chuquisaca school had flourished in the first century of Spanish settlement, the Potosí and Colla schools were to predominate in the period from 1650 to the end of the colonial period. Of the two, it was the Potosí school that was most influential and powerful in the 1650-1750 period. Just as the economic crisis was at its worst in the city, Potosí began a massive construction of churches and public buildings and also supported the most prominent colonial school of painters. The most outstanding of these Potosí painters, and the greatest of the colonial period, was Melchor Pérez de Holguín, who was born in Cochabamba in the 1660s and arrived in Potosí to begin his career in the early 1690s. From the last decade of the century until well into the 1720s, Holguín was the dominant painter in Potosí and spread his art through all the regular and secular churches, along with important private commissions for non-religious persons. A classic baroque stylist of extraordinary ability, Holguín had an enormous output which was to be found in all the major churches of the city and whose style soon influenced many of the other leading painters.

As for the Colla school of painting which also flourished after 1650, its primary center was not to be found in one of the provincial capitals, as with the schools of Chuquisaca and Potosí, but in a traditional peasant rural zone, most particularly the area around Lake Titicaca. This region was one of the primary centers of agricultural activity in Upper Peru and the heartland of Aymara settlement. The fact that churches of major artistic achievement were constructed in these small peasant villages, especially those which made up the provinces of Chuquitos (temporarily a part of Upper Peru), Pacajes, and Omasuyos, would seem to imply the existence of unheard-of wealth for rural and primarily Indian Upper Peru in this time of generalized crisis in the mining export industry. The existence of this wealth suggests the relative decline in the level of exploitation of the traditional free communities of this zone; the Indians in this area were thus able to retain their savings, which in turn were now available for investments in a major program of construction and artistic activity—almost all of it related to Church activity. That many of the artists in the Colla school were Indians and mestizos also implies an increasing specialization of labor in these areas, and this supports the idea of a relatively thriving rural economy which could permit such full-time artists to develop.

By the second half of the eighteenth century the pattern of artistic and architectural activity again shifted somewhat, as a generalized mestizo art style came to dominate most of the painting of the region, with the Colla and popular schools essentially melding together and the other two schools reduced in importance. Furthermore, in architecture as well, the baroque style largely ended by mid-century, and was replaced, as in Spain, by a neo-classical movement. Construction of these new-style churches predominated in Cochabamba and in Chuquisaca, which again became major centers of activity in the last days of the Audiencia, while the cathedrals of La Paz and Potosí were also built in this style.

Although art and architecture were somewhat tamed by the neo-classical movement, apparently sculpture in wood and stone and worked silver retained the extraordinary vigor of the so-called "mestizo-baroque" style until the end of the colonial period, with the Indian and mestizo artisans becoming dominant in these skills by the eighteenth century. In this mestizo style the themes of the baroque remained—mythic sirens, grotesque masks, and grotesques—along with pre-Renaissance Christian traditions. But now were added typical American flora and fauna as well as pre-Columbian motifs and figures.

Whereas the arts flourished in Upper Peru from the beginning and achieved extraordinary quality in all areas, the field of letters was very under-developed even by Latin American standards. There was some minor church music, most of which has not survived. There was some theater, including a vigorous religious and historical theater written in Quechua and Aymara by Spanish clerics desiring to spread the faith among the Indians. But there was little serious poetry and no major theatrical work of distinction that has survived. Even in historical and philosophical works, Upper Peru was a relatively backward area even in relation to Cuzco, let alone to the rest of America, until well into the eighteenth century. And in science the only major work of distinction remains the isolated classic by the parish priest Alonso Barba, the "Art of Metals," written in 1640, the most important metallurgical study composed in America in the seventeenth century.

But this relative backwardness of letters changed somewhat in the eighteenth century as the region seemed to partake more of the mainstream of ideas and developments experienced in the rest of the American colonies of Spain. Several major historians now appear, the most prominent of them being Bartolomé Orsúa y Vela, whose history of Potosí in 1724 was a major study, and Pedro Cañete, whose work on Potosí in the second half of the century was extremely important. There also appeared a group of famous statesmen who provided significant studies of the functioning of colonial society, with Cañete being the most prominent, along with such enlightenment writers as the intendants Francisco Viedma and Juan del Pino Manrique and the protector of the Indians, Victorián de Villava. Finally, the German-born scientist Tadeo Haenke spent most of his adult life in the region, recording its flora and fauna late in the century.

The university life at Chuquisaca also seems to have been quite vigorous by the eighteenth century, and many of the early memorialists and pamphleteers of the nineteenth-century independence movement received their education there. But on the whole in these areas, the output was quite limited. Neither the academy nor private individuals appear to have created a significant body of literature in any of the humanistic or scientific disciplines. Given the relative wealth of Upper Peru and the long tradition and regional importance of its university center at Chuquisaca, this lack of a more substantial output is difficult to explain. Factors that clearly must have influenced this output were the very low rate of literacy, and the very limited number of Spanish speakers within the entire population, which in turn delayed the introduction of a printing press until late in the eighteenth century. Clearly, Spanish remained a distinctly minority language throughout the colonial period and well into the next two centuries. But in the only form where language was unimportant, the arts, the Upper Peruvians flourished with an extraordinary creativity and output, marking the colonial period of Upper Peru as one of the great artistic eras in world history. The fact that this art was created by many Indians and mestizos along with Europeans also suggests that it was the only form of creative intellectual and cultural expression fully open to all persons within the colonial society, and therefore the form in which the greatest possible creativity was expressed without fear of racial oppression or class control.

Despite the important growth of the colonial economy in the period after 1750, which permitted a continuation of a very active period of new church and public construction throughout the highland cities, the Upper Peruvian economy was to show itself to be still very much affected by the long seventeenth-century crisis. It was to prove, in fact, extremely vulnerable to short-term changes in international market conditions, which in turn showed that the mining economy had relatively little reserve capacity to weather temporary trade crises or a weakening of governmental support.

This vulnerability became evident in the first decades of the new century. By the late 1790s the mercury supplies for Potosí were no longer coming from the defunct Huancavelica mines but were being shipped directly from the royal Almaden mines in Spain. The beginnings of the great international conflict known as the Napoleonic wars would soon lead to direct Spanish involvement, and a bitter dispute with England in 1796 led to open warfare between the two states and the effective disruption of Spain's sea routes to America. For Upper Peru this meant the halt of mercury deliveries and thus an immediate drop in local smelting. More important, the sudden collapse of the international trade routes created a temporary but quite severe depression in commercial markets in general with a consequent credit squeeze in the colonies. This in turn suddenly left the miners with little capital to maintain their costly enterprises, and, as a result, a rapid decline in production set in.

By the first years of the new century there was a general crisis in the mining sector, with production plummeting. Then, with its export sector severely reduced, Upper Peru was struck by a major series of harvest failures and epidemics between 1803 and 1805 which had a profound impact on both rural populations and regional markets. Thus, by the time of the French invasion of Spain in 1808, the Upper Peruvian economy was in a general state of depression, and the population was suffering from a temporary but severe loss of life. These conditions created an extremely tense atmosphere both in the rural areas and even more in the reduced urban centers.

Chapter 4 • Revolution and the Creation
of a Nation-State, 1809-1841

The nineteenth century began for Upper Peru with a severe long-term depression which was to have a profound effect on its literate urban populations and its mining export economy. This decline and the serious agricultural crises which erupted in the countryside in this same decade form a crucial background to the region's response to the collapse of the imperial government in Madrid. In late 1806 and all of 1807 Napoleon's armies slowly invaded Spain and eventually forced the abdication of the Bourbon monarchy. In May 1808 the Madrid populace rose up in revolt against the new French-controlled Spanish government, and the rebels eventually established a formal resistance structure which proclaimed itself to be the legitimate government of the Bourbons. Known as the Junta Central, and controlling part of southern Spain, the rebel regime claimed legitimacy, despite the abdication of Ferdinand VII, and demanded loyalty from the colonial viceroyalties. Such a situation of divided government had occurred once before in imperial history at the very beginning of the eighteenth century when the Bourbons and Hapsburgs had contended for control over Spain and fought a long and bitter conflict for the monarchy on Spanish soil. But at that time the colonies were passive and allowed all basic decisions about the fate of Spain and the empire to be made in Europe.

In 1808, however, the world was a different place. The two independence movements of former colonies, Haiti and the United States, had a profound impact on changing the dependent concepts of colonial American thinking. Moreover, the United States and England, both major powers, now provided both financial support for potentially rebellious movements, as well as places of refuge. But most important of all, Europe itself no longer possessed the same stable monarchic structure as had existed during the early eighteenth-century War of Spanish Succession: in 1789 the French Revolution had unleashed a new ideology and movement so unsettling that it affected every monarchy on the Continent and suddenly made republican governments a viable alternative.

The American colonies of Spain were not unaware of all of these developments, as the many small plots and revolts throughout the hemisphere showed. The ideology of the so-called "Atlantic Revolutions" spread throughout the Americas in the 1790s and the first decade of the new century. But the stability of the Spanish-American empire was such that the royal bureaucracy had little difficulty in suppressing these movements. In this activity, the bureaucracy was heavily supported by the white and mestizo classes because of their fears of potentially destructive social revolutions which might occur should the Indians be allowed entrance into the political debates of the whites or permitted to determine the fate of governments. In this respect, the Haitian experience was a warning not only to the slave societies of America but equally to those who lived off the labor of an exploited Indian peasant mass.

The disastrous collapse of the Spanish monarchy and the rise of a semi-popular revolutionary government in Spain created enormous problems for the local elites. They were suddenly confronted with several conflicting authorities, and each local group had to make fundamental decisions as to who could best guarantee its own legitimacy and stability. To the new monarchy of Joseph Napoleon in Madrid was now added a Junta government in the name of the abdicated Ferdinand VII; and another potential monarch was Ferdinand's sister Carlota, who arrived in Brazil in 1808 as the wife of the Portuguese monarch and who attempted as well to claim the allegiance of the American empire. Finally, with Spain in disarray and under French control, and with its European allies quickly succumbing to the armies of Napoleon, the English turned their energies toward their traditional interest in imperial expansion beyond Europe. They began providing strong support for potential revolutionaries and even to make plans for the formal invasion of Spanish America.

The arrival of the disturbing news from Spain slowly spread an ambience of crisis and indecision throughout the Americas in the months of July, August, and September. In each case the local royal officials were forced to make a series of unpalatable decisions. They also had to decide who should take part in the decision-making process. In most cases audiencias and governors or bishops made the decision for the status quo, which they defined as a wait-and-see attitude, with preference being given for the Junta government which was slowly retreating toward the peninsula of Cadiz. A few called open meetings of the citizenry (*cabildos abiertos*) to sound out local elite opinion as to which course of action should be taken. And a few decided to support actively either the French or Carlota's pretensions.

The divided loyalties, the threatening news, and the indecision of local officials created an extremely confusing and potentially conflictive ambience throughout the Americas, and in no area were all the Creole and Spanish-born elites fully content with any particular solution. This climate was conducive to local power struggles, conflicts between individual governors and their audiencias or bishops, and between these royal officials and the local municipal councils.

This background explains many of the strange events which took place in Upper Peru in 1808 and 1809. The region became the first area in Spanish America to be severely disturbed by all the conflicts developing in the imperial and international scene, and the first center of an independence movement. Partly because of its isolation from the sea, partly because it still formed an independent zone of economic power between two conflictive viceroyalties—those of Lima and Buenos Aires—and partly because of its traditional autonomy, the ferment of differing groups was allowed to develop for quite some time before being suppressed.

The first problems of control began with the arrival of the news of the Spanish crisis, which reached Upper Peru in September 1808. Immediately there developed a conflict between the Archbishop and the President of the Audiencia, on the one side, who demanded affiliation with the Junta Central, and the judges of the Audiencia, who refused to recognize the Junta's authority. Tensions grew quickly, and in late May the President of the Audiencia, Leon Pizarro, was seized by the independent judges, who feared their own imprisonment, and forced to flee the city. Though the Potosí intendent Francisco Paula Sanz opposed the movement, he offered no immediate resistance, so the semi-rebel judges proceeded to send emissaries seeking the support of the other cities. Despite the tensions and some limited mob action, the whole affair up to this time was confined to the bureaucracy and was almost exclusively a Spanish *peninsulares* affair.

This was not the case with the popular revolt which now occurred in the northern city of La Paz. On the sixteenth of July, also in 1809, popular unrest among the city's vecinos, many of whom included convinced revolutionaries, led to demands that an open town meeting be called to make some basic decisions about which regime to support. The fact that the local elite was demanding the right to make its own decisions on these events independent of what the central Audiencia bureaucracy had decided in Chuquisaca well reflected the growing power of La Paz itself. Now the largest city in Upper Peru, it based its authority on the wealth and population of its own agricultural hinterland and was relatively immune to the crises affecting the southern mining centers. It was now beginning to feel resentment toward southern domination, and thus the conflicts in both Spain and Chuquisaca provided an excellent opportunity for the local elite to express its own version of independence.

Being in direct contact with the representative of the rebel-like Audiencia, the local leaders in La Paz decided to go all out and carry through a full-scale revolution. Under the leadership of a vecino by the name of Pedro Domingo Murillo, the rebels seized the local governor and the Bishop of La Paz and declared themselves a *Junta Tuitiva*. They immediately voiced their opposition to the Junta regime of Spain and proclaimed an independent American government in the name of Ferdinand VII—a classic ploy used by all the later rebellious leaders in America to legitimate their independence movements.

This was the first declaration of independence by an American colony of Spain. It was to initiate the long period of American Wars of Independence, which would last from 1809 to 1825. But it proved only a short-lived revolt. The "shout" of independence by the rebel leaders of La Paz found no immediate echo among the Indians, nor positive response from the other urban Creole elites. Upon news of the revolt, the Viceroy of Lima ordered immediate reprisals and sent the President of the Audiencia of Cuzco, Goyeneche, to La Paz with 5,000 troops to suffocate the movement. Murillo and his supporters, for their part, were able to organize a local army of some 1,000 poorly armed men. But at this point Murillo and some of his co-conspirators grew concerned with the direction that the new Junta government was taking and attempted to negotiate with Goyeneche. The result was that Murillo and most of the more radical elements of the regime were seized by the royal troops while the rebellion continued. On the arrival of the Cuzco troops, the rebel army fled to the Yungas, where in November 1809 a major battle was fought at Irupana. The rebel army was defeated, and there followed the capture of all the former leaders, including Murillo. These men were tried immediately, and in January 1810 Murillo and eight of his fellow conspirators were executed, while over one hundred persons were exiled.

At the same time, the Viceroy in Buenos Aires appointed a new President of Upper Peru, Marshal Nieto, who also arrived with troops from Buenos Aires at about the time the Cuzco army arrived in the north, and in early December he took Chuquisaca. Nieto immediately arrested the rebel judges. By this action and by the execution of the rebels of La Paz, the independence movement of Upper Peru was formally brought to an end, and the first attempt at American independence crushed.

All opposition and violence did not end in Charcas, though, nor did this repression destroy Creole enthusiasm for independence. While the generation of 1809 urban leadership was effectively destroyed, a host of guerrilla leaders now emerged and established themselves in six important rural areas in little *republiquetas*. While the cities remained mainly in royalist hands, the guerrillas controlled an important part of the countryside and were effective allies in the various republican invasions which would come from the outside. From 1809 until 1816 these impromptu forces would obtain their support from all social classes in Bolivia, including the Indian peasant masses.

Despite the rise of a rural guerrilla movement, and the spread of the rebellion into the lower classes, however, the initiative for independence had passed out of the hands of the Upper Peruvians. Having been the first region formally to declare for independence, Upper Peru would paradoxically become the last region in South America to gain it. Moreover, it now became the battleground for more powerful forces to the north and the south, and lost its initiative in all the subsequent events to leaders and armies outside its borders.

Thus the history of Upper Peruvian independence shifts in the second phase of the independence movement to events occurring thousands of miles from the altiplano cities. The most important of these developments was the successful establishment of an independent government in the viceregal capital of Buenos Aires. After having crushed a British army of invasion in the Rio de la Plata region in 1806, the *porteño* leadership soon found itself contesting the power of its viceroy, and finally carried out a full-scale rebellion in May 1810. The euphoric Buenos Aires regime soon felt the need to spread its power throughout the old territory of the viceroyalty and viewed Upper Peru as a prime area for liberation. For their part, the liberals and guerrillas of Upper Peru viewed the developments in Buenos Aires as an extraordinary opportunity for re-establishing an independent local regime.

The initial response of the royalists led by Paula Sanz in Potosí and Nieto as President of the Audiencia was to break formal ties with the old viceroyalty and return Upper Peru to the jurisdiction of the Lima Viceroyalty. But this action could not prevent the spread of revolution. By September 1810 Cochabamba rose in support of the Buenos Aires regime, and in the next month an Argentine army had reached the region under the command of Castelli. Receiving tremendous popular support, the Argentine army was easily able to seize city after city, getting an enthusiastic welcome everywhere. By November Potosí was taken, and Castelli seized Paula Sanz and Nieto and executed them both. In the meantime the Cuzco President Goyeneche was forced to retreat, and soon Oruro and Santa Cruz rebelled against his armies and joined forces with Castelli, with the former defeating a royalist army. By April 1811 Castelli and his Argentine army had been welcomed in Oruro and La Paz, and the entire Upper Peruvian region was once again a free and independent zone.

But Castelli proved both an inept administrator and a poor general, and the popular support for his regime began to disappear. It became evident that the Argentines were not interested in allowing an independent republic to be established, nor in promoting Upper Peruvian interests at the expense of Rio de la Plata needs. Thus a defeat of Castelli's armies at Guaqui on Lake Titicaca in June 1811 turned into a full-scale rout that led to considerable urban bloodshed and civilian attacks by Upper Peruvians against the rampaging and retreating Argentine forces.

The defeat of the Argentines and the retaking of all of Upper Peru by the Cuzco royalists under Goyeneche did not end the rebellion within Upper Peru itself. In November Cochabamba again rebelled against the Crown and attempted to invade the altiplano. It took until May 1812 for Goyeneche to crush the rebellion, this time with considerable slaughter on both sides. Moreover, the desperate royalists were now turning to Indian support, and more and more kurakas were enlisted on both sides to provide Indian troops for the fighting. In turn the Indians began to obtain arms from all sides, with the result that the level of violence and social conflict escalated considerably by late 1811 and early 1812. Once reaching this state of mobilization, the forces unleashed by the independence movement proved difficult to contain, so the level of physical destruction and social dislocation became quite massive.

With Upper Peru now in the control of the royalists, Goyeneche decided, with Lima support, to push the struggle into northern Argentina and attempt to retake the Rio de la Plata region. But this effort collapsed in February 1813 at the Battle of Salta, when Manuel Belgrano led a successful northern Argentine army against the royalists. Thus began the invasion of Upper Peru by a second Argentine army under Belgrano, which had as little success as the Castelli adventure. Although Belgrano temporarily seized Potosí in the middle of the year, by the last months of 1813 royalist forces under the new leader Joaquin de la Pezuela had defeated the Argentines and retaken all of Upper Peru.

With the defeat of this second army and the subsequent invasion of northern Argentina by Pezuela, the leaders of the Rio de la Plata were convinced that Upper Peru could not be their main objective and eventually supported San Martin's decision to concentrate on a flanking attack on Chile as the best means to move against the center of royalist power at Lima. But this decision to strike elsewhere did not mean that Upper Peru would remain a quiet zone; for there now occurred within Upper Peru a series of small revolts and Indian uprisings, including an anti-royalist Indian revolt in mid-1814, which saw the conquest and sacking of La Paz by Indians from the Cuzco region. Meanwhile, the potential threat of a royalist Upper Peru was of concern to the Argentine republicans, so a small third Argentine army was organized and sent to Upper Peru in January 1815.

Again the invading Argentines found support from interior republicans. Upper Peruvian rebels seized Potosí and Chuquisaca from the royalists in April, and by May the Argentines once again were in control of these towns. But the Argentines could not take Oruro or Cochabamba and so in November 1815 suffered their worst defeat of the war, with their forces being totally destroyed. In the new year, the initiative shifted to the royalists, and Pezuela now undertook a massive attack on all the rebel forces in Upper Peru. The end was a resounding victory for Pezuela, with a massive destruction of the rebel forces. Whereas it is estimated that some 102 patriot caudillos operated in the rural areas from 1810 to 1816, after this date only some nine were left in control. Such famous rebel leaders as Manuel Padilla and Ignacio Warnes were executed, and even the intrepid Miguel Lanza was temporarily taken prisoner. Others such as Juana Azurduy de Padilla and Juan Antonio Alvarez de Arenales were forced into hiding. Of the six major republican zones under rebel control, only the republiqueta in Ayopaya (on the Cochabamba-Oruro-La Paz Cordillera frontier) survived, and it was totally isolated and neutralized.

Thus 1816 marks a major turning point in the history of the independence movement in Upper Peru. By this date both all external and all internal efforts to achieve independence, either under their own direction or with the support of the Argentines, had come to a disastrous end. Henceforth, Upper Peru would be isolated from the main events of the great struggles for continental liberation, while its final drives for independence would come from the very elite which had supported the royalist activities throughout the period. By 1816 many of the cities of Upper Peru had been sacked several times, and each retreating Argentine army had emptied the Royal Mint at Potosí. What was not destroyed in urban conflicts was destroyed in the rural rebellions. Haciendas were razed, isolated mines were destroyed, and the economy of the region was left in ruins. Moreover, the arming of Indian forces by both sides temporarily destroyed the Creole control of the countryside and created violent social tensions and urban fears, which led to further economic uncertainty and disorder.

Though 1816 marked the nadir in the wars of independence for the rebels, it was soon followed by a change of fortune. In that year Bolívar successfully re-established his revolutionary movement in Venezuela, while the Argentines felt strong enough to proclaim formally their total independence from Spain. With a few representatives from Upper Peru, the republican forces gathered in Tucuman and in July of that year declared the United Provinces of the Rio de la Plata as an independent nation. By 1817 the counter-offensive against royalist power had begun, and San Martin crossed the Andes into Chile and liberated the entire Capitaincy in the battle of Maipu in April 1818.

From 1816 to 1823 Upper Peru remained relatively quiescent after so many years of constant warfare, while its fate lay in events completely outside its control. In early 1817 the Argentines sent a quick expeditionary force to Upper Peru, its fourth and last such invasion, but this army remained mainly in the southern cities and had little direct influence over most of the region. Its only notable success, in fact, was the capture of a young royalist officer, a native of La Paz, by the name of Andrés Santa Cruz, who was sent back to Argentina by the republicans. Santa Cruz soon escaped, however, and eventually rejoined the royalist armies at Lima. But his experiences among the Argentines and his frustrations with the changing and vacillating policies of the Crown, which in 1820 was forced into a liberal position by the military revolt at Cadiz, led him to join forces with the rebels. Thus, in southern Peru in January 1821, he offered his services to General San Martin and his Chilean-Argentine army of invasion. After seeing considerable service in Peruvian battles, San Martin sent Santa Cruz with an expeditionary force to assist the Colombian troops under Sucre who were then in heated battle against the royalists in the Audiencia of Quito area. The result was that Santa Cruz and his troops now became fully allied with Sucre and broke their allegiance to San Martin.

All of this activity in Peru and Ecuador was in preparation for a new invasion of Upper Peru by republican forces, but this time from an entirely new direction. Both Argentines and Colombians no longer viewed the Charcas region as the main avenue to the taking of Lima, nor after so many years of warfare was it seen as a major financial center whose capture could lead to extraordinary wealth for the rebel cause. The Chilean and Ecuadorian routes proved to be the best gateways to the heart of royalist resistance, Lower Peru, with its vital center at Lima. In 1820 San Martin had landed troops in southern Peru, and by 1823 Sucre in alliance with Santa Cruz had arrived in the northern Peruvian region. At this point Santa Cruz was able to convince his Colombian and Venezuelan supporters that a major army of conquest could take Upper Peru in the confusion of battle for all the Perus. After a quick march from the coast, Santa Cruz led a successful invasion and captured his native city of La Paz in August. The royalist forces sent to oppose him were defeated (battle of Zepita), so he was able to take Oruro as well. Meanwhile the rebels under General Lanza seized Cochabamba. It looked as if liberation from royal control was finally at hand. But developments in Lower Peru left Santa Cruz's lines of communication exposed, and the existence of powerful royalist armies in central Charcas posed too great a threat. Thus, within a few short months of arriving, Santa Cruz was forced to evacuate La Paz, as the royalist armies successfully re-established control over the entire region.

The retreat of the republicans and the defeat of Lanza left the royalists in undisputed control of Upper Peru until January 1825. But Upper Peru as a royalist stronghold would prove to be a rather strange place indeed. For the commanding general of the royalist forces in the region, Pedro Olañeta, a native of Charcas, was an arch-reactionary who was deeply disturbed by the liberal revolution of Spain. Though fully supported by the Lima Viceroyalty, Olañeta and his aide and nephew, Dr. Casimiro Olañeta, were convinced that the Liberals threatened royal authority. Thus in January 1824 the Charcas general declared his unwillingness to send troops or supplies to aid his fellow officers in their desperate battles against the invading armies of Bolívar. For some twelve months the Lima regime cajoled, pleaded, and finally sent in regular forces to threaten Olañeta. But he refused to concede anything, while also refusing—despite the constant communications of his nephew with the various rebel armies—to join forces with the republicans.

Thus from January 1824 to January 1825 Upper Peru, though officially royalist, did not participate in any of the events affecting royalist power in the region and in fact succeeded in defeating several forces sent by the royalists to force their cohesion. At the same time Olañeta refused to become a rebel. The end result was the total isolation of the regime and the weakening of the defense of Lower Peru. In December 1824 the final fate of the region was sealed when the Spanish armies were destroyed at the battle of Ayacucho by Sucre and the royalist officers surrendered completely to the rebels. Though the royalists included Olañeta and his forces in the capitulation agreement, the latter refused to relinquish command or to endorse Bolívar. The result of this confusing state of affairs was that Sucre was finally forced to lead an army into Upper Peru to encourage the Olañeta troops to desert. This in fact occurred, and in January 1825 the old general was killed in a battle with his own mutinous troops. With this final death, the wars of independence both for Spanish South America and for Upper Peru itself finally drew to a close after almost sixteen years of bitter civil war, of serious loss of life, and of severe economic and social dislocation.

The military liberation of Upper Peru in December and January 1825 did not immediately resolve the question of the ultimate fate of the region. Just as the initiative for the war against the royalist forces had passed out of the hands of the local patriots after 1816, so too did control over their future destiny. It was in fact Bolívar and Sucre who would determine the destiny of the provinces of Upper Peru, since it was they who controlled both the army of liberation and the Peruvian Congress.

Initially, the idea that Upper Peru should be an independent republic was anathema to Bolívar and his plans for a continent-wide republic. The idea of allowing each region to form separate nations could only lead to the weakening of South America vis-à-vis its former European power and in the world order. But these initial ideas of unity were soon challenged by the reality of a growing conflict between his Gran Colombian state and the Peruvian regime which he had established. By 1825 Bolívar was already temporizing and was beginning to fear the growth of too powerful a Peruvian republic which in turn could threaten the existence and importance of his own base in Gran Colombia. Finally, the unqualifiedly hostile reception of Argentina to all his plans made the idea of a buffer state between Peru and Argentina a reasonable proposition.

Bolívar was truly uncertain what to do and in the end allowed Sucre—with much complaining on his own part—to decide the situation for himself. Transferring the authority to Sucre was in turn a positive step toward Upper Peruvian autonomy. For Sucre himself was not as concerned as Bolívar was with continental visions and at the same time was more influenced by local Upper Peruvian intellectuals, who were very much imbued with the idea of creating an autonomous state.

For the Upper Peruvian leadership, among whom General Olañeta's nephew Dr. Casimiro Olañeta was crucial, the idea of an autonomous state was a fixed idea. In this he and his other former royalist supporters were fully aided by the local urban elites in all the major centers, be they republican or royalist; for all Upper Peruvians had gone through a common experience during the war which rendered them essentially hostile to an amalgamation with either Argentina or Peru. To begin with, both sides were disgusted with the conduct of the four Argentine expeditionary armies that had invaded Upper Peru. Though the local republiqueta leaders had all loyally supported Buenos Aires, the Argentines had clearly shown their indifference to the needs of the local population and their willingness to sacrifice the entire region to their own exigencies. At the same time the royalists had now had almost fifteen years of government under the Lima Viceroyalty and were no longer tied to the Buenos Aires networks as they had been prior to 1810.

Thus both parties looked to Lima as the more natural zone of amalgamation, and in this they were supported by the logic of an economic and cultural unity. The southern highlands of Peru formed a natural region with the altiplano south of Titicaca, sharing both a common Quechua and Aymara background, as well as a similar ecology and an almost identical economic base. Equally, the commercial ties for all the Upper Peruvian cities, though greatly weakened by the constant shift of viceregal centers, were still essentially with Lima, which was seen as the most important zonal city binding together all of the regional networks.

The Peruvians, however, were in an uneasy relationship with Bolívar and his Colombian armies at this time, while the Lima elite was not prepared to push coherently for the incorporation of Upper Peru into its own national borders. They were more concerned with defining the jurisdictions of Puno and the Atacama coastal borders, especially the region of Tarapaca, than with binding the cities of the old Audiencia of Charcas into a unified state. The Peruvians also saw Upper Peru as a crucial buffer against the aggressiveness of the Rio de la Plata regimes and were thus on the whole relatively indifferent to the fate of Upper Peru so long as it did not become part of Argentina.

In this context of conflicting needs and demands by the external power centers which could decide the fate of the region, the local elite took the initiative in their own hands and pushed Sucre into formally declaring for an independent republic. With Lima uninterested if not hostile, and with their own long history of autonomous regional government, the Upper Peruvians were more than willing to assume responsibility for their own fate and make *de jure* what in fact had existed for some time, an independent regional government.

On February 9, 1825, when Sucre and his army arrived in La Paz accompanied by Dr. Casimiro Olañeta as his crucial adviser, he decreed the calling together of a constituent assembly of all the provinces of Upper Peru, which were to send delegates in April of that year to determine the future of the region. This decree was the final decision made by the external powers to allow the Upper Peruvians to create their own government. While Bolívar was initially furious with Sucre's decree, he did not disallow it and proceeded to accept Sucre's initiative. After some delays forty-eight delegates finally gathered together in Chuquisaca in July 1825 to decide the question, and with an overwhelming majority in its favor, the Assembly declared for formal independence. On August 6, 1825, a declaration of independence was issued, and the new state, in recognition of the ultimate necessity to obtain the leader's final approval, was named after Bolívar himself.

It was just at this time that Bolívar, fulfilling an old pledge to himself, was entering Upper Peru on a triumphal tour. The Chuquisaca Congress sent a formal delegation to him in La Paz requesting support for their actions and for the controversial decisions taken by Antonio Sucre. At first claiming that the Peruvian Congress still had to determine the ultimate fate of the region, Bolívar finally relented after his triumphal tour of the Upper Peruvian cities. In the end he ignored his own previous decrees and accepted the independence of the new republic. He even became its temporary president for a few months.

By the last months of 1825 an independent republic of Bolivia was finally created out of the old Audiencia of Charcas. To the rest of the world, Bolivia was still a mythical region of hordes of Indian peasants and incredibly wealthy mines that represented a treasure house of riches. But unfortunately for Bolivia the truth was otherwise. Upon entering its republican life, Bolivia was a war-weary and economically depressed region which was to experience, in the first years of life, an economic stagnation which lasted for close to half a century. From approximately 1803 to the late 1840s the Bolivian economy experienced a progressive decapitalization of its mining industry, a crisis in its international economy, and the greatest decline in its urban population since the last great depression of the seventeenth century. If anything, the early nineteenth-century depression was to be far worse than the previous great depression, leaving the Bolivian economy by the 1840s more rural-dominated and more subsistence-oriented than at any time in its past.

The very declaration of an independent republic for the region was, in fact, to have a profoundly negative influence on the national economy and was to deepen and prolong the crisis begun in the last years of the colonial era. Whereas recent historians have tended to downplay the impact of political independence on Latin American society and politics, in contradistinction to nineteenth-century liberal historians who saw it as a great turning point in national history, a reading of the economic crisis again shows just how important the events of 1825 proved to be. Twentieth-century historians are right to point out the persistence of traditional elites under republican disguises and to stress the continuity of social and political institutions until well into the nineteenth century, urging the 1880s as a period of fundamental change from the colonial structures. But it is also important to realize that the destruction of the colonial customs union which was the Spanish-American empire also had a profound impact

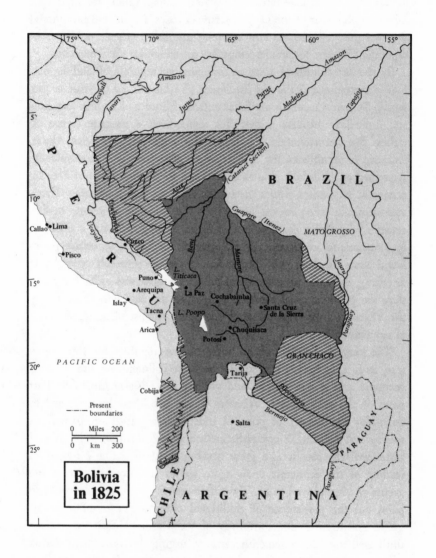

75° 70° 65° 60° 55°

5°

Amazon

Ucayali

Javari

Jurua

Purus

Madeira

Tapajos

P E R

Amazon

B R A Z I L

Cataract Section

Acre

Guapore (Itenez)

MATO GROSSO

10°

Callao• •Lima

•Pisco

Ucayali

Chuquibamba

•Cuzco

Beni

Mamore

Jauru

L. Titicaca

Puno•

•Arequipa

La Paz•

Cochabamba•

•Santa Cruz de la Sierra

Paraguay

15°

Islay•

Tacna•

L. Poopo

•Chuquisaca

U

Arica•

Potosí•

Paraguay

PACIFIC OCEAN

GRAN CHACO

20°

Cobija•

Loa

Tarija•

Pilcomayo

— · — Present
boundaries

0 Miles 200

•Salta

Bermejo

P A R A G U A Y

0 km 300

25°

Salado

ATACAMA

C H I L E

A R G E N T I N A

Paraguay

**Bolivia
in 1825**

on the national and international economy of the new republics, Bolivia included.

The creation of all the new South American republics in the early nineteenth century quickly led to a new era of mercantilism, as most of the new states initially rushed to set up tariff barriers against each other, if not always against the dominant English traders. For Bolivia this meant that its traditional markets in northern Argentina no longer represented a major source of trade. In fact, Bolivian independence was to have a negative impact and cause a long-term economic decline of the northeastern Argentine provinces. The end of intimate ties to Lima led to a serious credit crisis, which the few arriving foreign capitalists could not easily alleviate.

Transportation costs, which had always been a serious constraint on Bolivia's international trade, now became even more prohibitive as Peru, Chile, and Argentina charged Bolivia for the use of their ports. The creation of a Bolivian port at Cobija in the Atacama desert was little compensation for these new trade barriers, since even at its height only a third of Bolivia's foreign trade passed through this harbor and the overland transportation facilities were all controlled by foreigners.

Thus independence can be said to have seriously restricted, if not destroyed, most of Upper Peru's traditional economic ties and further pushed the economy toward subsistence. The decay in its mining sector, meanwhile, forced the republican government into an ever more negative economic role. As its own revenues from international trade declined, the Bolivian governments in the early nineteenth century were forced to rely increasingly on the manipulation of currency and on the forced monopolization of silver minting and export. Without the impetus of an expanding foreign trade, the common source for the increasing revenues of the more advanced states of the region, Bolivian taxation became increasingly regressive and a negative constraint on trade and production. A vicious cycle of decline, repression, constraint, and decapitalization set in with the establishment of a republican government, which in turn was no longer capable of drawing upon the capital, talent, or resources of an enormous imperial government to resolve the crises in local production.

The destruction of mines and smelters in the independence war, the government monopolization of minting and exports which severely reduced profits, the increase in transportation costs as a result of new tariff barriers, and the end of royal credit and mercury sales subsidization all led to a severe crisis in the mining industry. Whereas in 1803 there were forty *ingenios* (or silver refining mills) and several hundred mines in operation in Potosí, by 1825 there were only fifteen ingenios and fifty or so mines still functioning. Silver production, which in the last decade of the eighteenth century was averaging 385,000 marks of silver per annum, had dropped to 300,000 by the first decade of the nineteenth century, and declined further to an average of 200,000 marks in the 1810s, and finally to an all-time low of some 150,000 marks per annum in the 1820s. While production rose slightly in the 1830s, it was not until the 1850s that production again reached the 200,000 level.

This crisis in production was reflected in a decline in producing units. In an official census finally carried out in 1846, it was estimated that even at this late date there were some 10,000 abandoned mines in the republic. Nor were these mines abandoned for lack of silver ore. Rather, the wars, the destruction of capital and equipment, and the migration of technicians led to a simple process of abandonment. These still quite rich mines could be opened only with tremendous inputs of capital, and required the use of steam engines to remove the water from the flooded mines, a universal problem.

With its export sector in a long-term depression, Bolivia discovered that its urban Spanish-speaking populations declined as well. Potosí and Oruro, the two major mine centers, were so seriously affected that their combined urban population was estimated in 1827 by the British investigator J. B. Pentland to have fallen to below 15,000 persons (9,000 for Potosí and 4,600 for Oruro). Other mining-dependent cities were little better off, with Chuquisaca falling to 12,000 persons. Thus the wars and resulting independence most affected the centers, industries, and populations associated with the export trade.

But Bolivia was also inhabited by an estimated 800,000 Indian peasants in 1827. And just as the collapse of the export sector in the seventeenth-century crisis had been a positive aid to the more local regional agricultural markets and free Indian communities, the same would occur again in the early nineteenth-century crisis. Thus, in contrast to the decline of the mining centers and their satellite towns, the two key marketing towns of Cochabamba and La Paz continued to remain stable and/or grow in numbers. In 1827 the city of La Paz was unquestionably the most populous in the new nation and held some 40,000 persons, while Cochabamba was a close second with 30,000. Both were primarily farm center communities and both serviced hinterlands with large Indian peasant populations.

The fact that these cities grew, while the southern mine centers declined, demonstrates well the paradoxical problem of Bolivian growth prior to the twentieth century. The decline of the export sector reduced the level of Spanish exploitation and raised the income of the Indian peasants. The Indians were able to increase their internal trade because of their higher income, and in turn fully supported the regional economies and furthered the growth of the urban centers which serviced their needs. The war and the subsequent republican attack on Church properties was also crucial in seriously weakening the hacendado class throughout the republic. The lack of large urban markets (it was estimated that the new republic was over 90 percent rural) and the scarcity of capital meant that the hacienda system itself was in total retreat everywhere, with abandoned haciendas being a conspicuous casualty of the abandoned mines.

Just how important the Indian populations had become was revealed in the pattern of government revenues which became apparent in the new republic. Whereas the first republican assembly was forced to adopt Bolívar's Peruvian decrees outlawing the tribute tax collected by the royal government from all Indian males aged eighteen to fifty, the Bolivian government soon found that it could no longer afford the luxury of doing without it, and within one year it had reimposed the colonial tribute on all its Indians. This tribute tax, again collected at the same rate as in the colonial period, now accounted for some 60 percent of government income, whereas in the late eighteenth century it accounted for less than 25 percent of royal revenues. With a stag-

nant international trade, a declining silver production, and a bureaucracy incapable of systematically collecting land or business taxes from
the whites and cholos, the government came to depend on the Indian
head tax as its most lucrative source of income and was to maintain
that tax until the end of the century.

While such a tax was an obvious burden on the Indian population,
it nevertheless committed the Bolivian government to protecting the
free communities from white and cholo threats. The Bolivian con-
gresses gave ongoing legitimacy to the community governments and
their land titles, in contrast to official Bolivarian legislation which had
challenged their very right to existence. In fact, it was not until the
1860s, when the importance of the tribute tax seriously declined in the
totality of government revenues, that the central government finally
adopted the contemporary liberal ideology on land tenure and began
to challenge the legality of the corporate landholding structure of the
communities.

Just how disastrous an economic situation in Bolivia existed in the
early republican years is revealed by the failure of the first reformist
government to revive successfully a viable national and international
economy. The regime of Antonio José de Sucre, established in early
1825 and lasting until April 1828, was in fact a model of its kind in
Latin America and compared quite favorably with the reformist and
liberal regimes of Rivadavia in Buenos Aires and Santander in Colombia, from which it copied many of its own reforms. Sucre was a classic
eighteenth-century liberal with excellent ideas concerning the creation
of a viable economic and social order. He was also an ardent republican and attempted to provide the institutions for a representative and
relatively open regime. He even tried to undertake a serious reform in
the relationships between the Indian masses and the Spanish-speaking
state, in favor of the former.

Faced with the need to redevelop the war-torn economy of Upper
Peru, Sucre, with the support of Bolívar, began a thoroughgoing reorganization of the mining industry. With the resources of the Spanish
state no longer available to subsidize the miners, it was decided in
August 1825 to nationalize all the abandoned mines. Sucre then turned

to foreign capitalists to provide the desperately needed capital and invited both Argentine and, more importantly, British entrepreneurs to open the mines. This led in 1824 and 1825 to feverish activity, with several British engineers and representatives traveling to Bolivia to begin surveying the mines. A speculative boom also developed on the London money markets with the creation of some twenty-six mining "Associations" or companies established to develop South American mines. The most important of these new companies as far as Bolivia was concerned was the "Potosí, La Paz and Peruvian Mining Association," which was supposedly capitalized at £1 million but actually raised only 5 percent of that amount. The collapse of the London market in December 1825 led to a total collapse of almost all of these extremely speculative ventures, so that very little machinery, capital, or engineering staff ever reached Bolivia from England. What few miners did get through, from either Argentina or London, soon found that the costs of reopening the mines were prohibitive without the massive introduction of steam-driven pumping machinery on the one hand and a substantial lowering of costs on the other. Of these cost items, initially the most difficult to overcome was that of labor. For in July 1825 Bolívar had abolished the mita in all of the Peruvian area, and, once abolished, the new republican government found itself incapable of re-establishing the institution. Thus Potosí had to enter the free market for all its labor needs and was forced to offer high wages to attract peasants from agriculture. Such new costs were just too heavy a burden for the fragile industry to bear at this time.

While Sucre successfully resurrected both the *Casa de Moneda* (the Royal Mint) and the *Banco de San Carlos* (Minerals Purchasing Bank) on a sound footing and proceeded to get coin mintage up to reasonable levels, he could do little to reopen the abandoned mines and so ultimately was left with only local Bolivian miners as the providers of the silver ores produced for the Banco and the Casa de Moneda. Moreover, despite all his efforts, the introduction of steam engines—the crucial technological innovation needed by the silver mining industry—was still decades away, which meant Sucre was unable to deal with the crucial problem of mine flooding.

Even more revolutionary than his reforms in the mining industry were Sucre's attempts to introduce a progressive tax system to bolster the new republican regime. Accepting and supporting Bolívar's abolition of the repressive exploitation of the Indians, he pushed through the successful abolition of the mita and also temporarily rescinded the tribute tax. The hated royal monopolies were also attacked, and the tobacco industry freed from all restrictions. The famous sales tax (or *alcabala*) was abolished by Sucre, and such special taxes as those on coca production were reduced. All these disparate taxes, which either were regressive personal taxes against the poorest element in the society or were restrictive on trade and production, were now replaced by a single direct tax on urban and rural property and individual incomes. This "contribución directa" was truly a revolutionary reform and promised to modernize the tax structure of the state by establishing the most progressive tax structure then available.

But within one year of their implementation, the new direct taxes on wealth (landholdings and income) were abandoned. The state bureaucracy was incapable of effectively administering such a tax, which required a careful assessment of all the resources of the citizenry and their taxation by an efficient administration. No cadastral surveys were available, and no censuses, aside from the old Indian tribute lists, existed; nor did the regime have the ability to carry out these vital registrations: with the liberation from the Spanish empire, Bolivia had also lost the best part of its technically trained and well-educated governmental bureaucracy. It was a problem typical of all newly liberated ex-colonial areas: the Bolivians were left with the shell of the State and with few trained individuals capable of managing the needs of the government. Moreover, with revenue declining, the new state also found itself incapable of paying salaries that would attract the few able people that remained within Bolivia to its service. Thus Sucre's ambitious plans for a progressive tax system foundered on the inability of the state to carry them to fruition. The continued decline of foreign trade, which remained heavily taxed, deprived the state of a potentially expanding source of revenue—a source vital to all the more advanced and developing states of the region. Thus by the end of 1826 the administration was forced to abandon the direct tax and return to traditional sales, tribute, and other regressive taxes to support the finances of the State.

The failure of his fiscal reforms to generate capital helped push Sucre toward a confrontation with the Church in its role as an economic power within the State. Anti-clerical like most members of their generation, Sucre and Bolívar both sought to destroy the role of the Church in the new republic. In this, Sucre was assisted by a rather reactionary hierarchy within Bolivia which had supported the royalist cause to the end. The Church thus found itself with a weakened and discredited leadership when Sucre began his assault and so was unable to put up an effective resistance.

In fact the Sucre attack on the Church was one of the most radical in Latin America in the nineteenth century and unqualifiedly his most successful governmental action. He began by assuming control over the collection of the Church tithes, which probably amounted to some 200,000 pesos per annum. He then finished the earlier royal reforms of consolidating the credit structure of the Church and confiscated all the *capellanías* and pious works, which were either mortgages paying interest or annual payments from private properties granted to the Church to subsidize masses and benefices of clergy. Then the major rural and urban landholding organizations, the monasteries and convents, were challenged. The new government ordered the closing of all monasteries housing fewer than twelve persons and succeeded in reducing the monasteries in Bolivia from forty to twelve in number. Those that remained had their private estates confiscated and administered by the government, which then paid the remaining monastery residents their salaries. By this stroke some 3 million pesos in urban and rural property were confiscated. A similar attack was made against the convents, and their holdings were also now taken from them, and their numbers equally reduced. It was estimated that another 3.8 million pesos were thus confiscated from the female religious houses. With all these actions, Sucre probably brought under state control properties worth something on the order of 8 to 10 million pesos.

The confiscation of Church wealth was truly an awesome and revolutionary act from which the Bolivian Church never recovered. But in the end it did little for the regime financially, for in the depressed urban and rural markets the State could find few buyers for these vast properties. The State was forced to rent out most of these lands and houses to their previous renters and in turn collected no more than the Church had on most of these properties. Yet it now had to assume the responsibility for the salaries of the clergy and the maintenance of the remaining monks and nuns, a group probably numbering some 500 persons. It also had to pay its own administrators, and so the final returns to the State on income were quite small. It was able to use some of these properties to secure internal loans, but, given the state of the national economy, the internal capital market was not large enough or secure enough to provide a major source of income for the State. Most of the income generated from the rental or sale of former Church properties actually went for the establishment of social services and educational establishments in the urban centers of Bolivia. The six major cities (La Paz, Cochabamba, Santa Cruz, Oruro, Potosí, Chuquisaca, and Tarija) all obtained free primary schools and orphanages. But most of these institutions survived for only a short time and had little real impact on the economic or social structure of the society.

Thus the Church reform of Sucre was not the unqualified financial bonanza that it was expected to be. In fact it brought the state only temporary relief, and most of the income was absorbed either in maintaining Church personnel, starting a free education system, or in paying off militarily incurred debts. Little was finally made available for purposes of economic growth or the development of a vital communications infrastructure. But in political terms the Sucre Church reforms were a total success. Bolivia took over complete royal patronage powers, absorbed all the lands of the Church, reduced the monastic orders to an insignificant grouping, abolished the ties between laity and clergy by eliminating the *cofradías,* and even went so far as to take the Church silver from all the temples. All this was accomplished with no protests from the urban elites or the peasant masses. As a result, the Church became a dependent and passive actor in the affairs of the State for the rest of the century. Furthermore, Bolivia was spared the horrors of the religious conflicts which many of the republics of America were to experience and showed a religious toleration unusual by Latin American standards.

It should be stressed that the Church was not destroyed by Sucre, and in the late nineteenth-century revival of Roman power throughout the world Bolivia, too, would see the renaissance of an important Church. The reappearance of the Jesuits and the coming of the new orders, such as the Silesians, would revive the educational and religious powers of the Church. But its economic role was never restored, and the political power of the Bolivian Church remained muted and of little interest for either the traditional elite or the revolutionary masses.

Though a popular leader and an able military commander, Sucre finally found himself faced with an ungovernable situation. Revenues of the State were declining or stagnant in his two-and-a-half years of government. The burdens of a Colombian army of occupation of some 8,000 men also weighed heavily both on the treasury and on national political life. The process of fragmentation of the generation of victorious republican generals was having its effect in all the liberated territories, and Bolivia proved no exception. The disillusioned Sucre soon found himself opposing former comrades in arms. An assassination attempt and an aborted coup in Chuquisaca in August 1828 thoroughly destroyed Sucre's interest in remaining head of state. Recovering from his wounds, he resigned the government and went into voluntary exile, returning to his native Caracas.

The end of the Sucre government did not bring an end to the liberal and reformist regimes or usher in an age of anarchy as occurred in some of the other republics when their original leaders were overthrown. In fact, it was men who served with Sucre and were his loyal supporters who would now lead the successive governments of the republic for the next generation. Though the liberal generals who subsequently followed Sucre would in turn face the same problems as the first president, they held to the same goal of establishing a liberal and prosperous State.

Unqualifiedly the most important of these early leaders was Andrés Santa Cruz. A native of La Paz with a Spanish father and Quechua mother, Santa Cruz had entered royal military service at the beginning of the wars of independence, and after a long and successful career he finally joined the republican side in 1821 and became a leading officer in the ranks of San Martin's Chilean expeditionary army. In 1822 he was sent by San Martin to assist Sucre in his Audiencia of Quito campaigns, and thereafter wedded his cause with Bolívar, Sucre, and their Colombian troops. In that year he was elevated to a generalship by Bolívar and won a major victory in mid-1823 near the Bolivia border at the battle of Zepita, the most famous of his many conflicts.

Closely tied through his military father to the Cuzco upper classes, and long associated with the major Peruvian political and military developments, Santa Cruz was intimately involved in Peruvian affairs and was initially more interested in Peruvian than Bolivian politics. Elected by his native La Paz to the Constituent Assembly in 1825, he declined the honor and remained simply prefect, first of Chuquisaca during the time of the Constituent Assembly, and later in the Sucre regime as head of the La Paz district. But in September 1826 Bolívar recalled him to Lima and made him president of the Peruvian republic. His first presidency in Peru was shortlived, for by 1827 he was forced out. But the overthrow of Sucre, which in part was due to the efforts of his friend the Cuzco General Agustín Gamarra, who temporarily invaded La Paz, led to the decision to call Santa Cruz to the presidency of Bolivia. This was a move supported even by Sucre.

From the time the offer was made until his arrival, Bolivia was ruled by a series of temporary rulers, one of whom, General Blanco, unsuccessfully tried to seize the government for himself. But in May 1829 Santa Cruz finally returned to Bolivia and was sworn into office. The ten-year rule of Santa Cruz was to be a fundamental one in republican history, and the institutions which he founded were to provide the basic framework for the organization of civil life of the republic for the next two centuries. From 1829 to 1839, when he was overthrown by Chilean military intervention, Santa Cruz would prove to be one of the most able administrators Bolivia would ever know.

The primary accomplishment of the Santa Cruz regime was the creation of a stable political, economic, and social order. After almost a quarter of a century of uninterrupted wars and invasions, he was able to guarantee Bolivia something like ten years of peace. Given this stability, he was able to create a more viable state financial structure and to extract the most resources out of the economy. He could also use those resources to pay for a semi-professional army and to guarantee an active and responsible civil administration.

In economic terms, Santa Cruz was a determined mercantilist. Upon establishing his government he proceeded to set up important protective tariffs, even going to the extreme of totally prohibiting the importation of tocuyo cloths, the basic textile used in the country. He also decided that he would attempt to force all imports to go through Cobija, the only port left to Bolivia after the various treaties of territorial reorganization with Chile. Imports coming from the more natural ports of Arica and Tacna, now firmly in Peruvian hands, were heavily taxed, and incentives of lower taxes, a free port, and subsidies were provided for trade going to Cobija. It was estimated that at its most active, about one-third of Bolivia's international trade now passed through the city. Cobija went from a population of a few hundred to over a thousand, complete with its docks and warehouses. Also, a wagon road was built from Cobija to Potosí, while other internal routes were opened up to ease the crucial transportation costs.

Santa Cruz turned his attention to the usual areas of concern in mining. Again, typical of his manner of rationalizing the economic structure, he reduced mining taxes considerably. In 1829 the colonial 1½ percent "Cobo" tax was eliminated, and all other taxes reduced to a uniform 5 percent tax. The traditional 3 percent gold tax was eliminated altogether in 1830, and there appears to have been some increase in gold production, though silver production remained relatively stable throughout the period.

While Santa Cruz is credited with bringing economic stability, the normalization of customs and taxing arrangements, and the regularization of public credit, in fact relatively little basic change occurred. For despite all the specialized tariff protection, and some moderate construction of new roads, and the guarantees of peace, the economy would simply not respond to the mercantilist treatment accorded by the regime. For all the protection afforded the native textile industry of tocuyo cloth production, that production was estimated to have declined to one-quarter of its colonial levels. Thus by the end of the period the regime was forced to lift its total prohibition on tocuyo importations to meet the demands of the local market. Moreover, despite all the reduction of taxes, the lack of capital for mining prevented the expansion of production, and for the decades of the 1820s and 1830s production remained relatively stagnant for silver, the prime export of the republic.

Despite the considerable improvement in public credit and the rational protectionist efforts, actual government revenues stagnated in the first three decades of the republic. The figure of 1.5 million pesos per annum income seemed to have been one that no government could increase until well into the 1850s. Moreover, that figure hid long-term structural changes in the economy as well. As the famous statistician José María Dalence was to point out in 1846, every source of government revenue extracted from the economy declined steadily in the 1820s, 1830s, and 1840s. It was only the increase in rural population and the subsequent increase in the tribute tax which kept total income at a steady level. Thus the relative importance of the tribute income in total republican revenues had gone from 45 percent in 1832 to 54 percent in 1846, while customs receipts from both the internal and external tariffs, being the second most important item, accounted for just 22 percent of income.

The long-term stagnation of the mining sector was to prove fatal for sustained growth in the national economy, and greatly limited the availability of any serious government funds for the investment in basic infrastructure or the provisioning of credit for industrial growth. Despite his best efforts, Santa Cruz, like all the early republican presidents, found expenditures constantly outrunning income. While in the early years he did reduce military expenditures somewhat, the army still remained the all-engrossing monster which consumed the single largest share of government income. In a normal year army costs represented between 40 and 50 percent of total expenditures, with the costs of maintaining the clergy the next most important item in the budget. Add the costs of sustaining the bureaucracy, and there remained few funds left for investment. As Santa Cruz was to show, only additional taxes applied on internal trade could generate funds needed for capital expenditures.

This long-term squeeze on government budgets, which were almost uniformly in deficit in this period, led to the decision of Santa Cruz to issue a new debased silver currency. In 1830, by secret decree, a new silver currency was minted at Potosí which contained 18.05 grams of silver rather than the traditional 24.45 grams (in the old colonial *peso á 8*). While the decision to create the new devalued silver peso (*moneda feble*) was probably thought of as a temporary expedient to generate a windfall profit, it ultimately became a long-term liability for the economy, and its increasing production relative to the older "hard peso" is a good indication of the increasing crisis of the state financial structure. Whereas the regime in the 1830s issued only 3.5 million pesos of the debased silver currency as opposed to 16.5 million of the traditional one, by the 1840s the ratio had been reduced to 9 million and 11 million respectively. By the 1850s the new currency was overwhelmingly dominant, with 21 million pesos of it being minted as opposed to only 2.5 million of the old.

Given the fact that the regime attempted to collect in the old peso and pay in the new one, a general uncertainty was created within the national economy that increased with the years. Thus the long-term stagnation of the economy led to a long-term crisis in government financing, which in turn led to money manipulation that further accentuated economic uncertainty. Even the quite impressive growth of Cobija and its commerce under Santa Cruz quickly declined after 1836, when the creation of the Peruvian-Bolivian confederation once again made the port of Arica the legitimate port of Bolivia. The reduction of the discriminatory taxes against Arica allowed it to achieve its natural domination and virtually liquidate Cobija as a viable alternative.

While the long-range economic reforms of Santa Cruz may not

have ultimately reversed the stagnation of the national economy, his political and administrative reforms and the political peace which he did achieve were to prove of vital importance. Commissioning parliamentary studies and organizing special commissions, he finally enacted a major civil and commercial code modeled along the lines of the Napoleonic decrees. He also systematized local administration and successfully re-established the rural census-taking procedures which had been the basis for the success of the colonial tribute collection. While he approved a democratic constitution with a limited presidency, he also quickly obtained dictatorial powers, carried out complete press censorship, and readily exiled his opponents. It should be stressed, however, that by the standards of his day Santa Cruz was extraordinarily tolerant of his opponents and kept bloodshed to a minimum in political conflicts. Moreover, the tranquility of his rule from 1829 to 1835 was such that he received overwhelming popular support from the elite elements of the society.

While Santa Cruz was a dominant figure for Bolivia, Bolivia was not the exclusive concern of Santa Cruz. From his earliest involvement in the life of Cuzco to his presidential term in the mid-1820s in Lima, Santa Cruz was deeply involved in Peruvian developments. He was as committed a participant in the politics of southern Peru and Lima as he was in the intrigues of Potosí or Chuquisaca. At no point upon taking up the presidential reins in Bolivia did he give up his political ambitions in Peru. And the more chaotic the political situation in Peru became, the more appealing did the figure of Santa Cruz become for the Peruvians, especially those of the southern region.

By the mid-1830s the constant turmoil brought on by the intensive activities of the southern Peruvian leader Gamarra, who actively tried to intervene in Bolivian politics as well, along with the enfeebling of the crisis-ridden Salaverry regime in Lima, gave Santa Cruz the excuse for his followers in both states to invade Peru and establish a new regime. In June 1835 a Bolivian army invaded Peru, invited by one of the factions in the local civil wars. By August the Bolivians had defeated the army of Gamarra, and, after a long series of battles, Salaverry was finally defeated and executed in January 1836.

At this point Santa Cruz decided to reorganize Peru itself into two autonomous states, Northern Peru and Southern Peru, and join them with Bolivia in what became the *Confederación Peruboliviano*. After he had himself named as protector, he maneuvered so that all regional groups finally supported his unity idea, and the final Confederation government was established in October 1836. For all his astute political activity, however, Santa Cruz held a real power base only in Bolivia and Southern Peru, and in this latter area he was faced by the constant opposition of Gamarra.

For all the long-term uncertainties of the Confederation, there is little question that it brought both peace to Peru and respect for its power along the entire Pacific region. Though the population of Peru at this time was only slightly larger than Bolivia's—on the order of 1.5 million persons—the resources of the Peruvian state were potentially much greater. Unlike Bolivia, Peru had a multiplicity of powerful regional economies with strong native manufactures, plus a large variety of relatively easily exploitable resources which could be quickly developed for export into the world market. In contrast to the stable but stagnant Bolivian economy, the wealth of Peru could be more easily developed, so the potential for major growth was readily at hand. What was essentially needed to awaken fully this sleeping giant was a stable political system and a controlled and responsible bureaucracy.

Such a situation was ideal for Santa Cruz, whose fame justly rested on his excellent administrative skills. Immediately, he established civil and commercial codes for the new state, while statistics were collected, customs reorganized, protective tariffs introduced, and the bureaucracy reorganized and refinanced. The army was also quickly provided with funds and support and so became a major ally of the regime.

Unfortunately for Santa Cruz his potential to make Peru a major power was also recognized by the Chileans. They saw their own expansion as being one of northern movement along the disputed territory of the Pacific and were competing actively with Peru for the same European markets. Thus a revitalized Peru under Santa Cruz could not be accepted. As a result, Chile gave active support to dissident Peruvian politicians, to the extent of both arming them and transporting them back to Peru. They also "disguised" their own troops as Peruvian rebels and then made a major bid to defeat Santa Cruz through constant incursions.

The end result of these Chilean-inspired invasions and subsidized revolts was a serious weakening of the Confederation government. While Santa Cruz won several important battles, the long-drawn-out conflicts finally took their toll. By 1838 the Chileans put a regular army into Peru, and in a major battle near Lima in January 1839 both the Confederation government and the political career of the remarkable Santa Cruz were brought to an end by Chilean arms.

Forced into exile in Ecuador, Santa Cruz by necessity had to abandon the Bolivian government as well, so his local representative General José Miguel de Velasco assumed control over the new independent state. But the Velasco regime proved a difficult one. The former ally turned himself into a bitter foe of Santa Cruz and confiscated all his personal goods. But he soon found himself in constant conflict from another one of Santa Cruz's generals, José Ballivián, who attempted several major revolts in the few short years of the Velasco regime. Velasco was able to carry out some reforms, rewriting the constitution to provide for a more controlled presidency and even renaming the city of Chuquisaca after Sucre, but he was unable to calm the political situation. Finally, after some two years in office, a pro-Santa Cruz revolt brought down the Velasco regime in June 1841.

The overthrow of a Bolivian government was not considered a local event in the context of contemporary international politics. Since the fall of Santa Cruz, the Lima government had been under the control of Gamarra, his oldest enemy. Peru, Chile, and even Argentina had closely monitored local Bolivian developments, and, when it became clear that Santa Cruz had finally won, Gamarra announced his intention to invade the republic to prevent the feared Santa Cruz from returning to power. In July a Peruvian army began to cross the frontier, and by October it had taken La Paz without a major battle. It was now made clear to all that Gamarra hoped to annex a good part of Bolivia to Peru. Other neighbors of the republic saw this as a potential opportunity. Argentina supported an army under Velasco in the south, while Ballivián seemed to be wandering between various camps, first supporting Gamarra and then finally deciding to seize the government for himself and oppose the Peruvian invasion.

In all the intrigues and maneuverings, it was Ballivián who finally emerged as the leading figure. With three separate internal rebellions going on at the same time and with an invading army threatening the very existence of the state, all the factions finally decided to cease supporting the return of Santa Cruz and switched to Ballivián as the most capable general for establishing a defense. In many ways this turned out to be a vital decision in the international affairs of the new republic.

Ballivián met Gamarra in battle at the town of Ingavi in November 1841 and totally defeated the invading forces of Peru. As a result of this action, the Gamarra government fell in Peru, Bolivia was relieved of its economic obligations to Peru which had been imposed as a result of the fall of the confederation, and the close connection between Peruvian and Bolivian politics was definitely broken. After Ingavi, Peru never again thought to involve itself in Bolivian affairs, and no Bolivian political leader ever again became a potential contender in Peruvian politics. Moreover, the end of the Santa Cruz threat meant that Chile and Argentina now both gave up their intense involvement in Bolivian internal affairs and allowed Bolivian politics to return to primarily national concerns and national issues. On the other hand, the end of the Santa Cruz era marked as well the end of Bolivia as a major power of contention in the Southern Hemisphere of Latin America. It also ended the most brilliant epoch in terms of extraordinary leadership which the new republic was to obtain. While the economic stagnation of the republic had ultimately limited their scope of action, the regimes of both Sucre and Santa Cruz represented the best of the revolutionary ideology of the great liberation movements. Both men showed an essential humanity and toleration in their political dealings which ultimately would stand in sharp contrast to the next group of leaders who would govern the republic.

Chapter 5 • The Crisis of the State, 1841-1880

The post-Santa Cruz period began under the rather unusual leadership of José Ballivián. Born in La Paz in 1805, Ballivián came from an upper-class family, his uncle being the high royal official Sebastián de Segurola, who led the suppression of the Túpac Amaru rebellion. Yet despite his class background, Ballivián was a relatively uneducated individual, having entered the royal armies at the age of twelve and knowing nothing but a military career for his entire life. An important leader in the independence armies, he was to rise to the highest ranks in the armies of Santa Cruz. But his own lack of education and political sophistication, plus his strong personality, created an ambience in which revolt, massacres, and needless executions became a set pattern.

Nevertheless, the Ballivián era from 1841 to the end of 1847 was a calm period of rule for Bolivia and is considered the last stable regime of the early caudillo period. Under Ballivián, Congress was active in organizing society, and many able civilians came into the central government. Slowly, but steadily, population and government income began to rise as the nation attempted to reorganize its internal space in the light of changed international conditions.

Though a confirmed militarist, Ballivián recognized the absurdities to which previous regimes had stooped in their thirst for international power. After attempting to invade Peru and failing, Ballivián settled down to governing Bolivia. At this point he faced an overinflated army that absorbed almost half of the national budget and had one general for every hundred soldiers. Establishing special land grants and pension acts, Ballivián attempted to dismantle the Bolivian war machine and reduce its weight in national politics. The number of troops and officers was reduced, and even some "military colonies" were established in the eastern lowlands. Nevertheless, the costs of pensioning off this army created a new and heavy burden of public indebtedness and the overall expenditures for the army changed little.

In other areas the regime was a bit more successful. Though the national budget continued its traditional deficit, revenues were pushed up from their 1.5 million peso figure of the 1820s and 1830s to something close to 2 million pesos by the late 1840s. Though modest, this still was an increase. Nevertheless, even here, the long-term structural restraints were still evident. Indian tribute income still provided its steady 40 percent of total income, and customs revenues still fluctuated quite widely from year to year. Now, however, the state had organized some important internal tariffs and taxes which were paying more steady incomes. The tax on coca production, an item consumed exclusively by Indians, was now producing an annual average of 200,000 pesos, and the newly revived export of Peruvian bark (*cascarilla*) for the manufacture of quinine was yielding an equal amount and providing an important secondary export along with silver.

The government also turned its attention toward the eastern lowlands. The department of the Beni was formally established, military colonies were organized, and even various unsuccessful European colonizing companies were attempted. There was also considerable discussion of opening up new river and canal routes in the eastern lowlands in order to develop an Atlantic outlet for Bolivian production. Just as the government was beginning to look eastward for the first time, it also finally recognized the changed reality of Bolivian population and resources by calling for an independent bishopric for Cochabamba, now the second largest city in the republic. In 1843 Congress decreed the establishment of this fourth major ecclesiastical district, which was finally approved by the Vatican in 1847. Thus Bolivia now had bishoprics in La Paz, Santa Cruz, and Cochabamba and an archbishopric district in La Plata (Sucre).

Finally, in 1846, came Bolivia's first national census, carried out under the able statesman José María Dalence. It was discovered that the population had risen steadily to some 1.4 million persons, with an additional estimated 700,000 ungoverned Indians scattered through the eastern lowland territories. But despite the growth of the population in the almost quarter-century of republican life, there had been little change within the social and economic organization of the society. La Paz was still the largest city but now held just 43,000 persons, while Cochabamba—the second largest center—held only 30,000. Counting together the population of all eleven cities and thirty-five *villas* (or towns) of the republic (those living in towns of approximately 500 persons and above) still produced an urban population of only 11 percent, a figure not much different from the estimates of Pentland in the mid-1820s.

As could be expected from the lack of government investments and the general stagnation of urban life, the educational level of the society was extraordinarily low. Only 22,000 children were attending school in 1847, or 10 percent of the number of school-age children in the republic. This would seem to imply that little change in literacy could be expected in the future, for Dalence generously estimated that there was a maximum of only 100,000 persons literate in Spanish in the republic, which meant just 7 percent of the censused population. Without a major increase in school attendance it was evident that the next generation would be little more literate than the one of 1846.

Nor had the economy changed greatly, despite the relative peace now ensured by the Santa Cruz and Ballivián periods. Although silver mining had dropped to 156,000 marks per annum in the 1820s, it increased only moderately in the 1830s to 188,000 marks, and to just 192,000 marks in the 1840s, or exactly one-half of the peak production of 385,000 marks in the 1790s. Moreover, Dalence estimated that there were 10,000 abandoned silver mines in the republic, two-thirds of which still retained silver but were now under water and could not be developed without pumping machinery. There were, in fact, only 282 active mine owners in the republic in 1846 who employed only some 9,000 miners, most of whom were part-time specialists who worked in agriculture as well.

As for the rest of national industry, Bolivia was the homeland of a large artisan society which essentially satisfied the needs of its population. Woolen textiles for home or local consumption was a major industry, along with food processing. The one area which the government attempted throughout the early years to develop—cheap cotton textiles—just did not survive. Despite sporadic prohibitions and continually heavy tariffs against cheap English cottons, the tocuyo cotton cloth industry, centered in Cochabamba, never regained its eighteenth-century importance. Whereas in the colonial period it was estimated that the tocuyo cloth industry of Cochabamba had several hundred *obrajes* (factories) producing cloth, these numbered just 100 by 1846, and their value had declined from an annual production estimated at 200,000 pesos to some 60,000 pesos in the 1840s. The cheap cotton textile needs of the Bolivians were now filled by British cloths which dominated the market.

Bolivia thus remained an overwhelmingly rural society. Outside the cities and hamlets lived 89 percent of the population, who produced over two-thirds of the national product (estimated at 13.5 million pesos worth of goods, compared to 2.3 million pesos in minerals and 3.9 million in manufactured products in 1846) and who remained not only totally illiterate but largely ignorant of even the national language. While no figures are available on languages spoken, it would not be an exaggeration to estimate that no more than 20 percent of the national population was either monolingually or bilingually conversant in Spanish. Quechua remained the predominant language of the republic, with Aymara running a close second. Spanish thus was a minority language in the republic, though the only language of national political and economic life.

Within rural society, the balance of control between haciendas and *comunidades* (free Indian communities) remained rather much as it had existed in the late colonial period. In 1846 there were over 5,000 haciendas valued at 20 million pesos and some 4,000 free communities valued at only 6 million pesos. But while the relative value and numbers seemed to favor the haciendas in the rural areas, in fact the majority of the work force lived on the free communities. Dalence estimated that there were only 5,135 heads of families who were hacendados, with some 138,104 heads of households living on the comunidades. Accepting Dalence's own estimates of four and one-half persons per family as a multiplier means that over 620,000 Indians lived on the communities, and they made up a total of 51 percent of the total rural population. The hacienda population of yanaconas (or landless laborers) probably numbered between 375,000 and 400,000, and the other 200,000 persons of the rural population were probably freeholders in the southern regions or landless migrating workers who rented lands from either the communities or the haciendas.

While the haciendas had obviously had the more commercially valuable properties, they nevertheless were in a relative state of stagnation, except for the two exceptional areas of the Yungas and the Cochabamba Valley. The former was the major source of coca production, which was on the increase along with the increase in the Indian population. As for Cochabamba, it had seemingly recovered from the economic shock of the late colonial crisis and was now the principal national producer of the two basic grains, wheat and corn, and had now returned to its pre-eminent position as the granary of Bolivia. Elsewhere, however, the haciendas remained relatively quiescent and posed no serious threat to the densely populated regions where the free communities predominated.

Within the free communities themselves there were, however, ongoing changes and much internal stratification. The elimination of the mita obligation had clearly favored the *originarios*, or original members of the communities with the greatest access to lands. With the onerous labor obligations removed, their numbers seem to have grown or at least stabilized and in the 1840s were estimated to represent 35 percent of all heads of households on the free communities. The *agregados* with land (or later arrivals with lesser land holdings in the communities) represented 42 percent of the communities' population, and a new and important group of forasteros without any land now accounted for 23 percent of all Indian families. Evidently, the slow growth of population was beginning to create a landless class of Indians on the free communities themselves.

While there were some changes going on within the dominant rural world, the stagnation of the mining industry and the failure of national manufactures to meet local demands meant that for the first quarter-century of its existence Bolivia was in the unusual position of being in a constant deficit in its balance of trade. In each year from 1825 until well into the 1850s, Bolivia showed a deficit in its legal trade account, which could be met only by the illegal exportation of silver and by a very active contraband trade. Thus the government Minerals Purchasing Bank was having a harder and harder time collecting all the silver being produced in the country, while government losses on illegally exported items seem to have been quite high. Finally, government deficits were a constant phenomenon, as expenditures, especially of a military nature, far outstripped the resources of the state treasury.

Thus, by mid-century, Bolivia was, if anything, in worse condition than it had been at the beginning of its republican life, and it appeared that things would only deteriorate further. This expectation would seemingly be reinforced with the fall of Ballivián and the beginning of Bolivia's most chaotic period of caudillo rule from 1848 to 1880. But, paradoxically, it was precisely this period of greatest political turmoil that was to prove the great age of expansion of the Bolivian economy. It was in the 1850s and 1860s that the successful implantation of steam engines into the altiplano mine industry began. It was also largely merchants and hacendados from the area of Cochabamba and some of the more advanced grain-producing regions who now provided the capital with which to open the major mines. Extracting their wealth from interior commercial operations, these new merchant-miners were able to begin to invest seriously in new mine technology.

Along with the slow development of altiplano mining, the 1860s and 1870s would see the very rapid growth of mining on the Pacific littoral of Bolivia. The silver mines of Caracoles in the 1870s, as well as the older mines on the altiplano, would now come into full production. In turn the growth of modern mine companies attracted international capital and in turn provided the resources to expand new mining ventures even further.

All of this renewed economic activity would occur in the midst of the most politically violent and chaotic period of republican political history. But the chaos of political violence seems to have had little impact on the slow but steady growth of a modern export sector. If anything, the regimes that came in the 1860s and 1870s responded well to the demands of the new mining elite and met its most immediate concerns, which were primarily related to ending government monopoly positions in the purchasing and trading of metals.

But the cause of this paradoxical growth still remains to be fully determined. To begin with, it is evident that a series of events external to Bolivia played a decisive role in awakening the mining giant. The increasing productivity and declining costs of the steam engine in Europe and North America in the first half of the nineteenth century meant that the steam engine of the 1850s and 1860s was a far cheaper and more readily available and reliable item than it had been in the 1820s. Thus the costs of opening up a flooded mine were considerably reduced. Moreover, the growth of Peruvian and Chilean mining in this period provided a general regional background of capital and technical expertise which could be readily exported to the incipient Bolivian industry and also provided a ready market for Bolivian exports. Finally, the decline of international mercury prices reduced a major traditional cost item for silver extraction.

But these factors explain only the general international conditions which provided a much larger pool of engineers, machines, and mercury at much lower cost than previously for the altiplano miners. The initial capital placed in Bolivian highland mining came from Bolivians themselves. And the key question remains: Where did this capital come from, given the relative stagnation of the economy for the first quarter-century of republican existence? From an analysis of the early mining companies in Potosí and Oruro, it is evident that a disproportionate share of the capital stock came out of the merchant and landed aristocracy of the Cochabamba Valley. It would thus appear that the steady but unspectacular growth of the national population, despite some rather severe epidemics in the 1850s, created an expanding internal market for agricultural production, especially for corn and wheat, which was the core of Cochabamba agriculture. From this growing internal market, the Cochabamba elite was able to extract surplus capital. Cochabamba seems to have had, too, a class of incipient entrepreneurs who were more than willing to undertake the risks of heavy capital investments in the traditionally quite unpredictable mine industry. The fact that the Cochabamba region was the heartland of the most advanced cholo population in the republic and also had the most active rentier class of freehold peasants, the bulk of whom were bilingual in Spanish and Quechua, also helps to explain some of the evident entrepreneurial skill available.

Starting in the 1830s it had become popular to establish national joint stock companies to begin mining operations. Usually selling a large number of shares at low costs per share, these companies on average would produce something on the order of 10,000 pesos of working capital. Among the numerous companies formed in this pioneer epoch, the most important was the Huanchaca Mining Company, which worked the Porco mines in the province of Potosí, founded in 1832. Like all such ventures, these early companies barely met costs and spent many years building drainage and new mineral shafts so as to get the mines working, using the most readily accessible surface silver deposits to pay for ongoing costs. Many of the companies went bankrupt before they could complete the operations, and by 1856 the Huanchaca Mining Company was typical of these in having spent some 180,000 pesos on basic infrastructure and having as yet to produce a profit for any of its shareholders. The same year the merchant Aniceto

Arze bought into the company for 40,000 pesos and quickly began to provide the crucial capital needed to get the company going. Similarly, in the mid-1850s the Aramayo family bought out the bankrupt Real Socavón Mining Company of Potosí. Finally, in 1855 the merchant Gregorio Pacheco took over the Guadalupe mines from one of his debtors in the Chicas district of Potosí province.

Thus within a few years of each other, the three major silver mining dynasties were implanted in the mining districts of Potosí. With new infusions of capital and leadership, the reorganized companies began to prosper. By the 1860s the three leaders were well into rationalizing their operations and undertaking long-term structural changes in the industry through the introduction of modern machinery, pumping operations, and shaft reconstructions. By the 1870s foreign capital began to arrive in ever-increasing amounts, and by the second half of the decade the Bolivian silver-mining industry can be said to have reached international levels of capitalization and technological development and efficiency. Bolivia was once again one of the world's leading producers of refined silver, and a thriving and vital export industry had revitalized both the internal economy as well as Bolivia's international commerce.

It was this increasing economic tempo of the 1850s which in many ways explains the rather strange configurations of governments that arose on the political scene. With the fall of the Ballivián regime, another *paceño* of his generation (born in La Paz in 1811), General Manuel Isidoro Belzu, emerged as the new political activist. Of humble origins, though apparently of Spanish extraction and, like Ballivián, primarily and exclusively a military officer from his youth, Belzu had been involved as an important officer in the Santa Cruz armies. Once Ballivián had taken over, he had played a key military role in the new regime. Shifting alliances constantly, as had Ballivián before him, he emerged as the strongest opposition general demanding a place in the government.

After the fall of Ballivián in December 1847, Belzu emerged as the most powerful figure. He took the presidency formally in 1848, holding on to power until 1855 when he voluntarily retired—the first Bo-

livian president to do so since the time of Sucre. But the continued
chaos of government finance and the progressive weakening of loyalties and the emergence of contending personalities left the political
scene filled with unpaid and unsatisfied generals, all of whom wished
to be president. Without an established political party system to chan-
nel demands or aspirations or control appetites, national politics was a
gruesome free-for-all in which any small-time regional leader could
play. The result was that Belzu had to face something on the order of
thirty to forty different revolts in his six years in government. In the
end, the countless battles, assassination attempts, and intrigues exhausted even this indomitable warrior, so he voluntarily resigned his
position.

Below the level of intrigue, however, certain very important changes
were occurring which Belzu accurately reflected. The Belzu regime
has been taken as an aberration by many Bolivian historians, with the
epithets of "demagogue" and "socialist" being freely applied to him.
There is no question that Belzu expressed a frank hostility to the upper aristocracy of Chuquisaca and the other provincial elites, or that
he expressed himself in favor of some type of scheme to confiscate the
wealth of the rich. He was also quite an imaginative populist who
liked to declare himself a representative of the cholos and lower classes
of the cities, and expressed himself in terms of Christian socialism and
attacked the legitimacy of private property and class structures. Often,
he distributed monies to the urban poor in quite classic demagogic
gestures. But a close look at the Belzu regime will show the president
and his leading civilian advisers to be the last representatives of the
traditional mercantilist position.

The profuse legislation which Belzu enacted in the economic area
involved protective tariffs against English manufactures, promotion of
artisanal industries within the country, tax incentives to national products, the creation of state monopolies for the promotion of the national
economy, and even laws prohibiting foreigners from operating in national commerce. These were efforts which were directly opposed by
the merchants and their new mining allies, all of whom very much
favored free trade and an open economy. Just as the free trade move-

ment was beginning to gain important economic adherents, the traditional classes struggled to prevent the dismantling of the old mercantilist scheme. Belzu proved hostile to the new silver miners, even going so far as to set up several more minerals purchasing banks and a monopoly bank for the purchase of quinine bark. For this he was bitterly attacked by the new mining and commercial elites, while at the same time he received wide popular support.

Just how extensive popular support was for Belzu became apparent very early in his regime. In March 1849 an early attempt by some generals to overthrow his government led to popular uprisings in the cities of La Paz and Cochabamba—the most advanced and populated in the republic—in support of the regime. For several days in both cities lower-class mobs took over and led a rather systematic attack against the local elites. Moreover, popular support was so powerful that an almost successful assassination attempt upon Belzu in September 1850, followed by a long convalescence, did not lead to an overthrow of his regime.

Just as the upper classes were opposed to Belzu for his popular support and his hard-line mercantilist ideas, foreign states were embroiled with him as he tried to prevent the penetration of foreign goods into the national market and restrict the role of foreign merchants. This conflict even led to the expulsion of the British diplomatic representative and resulted in the often-told but untrue tale that Queen Victoria eliminated Bolivia from the map in retaliation.

The increasing economic power of the free trade opposition and the declining power of the artisans and local manufacturers did eventually erode the support of Belzu and fully financed his opposition. Tired of putting down another rebellion of his troops fomented by his opponents, Belzu declared his intention to retire and ran his docile son-in-law General Córdova for president. This controlled election in 1855, which saw some 13,500 electors voting, led to the establishment of what proved to be a transitory but moderate government before the final victory of the free-trade and pro–foreign capital advocates.

Córdova lasted two years and was replaced by Bolivia's first essentially civilian president, José María Linares, in 1857. The Linares regime, for all its problems, would clearly mark the shift of power to the newer elements in the economy and the end of the government's monopoly role in the mining industry. Whereas Belzu and Córdova had been indifferent to the demands of the mining industry, Linares made this the primary concern of his government. Though born in 1810 in Potosí, and thus very much a member of the generation of all the presidents since Santa Cruz, Linares was unique in that he never followed a military career. A son of an upper-class Spanish family, the well-educated Linares had quickly risen in politics and civil government and had played a role in secondary education in the capital of Chuquisaca. He had initially been a loyal supporter of Santa Cruz and had served as prefect, legislator, and central government administrator during the years of the Confederation. Eventually opposing the Confederation, he found himself on the outs with Ballivián, went to live in Europe during the Ballivián and early Belzu periods, and practiced law in Spain.

Returning to Bolivia in the later Belzu years, he was constantly involved in plotting against the old general and even ran against Córdova in the elections of 1855, winning some 4,000 votes. But his defeat at the hands of the government, which fully controlled the elections, committed him to a violent overthrow of the regime.

The Linares government, which lasted from 1857 to his own ouster in 1861, showed itself much more receptive to the ideas of free trade. The tariffs protecting the native cloth industry were lowered, the quinine monopoly was ended, and all ores but silver were now permitted free entrance to the marketplace if they were refined in Bolivia. The regime, however, did not go as far toward free trade as the miners wished, and in fact it tightened up on mercury sales, making the industry a temporary state monopoly and increasing the control over minting. Nevertheless, the Linares government encouraged the miners to form a powerful government-supported *camara,* or interest group, to push for their demands.

Just how important these new mine owners had become was evident in the early years of the new regime. Whereas total government revenues still hovered between 1.5 and 2 million pesos per annum, the major mine companies, like the Aramayo-owned Real Socavón Mining Company of Potosí, for example, had invested 281,000 pesos between its organization in 1854 and 1861. Pacheco's companies from 1856 to 1861 had invested 333,000 pesos, with a like sum being spent on the Huanchaca Mining Company. The use of steam engines, railed carts, and modern refining machinery was already common in the mining zones, and by the mid-1860s these companies were going overseas for their capital needs. Thus the investment in just the three largest of these companies was close to the total income generated by the national treasury in any one year.

Along with the steady growth of the traditional mining zones, the littoral province of Atacama along the Pacific coast was finally beginning to take on some significance. In 1857 the first nitrate deposits in the Mejillones region had been discovered. This led to the slow but steady growth of the port of Antofogasta, which was soon rivaling that of Cobija as the principal Pacific port of the state. This growth, however, was all under the control of British and Chilean capitalists, who worked out rather favorable contracts with the Bolivian government, which essentially added little real income to the central treasury.

In the budget of 1860, for example, the tribute tax was still double the income of any other source of national revenue and accounted for 36 percent of the budget. Furthermore, the once quite lucrative income from quinine exports had totally disappeared. A major source of government revenues and of exports in the 1840s and early 1850s, the monopoly of Bolivian quinine production was broken by Colombia in 1855 and thereafter production declined to relative insignificance. Finally, despite Linares's attempts to control the military, and the reduction of the army to just 1,500 men, the armed forces still absorbed 41 percent of the national expenditures.

Although incapable of revising government incomes and expenditures, Linares made a successful effort to refund the internal debt and to restore some semblance of normality to the government minting of silver. He also attempted to reorganize the national administration and to provide for more efficient local government. He appears to have been able to get some successful funding provided for local education.

Thus, while the Linares administration did not overwhelmingly change the public economy, it did initiate some long-term changes in the direction that was to mark the ultimate victory of the free trade ideology. It also began a thoroughgoing reorganization of public credit which was to prove a most important precedent for the regimes of the 1870s and 1880s.

The very strict reformism and harsh rule of Linares, who even established a formal dictatorship after September 1858, was to prove too much for many of his followers, though. While his most ardent supporters, among them Tomás Frías and Adolfo Ballivián, formed themselves into a powerful supportive group that later would take on the sobriquet of the *rojos,* his opponents mobilized large-scale support for his overthrow. In 1860 the regime had massacred Indian rebels at the shrine of Copacabana on Lake Titicaca, and at the same time was forced to head off a major revolt attempt. These actions weakened the dictator, so Linares was forced into exile in January 1861 by three of his most important ministerial appointments.

In the resulting politicking, a new congress was elected in which many of the rojos were represented. Nevertheless, General José María Achá, one of the three conspirators, was selected president of the republic by Congress, and Linares and his supporters were excluded from power. The new regime in many ways continued the basic policy decisions of the Linares period, in fact carrying out a further freeing of the economy. The mercury monopoly created by Linares was abolished and the fiscal reorganization continued, though the strong centralized budgeting arrangements carried out by Linares were abandoned.

While the new regime continued the economic direction of the Linares period, it was to have the unique distinction of being the most violent of the nineteenth-century governments in terms of the repression of its opponents. In 1861 in a typical episode of political maneuverings, some seventy supporters of Belzu, including ex-President Córdova, were taken into custody in La Paz by the local commander Colonel Yañez. Using the threat of a Belzu uprising as his excuse, Yañez ordered the execution of these leading politicians—the single most bloody reprisal in republican history to that date. Thereafter the regime was faced, as usual, with constant political unrest, with the future presidential contenders testing themselves out in a series of power plays and military revolts. What is impressive about all these revolt attempts is the slight impact they had on the general economic and social structure of the state. While the Bolivian army under Sucre and Santa Cruz had numbered between 5,000 and 10,000 troops, the Bolivian army was reduced to a force of between 1,500 and 2,000 men in the post-Confederation period, and especially after the end of the Peruvian threat at Ingavi in 1841. This was an army which supposedly controlled a society which numbered some 1.8 million persons in the 1850s.

Thus the constant attempts at revolt and the marching back and forth usually involved only a few hundred men on each side and in effect produced little serious disruption of the economic or social life of the society. Moreover, so long as the military regimes reflected the increasing power of the new mining oligarchy, they were more or less ignored by the new miner capitalists. Deeply involved in establishing their companies on a viable economic base, they had little time for politics if their basic needs were satisfied by the government. And until the military caudillos finally fell into a serious war with these miners' closest allies and supporters, the Chileans, they felt no need to intervene.

Given the indifference of the new and old economic elites, the civilian politicians found themselves incapable of controlling the generals or the troops. Linares had been their best hope, with the result that the constitutionalist, or rojos, faction continued to offer a strong appeal for those committed to a powerful civilian-dominated regime. But the majority of factions, from those of Santa Cruz to those of the followers of Belzu, continued to find a convenient general or colonel to lead their cause and declare for their candidate. Until these other political and oligarchic factions would agree to press their claims in a different arena, the pattern of military revolts followed a precise and well-worn pattern.

While the Achá regime conformed to the typical model, and also reflected the new economic interests, there was a new factor that was beginning to make itself felt in the Bolivian political and economic scene. In 1863 the Achá regime was forced to deal with the first major aggressive step of Chile in the Atacama mining region. In that year a dispute between a Chilean- and Brazilian-financed mining company was taken to the Bolivian courts for arbitration. In this conflict, the Chilean government refused to recognize Bolivian jurisdiction and in 1863 extended its territorial claims to include the Mejillones nitrate fields. While Achá sent Friás to negotiate, and Congress in 1863 voted for war, the Bolivian government found itself impotent against its southern neighbor and was forced to accept Chilean demands for rights to these extraordinarily rich fields.

As the term of Achá drew to a close, the General attempted to establish free elections. The two most powerful civilian movements proved to be those of the rojos supporting the old Linares line of moral civilian rule and the Belzu populists. But before the elections could be held, a close relative of Achá's, General Mariano Melgarejo, seized the government in December 1864. Thus began one of the longest and most bitterly contested dictatorships in Bolivian history— a regime that has caused great debate in Bolivian history.

Like Achá before him, Melgarejo was of Cochabamba background and had participated in a series of military occupations, revolts, and constant political machinations. He differed from his predecessors primarily in age, having been born in 1820, and in his total lack of class support. Unlike all of his predecessors except Belzu, he was totally alienated from the upper classes. He was illegitimate and had made his successful career through military prowess alone. At the same time, he had none of the revolutionary ideology of Belzu and so made no serious intellectual or political attempt to reach the popular classes.

Yet despite the term of "caudillo bárbaro," with which Bolivian historians labeled him, Melgarejo in many ways represented the coming to full power of the mining elite of the country and the triumph of its policy of free trade. The economic policies of the regime represented a coherent continuation of policies that had been set in motion as early as the Linares period. Moreover, despite his notorious "drunkenness" and dissolute living style, Melgarejo received important support from the new mining elite for much of his term in office. His regime would also see the first serious attack on the land question since the early days of the republic. Nor did his attack on the legal rights of the free communities differ from his support of the mining elite, since both activities were of a kind in the movement to adjust the Bolivian economy and society to the re-emergence of a powerful silver-mining export industry in Bolivia.

The Melgarejo period must be seen in the context of the international economy to be fully understood. The years 1864 to 1873 were an extremely prosperous time and the first great era of capital exports from Europe to the developing world. The same period saw the great boom in the Pacific coastal exports industry, first guano and then nitrates, and the entrance of English, North American, and continental European capital in general into the local mining industries in alliance with Chilean and Peruvian capitalists. All of this feverish investment activity also greatly affected the whole southern Atacama region known as Mejillones, which, though disputed constantly by Chile, was still under nominal Bolivian control. Here were major deposits of guano and nitrate, and in addition important deposits of silver would soon be discovered in the nearby Carracoles region.

What few Bolivian capital resources existed were totally tied up in developing a modern silver industry in the traditional altiplano mining centers. Therefore all of these new zones acted as magnets for Bolivia's neighbors. For the altiplano miners, this interest was a welcome event, for it spread over into interest in supporting highlands mining growth. For the always penurious Bolivian government whose income had remained virtually stable for almost fifty years, this interest in its coastal resources was an unexpected cornucopia which could lead only to unheard-of personal wealth. Whereas all the previous rulers of Bolivia tended to die in poverty in exile abroad, the current leaders suddenly found themselves courted by foreign governments and foreign capitalists, and proved to be unwilling and unable to resist the temptations.

Bolivian historians and writers have justifiably condemned the Melgarejo government for consistently selling the nation to the highest bidder. But could other regimes have successfully resisted these blandishments after some fifty years of stagnant fiscal revenues and an officer corps that proved insatiable in its demands for power? Moreover, one can seriously question whether the new mining elite was at all concerned with the huge concessions granted to Chilean capitalists or other aspects of government policy which essentially ended all attempts at mercantilist control either in terms of the mining industry or in terms of protecting national industries.

Whether Melgarejo and his extremely hungry generals were any better or worse than others is not the issue, but they certainly were more active. For the first time since the British speculations of 1825 and 1826, there was a rush of foreign capitalists into Bolivia with schemes to make everyone rich. Such classic North American entrepreneurs as Henry Meiggs and Colonel George E. Church were on the scene, along with such venerable Chilean houses as Concho y Torres, and such classic British companies as Gibbs & Co. The primary source of potential wealth was the Mejellones nitrate and guano fields. In a treaty of 1866, Chile and Bolivia had agreed to share the resources of the Mejillones region and had redrawn the frontier to give Chile direct control over everything below the 24th parallel. This was a real source of income, and foreigners, mostly British and Chileans, entered into long-term export contracts and special railroad concession arrangements.

Since the Melgarejo regime was faced with a deficit budget from its first days in office, it was desperate for hard money and was ready to give extremely generous long-term contracts for immediate but relatively small amounts of funding. Many of these contracts were worth several millions of pesos, taken on the worst terms for Bolivia and tying up invaluable resources for long periods of time with onerous commitments. Many of these contracts, in fact, would become quite binding on the government and would eventually provide the crucial background to the commercial conflicts which led to the War of the Pacific.

But the altiplano government was essentially indifferent to all these long-term problems. In the first days of the new government, Melgarejo had resorted to forced loans to generate income for the treasury, and he never really caught up to his expanding expenses. Thus anyone offering a few hundred thousand pesos of income could obtain millions in long-term concessions. Moreover, one had the impression that for the altiplano politicians the whole coastal boom market was an unreal world over which they had little control and over which they were willing to concede virtually anything these industrious foreigners wanted. It is also well worth noting that, despite complex guano and nitrate export contracts, Pacific coastal railroad schemes, Amazonian river boat and Belgian colonizing companies, and other real and imaginary speculative proposals, there was no attempt to allow foreign operators to enter into the highland mining industries. These remained firmly in the hands of national investors.

With its new wealth on the coast and a whole wave of speculative capital coming from Europe and North America, even nearby governments were willing to get involved with the overly generous Melgarejo regime. Thus Bolivia signed commercial and territorial treaties in the late 1860s with every one of its neighbors. In 1865 a special treaty with Peru went into effect whereby Bolivia, for obtaining free port rights at Arica, virtually became part of the customs union with Peru. Bolivia ended up by charging Peruvian customs taxes at Cobija and in turn was granted a fixed income of 450,000 pesos per annum from the customs houses of Arica and Tacna. By this treaty, Peruvian manufacturers entered Bolivia without restrictions. It was this fixed income coming from the more responsible Peruvian government which the Melgarejo regime quickly mortgaged to foreign interests for short-term loans.

Next came the Chilean treaty of 1866, which not only resolved the Mejellones and previous occupations in favor of Chile but also provided that the local Pacific ports could export mineral products free of Bolivian taxes and that Chilean goods could come into such ports also free of the usual tariffs. By these two acts alone, the whole mercantilistic program of protective tariffs was completely destroyed and Bolivia was now in a virtually free-trade arrangement with Chile and Peru. Bolivia then negotiated away its part of the joint guano output from these treaty areas, and did so with foreign firms on disastrous terms and in a manner which could only incite continued Chilean pressure. Finally, Melgarejo offered the Chilean diplomatic representative, whom he had grown to like during the treaty negotiations, the post of Minister of Finance in his own government. When this offer was rejected, Melgarejo then made him his own diplomatic representative before the Chilean regime!

Next came two treaties with Argentina and Brazil in 1868 which provided for free fluvial rights to the Atlantic for Bolivian shipping in return for further special concessions in relationship to the importation of the products of both of these nations. Moreover, in the Brazilian treaty a territorial "adjustment" of some 40,000 square miles was made in favor of Brazil. Thus all the treaties—despite their excessive concessions of income and even territory, as in the Chilean and Brazilian cases—went far toward totally dismantling the carefully constructed edifice of protective tariffs which had been the hallmark of Bolivian political economy up to that date. All of this was directly related to the new altiplano mining elite's great desire to allow free trade to become the operating principle of the national economy.

In the internal economic sphere, Melgarejo also attempted some fundamental reforms. While the regime went to great excesses in minting devalued currency, it carried out the basic reform of the old colonial currency and gave up the peso for the new decimal-based currency of the *boliviano* in 1869. More importantly, it attempted to destroy the land-owning rights of the free communities. This extraordinary decree of 1866 was the first really sustained attack on Indian communal property rights since the Bolivarian decrees of 1824 and 1825, which were left in suspense by the Sucre decision to return to the tribute as a basic form of taxation. With the sudden wealth being generated by the Pacific mineral and guano deposits, the relative importance of the tribute income in the total revenues of the State began to decline. While the actual amount of tribute remained stable—at 800,000 to 900,000 pesos per annum—its relative importance was slowly declining, as income from mineral exports and mining taxes was beginning to become as important. In addition, the slow revival of the mining industry was having its impact on the growth of urban markets and the consequent increase in the tempo of commercial agriculture to supply those markets. Thus the 1860s saw the first stirrings of revived interest in the rural haciendas and the beginnings of a sustained attack on the property holdings of the communities.

By the terms of the confiscation decree, it was declared that all community properties were really State-owned lands and that Indians residing upon them were now required to purchase *individual* land titles at the sum of no less than 25 pesos and no greater than 100. The Indian who did not purchase his title within sixty days of the decree would be deprived of his lands, and the State would auction them off to other purchasers. Moreover, it was provided that holders of the State debt obligations could use these in payment for land. If no one purchased the lands in public auction, then the Indians who worked them would be allowed to retain these lands as renters and would be forced to pay a rental tax to the State. Even if the Indian should be able to purchase his lands, ultimate possession still resided with the State so that the lands would have to be repurchased all over again after five years.

At the end of the Melgarejo's period in 1870, over 1.25 million pesos of land had been "sold" to whites and mestizos, the majority of which was paid for in debt obligations from the State. The outcry of the anti-Melgarejo forces and the fact that Indian protest was so violent and bloody had their impact on terminating this initiative before the community lands could be effectively confiscated, and the succeeding government actually restored most of the lands taken. But it was the fact that Melgarejo had anticipated the market too soon that really explains the "failure" of his confiscation scheme. For, in fact, the demand for community lands would grow enormously so that by the end of the next decade the Bolivian government would carry the entire confiscation program of Melgarejo through to fruition.

Melgarejo also completed his assault on the protectionism and mercantilistic ideology of his predecessors by emasculating the entire silver monopoly arrangements which had been the key issue of contention between the new silver miners and the government. During his regime, the largest silver-mining companies such as the Huanchaca enterprise of Aniceto Arce received exemptions and were allowed freely to export their silver to the international market. Thus from the late 1860s onward the percentage of mined silver being purchased by the *Banco de Rescate* (Minerals Purchasing Bank) went into sharp decline, and the effective control of the government in setting prices for national silver production was ended. By these actions, Melgarejo satisfied the most important demand of the new mining elite.

The political overthrow of Melgarejo when it came in 1870 brought no serious change to any of the policies which had been initiated in his six years of office. While the new regime of General Morales (1870-72) desperately renegotiated some of the more extravagant contracts and temporarily restored the Indian lands, it actually furthered the general policies initiated or fully developed under Melgarejo. With the opening up of the Pacific coastal Caracoles silver mines in 1870— which in two years had a total invested capital of $US 10 million— and the continued boom of the Mejillones region, there was now even more money available to the central government. This meant it could afford to undertake the essential reforms that the extremely hungry Melgarejo government was unwilling to make. In 1871 and 1872 the government finally abolished the monopoly on silver purchases for all companies and declared a free trade. It also terminated all minting of the famous debased currencies which went back to the days of Santa Cruz. The semi-private, but powerful new *Banco Nacional de Bolivia*, created in 1871, was given charge of redeeming this money and reorganizing the national currency.

Nor was the new government adverse to continuing many of the essentially corrupt loan arrangements which Melgarejo had begun. The Church contract for a steamship company on the eastern rivers eventually raised £2 million, of which the government got practically nothing and under which no boats were ever delivered to Bolivia. The first successful railroad concession was granted to Meiggs and other foreign capitalists, also in 1872, and at least there was some success in this. The Nitrates and Railroad Company of Antofagasta was established that year with a heavy Bolivian subsidy and began the construction of a railroad from Antofagasta and the Mejillones fields through to the new Caracoles silver mines. Thus was begun the era of railroad construction in the republic, though as yet no railroad was successfully begun to the altiplano from the coast—a move which was the next major demand of the new altiplano silver miners.

The overthrow of the Melgarejo regime essentially brought the old Linares civilian constitutionalists—or rojos—back to power. While General Morales won a very controlled election in May 1872 with some 14,000 votes cast, his apparent derangement and eventual assassination prevented this potentially despotic ruler from seriously threatening the domination of the rojos. In a new election in May 1873 their primary leader, Adolfo Ballivián, the son of the former president, was elected in a rather free and wide-open electoral campaign in which some 16,674 votes were registered. An urbane, well-educated, and traveled figure, Ballivián successfully led his followers to power and was replaced on his death by illness in 1874 by Dr. Tomás Frías, the second leader of the party and head of Congress. Thus from late 1870 until 1876 the central government was essentially under the control of the old Linares party leaders and reflected the most advanced elements of the civilian leadership of the period.

But the inability of the rojos to control the army and their continued corruption and relative innocence in international contracts and negotiations—differing little from the Melgarejo patterns—meant that the civilian regimes—the first such regimes since the Linares dictatorship itself, and only the second episode of non-military rule since the founding of the republic—could not successfully maintain itself in office. These civilians, moreover, were still not directly related to the now-dominant mining elite of the altiplano. While Ballivián, Frías, and the other policy-makers fully accepted the free-trade ideas and the strong currency advocated by the altiplano miners, they were not fully integrated into this elite. The mine-owners were now in the midst of their greatest phase of organization and paid little direct attention to politics. All this in turn weakened the civilians and made them vulnerable to the traditional military maneuverings.

General Hilarión Daza emerged under the civilians as the chief military figure in the republic, heading the elite Colorado battalion which had been formed in the time of Melgarejo. In the same mold as Melgarejo and Morales, Daza overthrew the government in 1876. Upon seizing power, Daza soon found himself badly in need of funds and plundered the national treasury to pay his restless officers and maintain himself in power. Thus the fiscal reforms carried out by the civilians at the beginning of the decade were undone in the last half of the 1870s by Daza. The collapse of the central treasury in turn led to the wild extravaganzas of more fictitious loans, special entrepreneurial concessions, and further raids on the national treasury by foreign and national speculators. All this made for a potentially explosive environment as the conflicting concessions policies and changing taxation rules created a tense situation among foreign companies operating with Chilean support on Bolivia's coastal territory. It also encouraged the Chilean belief that the Atacama territories were theirs for the taking.

Thus the short-lived civilian rule after the overthrow of Melgarejo brought little serious change to government policy or to national political organization. But the satisfaction of all the basic demands of the altiplano mining elite by Melgarejo and his successors allowed that elite to enter into its most expansive phase of operations and reorganization. The period from 1873 to 1895 is considered the great age of nineteenth-century altiplano silver mining. By the end of the decade of the 1870s Huanchaca alone was generating more income than the central government itself. Moreover, all the other major firms were now completely reorganized with heavy inputs of European and Chilean capital. The growth of Bolivian silver output in this period was phenomenal, as can be seen from the production statistics. The mines, which in the period of the 1860s had still averaged only 344,000 marks per annum, moved toward an average of 956,000 marks in the 1870s, then jumped to 1.1 million marks in the 1880s, and reached some 1.6 million marks per annum in the 1890s. The peak of nineteenth-century silver output occurred in 1895, when some 2.6 million marks were estimated to have been produced.

The Bolivian mine-owners put no effort into guaranteeing control by the civilian elite of the government, for the return of military rule under Daza seemed in no way to threaten their fundamental interests. In fact, Daza supported them by continuing all their pet projects, promoting their Chilean interests, and even ruling with a civilian parliament that wrote the very important constitution of 1879, which provided a fundamental liberal charter for the national government and stressed private property rights.

But the political indifference of the altiplano elite would not last, for the very weaknesses of the military regime would carry Bolivia into a full-scale war with Chile, which in turn would create serious political and economic problems once again for Bolivia's mine-owners. The Pacific War of 1879 appears from the Bolivian perspective almost as a Greek tragedy. Though Bolivia had protested Chilean expansion from the beginning, it had allowed de facto control of its Atacama territories to pass into the hands of both Chilean capitalists and Chilean workers and settlers from the earliest period of guano discoveries in the 1840s and 1850s. Ever since 1863 the pressures internally and externally were building to their inevitable climax. The increasing tempo of guano exports led to the Chilean military occupation of that year and the treaty of 1866, which gave legitimacy to Santiago's wildest claims. The first nitrates were discovered in the joint area near Mejillones, and a new period of intensive penetration began, quickly followed by the establishment of the port of Antofagasta in 1868, with the consequent abandonment of Cobija. The silver strikes at Caracoles in 1870 were followed by the British-Chilean Nitrates and Railroad Company in 1872. This mining concern soon controlled the nitrate fields and succeeded in dominating the more interior desert mining camps at Carracoles as well, once its railroad had been completed. With the coastal region made up of two-thirds Chilean citizens, the province was for all intents and purposes a colony of Chile.

Bolivian authorities had allowed this unusual state of affairs to develop because of their need for funds and the total inability of national capitalists to develop these previously empty deserts. But the military leaders became increasingly desperate once they had emptied the treasury and found that their source of new income could come only from

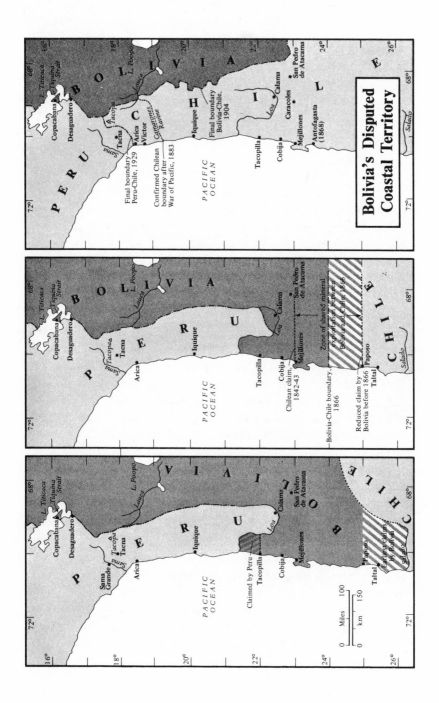

Bolivia's Disputed Coastal Territory

Final boundary Peru-Chile, 1929

Confirmed Chilean boundary after War of Pacific, 1883

Final boundary Bolivia-Chile, 1904

Zone of shared mineral exploitation between Bolivia and Chile, 1866

Bolivia-Chile boundary, 1866

Reduced claim by Bolivia before 1866

Chilean claim, 1842-43

Claimed by Peru

Earliest claims by Bolivia

these same coastal centers. For on the altiplano the immediate power of the Oruro and Potosí miners prevented the military from increasing their exactions, lest they succumb to a direct political confrontation which would lead to their immediate overthrow. The coastal territories, on the other hand, were distant and indifferent to the actual politics of the altiplano cities, so that the generals felt less inhibited in trying to rearrange concessions or renegotiate taxes.

It was in this context that in 1878 the Bolivian government initiated a new minimal tax on nitrates exported by the Nitrates and Railroad Company of Antofagasta. The English director, with the full backing of the Chileans, refused to pay this "unjust" and "illegal" tax. When Bolivian authorities attempted to arrest the disobedient director, he escaped to Chile. After the government announced it would confiscate company property to pay indemnity, the Chileans made their long-planned and carefully prepared move. In February 1879 Chilean troops made a successful landing at Antofagasta in support of the local Chileans, two days later seized Caracoles, and in March finally fought a major engagement with the Bolivians at the Calama oasis. In April came a formal declaration of war, and the involvement of Peru on the Bolivian side. But by this time, the entire coastal territories, including Cobija, had been seized by the powerful Chilean navy. Thus within two months of the beginning of the conflict, the entire Bolivian littoral territories had been seized by Chile.

The War of the Pacific was just beginning, for the Chileans were intent on seizing not only the Bolivian territories but also most of the Peruvian coastal mining regions. Using as an excuse a so-called "secret" treaty of mutual support signed between Bolivia and Peru in 1873, the Chileans in fact had prepared for a long naval war with Peru. Chile deliberately provoked Peru into aiding Bolivia and then proceeded to concentrate all its efforts at destroying the military power of Peru. Within hours of the formal declaration, it was blockading southern Peruvian ports.

By the time Bolivia was able to mobilize an army of 4,000 troops and get them to the coast, the Chileans were already attacking Peru's ports of Iquique and Tacna, and the Bolivian forces in joint operations with the Peruvians were destroyed piecemeal by the Chilean forces. By the end of the year Daza was at the head of the Bolivian troops on the Peruvian coast, but he proved an even worse general than a politician. Despite all the efforts of the troops, the miserable quality of Bolivian generalship led to inevitable defeat, as the Chileans by now had complete control of the seas and could strike at will along the coast.

Though the Bolivian government thought that a highland invasion was imminent after the defeat of its major armies by the end of 1879, in fact the Chileans had no intention of crossing the Andes. They were totally indifferent to the altiplano and recognized that a campaign in Bolivia's heartland would be a bitter and very costly affair resulting in few gains. Thus the Bolivians now became largely minor partners of the Peruvians and essentially passive spectators of the massive warfare going on in Peru. The shock of the war, the total unpreparedness of their troops, and the disastrous campaigns of Daza as a military leader led to widespread popular discontent. In December 1879 both the citizens of La Paz and the troops on the Peruvian coast rose in rebellion against the government and drove Daza from the presidency.

After intense negotiations and constant maneuverings, the rebel leaders finally agreed to appoint the one general who had not participated in any of the rebellious activities and who was unqualifiedly the best-trained officer in the Bolivian army, Narcisco Campero. With great reluctance, Campero took office in January 1880 and agreed to lead the nation in its continued struggle with Chile. An engineer trained at St. Cyr in France and at other leading European military centers, Campero was totally committed to the elimination of the worst aspects of militaristic rule and to the establishment of a stable civilian regime. He quickly put down the worst of the old officers, brought in the able liberal General Eliodoro Camacho to support his efforts, and then immediately called into session a special Congress to give him support.

The fact that the Congress of 1880 contained among its extraordinary members not only every leading political leader of the country

but such mine-owners as Gregorio Pacheco and Aniceto Arce indicated that the indifference of the new mining elite to national politics
had ended. The Pacific War had disrupted their traditionally close
links with Chilean capital, interrupted their exports, and forced them
to recognize that their long-term interests now required the establishment of a stable and financially sound government. Equally, the industry would soon find its expansion dependent upon the creation of
a modern communications infrastructure now perceived as a basic
necessity for future mining growth. Only a politically stable and economically viable regime, it was thought, could provide the funding
for roads and railroads, now that the chimerical wealth of the Pacific
coast was lost forever. The discrediting of the old military leaders, the
disaster of the state financial structure which had led directly to the
costly war, and the loss of all the wealth-producing coastal centers
combined to force the miners and the altiplano elite to participate directly in politics. The Pacific War disaster destroyed the power of the
army and also gave the civilian politicians the justification they needed
for finally and effectively bringing the national political structure into
some kind of coherent relationship with the changing nature of the
export and urban economies. The result was the ending of the era of
military caudillo rule and the beginnings of a modern parliamentary
structure with limited political participation that was dominated by
civilians. Thus, some fifty-five years after establishing an autonomous
republican government, Bolivia finally was to enter the age of classic
nineteenth-century civilian rule.

Chapter 6 • The Ages of Silver and Tin, 1880-1932

The year 1880 marked a major turning point in Bolivian history. To contemporaries the most dramatic event of this year was the utter defeat of Bolivian arms at the hands of the Chilean invaders and the loss of its entire coastal territory in the War of the Pacific. Less dramatic but equally important was the establishment of a new government to replace the previous caudillo regime. Though the replacement of governments by military coups was not an uncommon feature of political life in the republic since its creation fifty-five years previously, the new regime did in fact mark a fundamental change in national political development. It represented the first viable republican government of a civilian oligarchic nature, which would become the norm of political life until 1934. Though the loss of its direct access to the sea would remain the most intransigent of Bolivia's international problems from 1880 to the present day, the establishment of a modern political party system and a civilian-dominated government would cause long-term political, economic, and eventually even social and cultural changes within Bolivian society, changes that were profoundly to shape its historical evolution.

The fundamental stabilization and maturation of Bolivian politics after 1880 was not the result of the war with Chile but rather derived from basic changes within the Bolivian economy that had begun at least thirty years previously. Starting approximately at mid-century, the silver-mining industry had broken almost half a century of depression and had begun to reorganize on a massive scale. That reorganization involved the introduction of capital into mining in the form of modern machinery, the consolidation of many mining companies, and the liberation of production and minting from governmental control. All these developments took considerable time, since most of the capital was internally generated, and a new generation of technicians had to be created to develop the industry. By the 1860s and 1870s Bolivian mines were reaching world standards in terms of both output and technology. This in turn led to greater needs for capital and an opening up of highland Bolivian mining to Chilean and European capital.

Having initially organized themselves politically to break government monopoly over foreign sales and forced local purchases, the new mining elite began to operate as a coherent pressure group to obtain a government even more pliable to its interests. These interests were primarily focused on creating stable governments which could help finance the vital railroad linkages so desperately needed by the mine-owners. Coming into full production just as a long-term secular price decline in silver was beginning on the world market, the new elite was constantly forced to lower costs and increase productivity. This involved the increasing use of machinery and electricity and, above all, the mechanization of transportation.

While mechanization of the mines and their electrification would be the exclusive concern of Bolivian mine-owners, the problems of transport were beyond even their resources. Yet this was a cost item which had become a major obstacle to continued Bolivian expansion. For this reason government subsidies and international financing were imperative, and only a stable government responsive to their needs could provide the mine-owners with what they wanted. For them the war was a terrible shock which they desired to terminate as quickly as possible and turn into an advantage for Bolivia. Closely tied to their new Chilean capitalist links, they saw the war as a fatal break with their sources of new funding as well as a serious disruption in international trade. They also held the incompetence of the preceding military regimes as the primary cause of the war. The end result was that the miners formed a powerful peace party and threw their weight to the enlightened General Campero, who had helped overthrow the Daza military regime in December 1879.

Thereafter they sought a rapid end to the conflict with Chile and indemnification for all lost territories to be used exclusively for railroad construction. To accomplish these ends they created a formal political party known as the Partido Conservador. Constructed along the lines of such movements elsewhere on the continent, Bolivia's Conservative Party was in fact not formed in the traditional mold. While formally they defended Church interests, the primary concern of the Conservatives was with the creation of a powerful parliamentary regime, a civilian presidency, and a government dedicated to massive support for the construction of a communications infrastructure. Given the role of the Church as a weak and eventually apolitical institution, a powerful and coherent anti-clerical movement never developed in Bolivia. Thus the Conservatives, unlike most of their contemporary American counterparts, were able to concentrate all their energies on the political and economic modernization of Bolivia.

The development of a modern export sector had a major effect on the nation's social as well as economic and political structure. The growth of the mines in Oruro and Potosí created new demands for foodstuffs and labor, and, as a result, the population of some 2 million Bolivians was deeply affected by the changes. A dynamism entered the area of commercial agriculture, and the opening up of railroad links created new markets for hitherto marginal areas.

All of this growth meant that the hacienda system, which like mining had been restricted for almost half a century, was able to recover and expand. At the same time, the decline in the importance of the Indian head tax, at one time the government's major source of revenue, meant that the national government no longer had a vested interest in protecting the free communities in their lands. While the land titles of the free communities had been challenged as early as the Melgarejo period in the 1860s, Indian resistance had nullified this attack, so the communities had effectively retained their control over the lands. But by the 1870s the whites and cholos were increasing their pressure, and the new urban and mining camp markets provided the economic incentive for the landed elite to undertake a full-scale attack. Accepting the self-serving thesis that the communities were an anachronistic system of land tenure and a barrier to social integration, the elite used classic nineteenth-century liberal ideas of the need for a free peasantry holding title directly to the land. They forced upon the communities in the 1880s a system of direct land purchase in which the titles to the land were held by individuals and not by the corporate group. The creation of an individualistic Indian "peasantry" holding de jure title gave the hacendados the power to break up the de facto control of the communities by purchasing a few small parcels and thus destroying the cohesion of the community. The rest was simple, with fraud and force being as common as simple purchase, and soon there was a major expansion of haciendas throughout the highlands and the adjacent sub-puna valleys.

The Melgarejo attack of the 1860s on the communities had been based on these same "liberal" ideas. But the 1870s and the 1880s were a period in which new capital was made available to make the attack an effective one. Thus the period from 1880 to 1930 saw Bolivia's second great epoch of hacienda construction. Still holding half the lands and about half the rural population in 1880, the communities were reduced to less than a third of both by 1930. The power of the free Indian communities was definitively broken. Only the marginality of the lands they still retained and the stagnation of the national economy after the 1930s prevented their complete liquidation.

This progressive decline of the community meant the loss not only of land title but also of social cohesion. While many of the haciendas had re-created the political and social organization of the free community governments, the hacienda ayllus were often powerless to protect their members from expulsion from the estates. Moreover the need for laborers on the estates was less than the requirements had been for the former free communities. The result was an increased breakdown of Indian social norms, migration to cities, and an expansion in the urban and rural mestizo populations. The only thing preventing a total destruction of Indian culture was the continued growth of the Indian peasant populations throughout the nineteenth century. Though a series of epidemics at mid-century had slowed that growth, the disappearance of such communicable diseases as cholera by the last quarter of the century allowed for the continued strong rates of growth. In addition, the absence of public education in the countryside prior to the 1930s meant that the languages of the rural areas. for all classes and groups remained the indigenous ones.

Bolivia remained predominantly a rural and Indian peasant nation well into the twentieth century, despite the growth of a modern export sector, the dramatic expansion of the commercial agricultural network and the hacienda system, and even the growth of modern urban centers. It was estimated in the 1846 census that indigenous people represented 52 percent of the national population and still accounted for 51 percent of the national total by 1900. Even by a generous definition of urban, Bolivia in 1900 still claimed 73 percent of its population as rural. Finally, not only was Spanish a minority language in the republic but the illiteracy rate even among Spanish speakers was extraordinarily high. With the population of seven years or older as the base, it was estimated in 1846 that only 10 percent had received some schooling, a figure that had increased to only 16 percent by 1900. If anything, these figures probably overstate the actual literacy rates of the period.

Thus the republican governments established after 1825 were constructed on the base of a small percentage of the national population and for all intents and purposes were representative of only the Spanish-speaking literates of the republic, at best only a quarter of the national population. Given the literacy requirements for voting, let alone the financial restrictions for holding office, the Bolivian regime was in every sense of the word a limited-participation political system with the electoral base ranging from 30,000 to 40,000 persons in the period to 1900.

In terms of the Indian peasant masses there was nothing democratic or participatory about the republican governments that existed after 1880. In this respect the regimes if anything were more exploitative than the previous caudillo rule, if only because the economic expansion of the white elite was always at the cost of the Indians, either as miners or as landed agriculturalists. Nor was there any dispute about this among the elite, who were deeply concerned about keeping the Indian masses out of politics and denying them access to arms or any other effective means of protest. The army, especially after its professionalization and modernization, became an indispensable tool to maintain Indian submissiveness and was constantly called upon to suppress periodic Indian uprisings.

The elite divided into political parties and even resorted to arms to overthrow governments. But such acts of conflict and violence were quite circumscribed and largely urban and intra-class affairs. Appeals from the elite to non-elite and non–Spanish-speaking groups were extremely rare. Political life for the period 1880-1934 was largely carried out within strictly defined rules. Only once, in 1899, would Indian peasants be allowed to participate even temporarily in a national political conflict, and this intervention ended in total suppression of the Indian kurakas. For the Indian rural masses, political expression was confined to traditional village elders or temporary leaders of revolts who led them in their conservative "caste wars." These were uprisings confined to small communities and were exclusively defensive in nature, protesting either increases in exploitation or attacks on land rights. Thus, until well into the twentieth century, politics was the exclusive concern of only 10 percent to 20 percent of the national population even as participant observers, let alone formal actors.

This impact of economic change on the political and social life of the nation also had its counterpart in national culture. Cultural life under the republic was a much debased aspect of national existence. Social and intellectual isolation as a result of independence had its impact on elite thought and activity, just as the collapse of great centers of wealth reduced the patronage for popular art which had so flourished in the colonial period.

Although new universities had been established in the early decades of the century, the Universidad de San Francisco Xavier in Sucre continued to be the dominant intellectual center of the nation. But students from Chile and the Rio de la Plata no longer came to study, while the fields of activity remained the traditional ones of theology and law. In addition, the loss of metropolitan cadres, combined with the general decline in Bolivia's international trade and contacts, meant the loss of immediate European stimulation. Now Bolivia received European currents filtered through the experience of its American neighbors. In the first decades of the century Bolivia reverted to a level of intellectual activity much less intense and cosmopolitan than at any other time in its history.

There were of course some exceptions to this general pattern, but these were isolated individuals who were educated abroad and wrote their works outside Bolivia or worked within the country in a totally isolated environment. Also, a few distinguished foreign intellectuals such as José Joaquin de Mora, Bartolome Mitre, and Ramón Sotomayor Valdez wrote significant poems, novels, histories, or other literary works during their residence in Bolivia. There was, of course, an active pamphlet literature produced in this period which focused on immediate political or economic issues, but few of these works showed outstanding originality or had more than an ephemeral impact. The only exception to this general picture of pre-1880 literate culture was José María Dalence, whose statistical work on national society clearly earns for him the title of the father of the social sciences in Bolivia. His efforts at the systematic reconstruction of the social and economic structure of the nation in the 1840s were unique, and the intelligence and sophistication of his work mark him as a social analyst conversant with the latest European developments.

In the fields of literature and the arts, little was accomplished. The first novel which was written by a Bolivian did not appear until the 1860s, and the first ephemeral literary journals until the end of that decade and the beginning of the 1870s. The poetry and drama of the time are considered by national critics to be of the poorest quality. The only exception was Nathaniel Aguirre, considered one of Bolivia's most important novelists of the modern period. Though Nathaniel Aguirre did begin his formal education and early writing before 1880, his major work appeared afterward.

After 1880 intellectual life revived under the combined impact of stable civilian government, increased national wealth, the professionalization of the occupations, and the establishment of modern curricula in the schools. Individual writers found kindred groups, while individuals of good families now had ample opportunity to write and live abroad and participate in the latest Latin American or European cultures. Thus the Bolivian poet Ricardo Jaimes Freye joined Rubén Darío in Buenos Aires and was a powerful voice in the modernist movement which swept through Latin American and Spanish letters. Such national writers as Gabriel René Moreno, Bolivia's leading historian, found employment in the libraries and archives of Chile, and novelists and essayists such as Alcides Arguedas, living in Paris, became known throughout the Americas for their new realistic approach to letters. Given the increased tempo in the writing of poetry, literature, and the humanities in general, Bolivians came to term the writers who came of age in this period as the "generation of the 1880s." This was the first literary generation to appear in republican letters and provided an important base upon which all later cultural developments could occur. The period from 1880 to 1920 was in many ways a golden age for national literature.

In the sciences the traditional structures of the national universities prevented any serious changes. Although Bolivia by the 1880s was as technologically advanced in mining as any nation in the world, all its machines and technologists were imported. Foreign engineers from the best schools in Europe and North America established the latest in plants and mines, but no significant discoveries even in metallurgy occurred in Bolivia. The problem in what Bolivians called the "exact sciences" was the lack of an infrastructure. Low budgets and part-time teachers prevented the development of scientific laboratories or systematic research. Whereas novelists, humanists, and social scientists could develop out of the traditional professions of law, theology, and medicine, this was not possible for the sciences or technology. Although Bolivians trained and working abroad did participate in the development of modern science in the advanced countries, until the present day Bolivia has remained an importer of science and technology.

In the plastic arts, the economic stagnation and the concurrent decline of the Catholic Church in the first decades of the nineteenth century served to bring to an end the great age of creative artistic activity of the colonial period. Sucre's elimination of tithes and confiscation of Church incomes and properties had brought church construction to a halt. With the Church and wealthy pious citizens no longer available for patronage, the demand for paintings and carvings also declined. The nineteenth-century Church also became less tolerant of folk Catholicism, more timid in its acceptance of native mestizo and Indian art styles, and archly conservative in its overall artistic taste. Thus when Church revenues again became significant after the victory of the Conservatives and major construction resumed, the clerics and the white elite rejected Bolivia's rich colonial artistic heritage and slavishly adopted the most reactionary of European models. The result of these factors was the stagnation of Bolivian plastic arts from the first decades of the nineteenth century until well into the twentieth century and the elimination of the Indian and cholo masses from significant participation in the cultural life of the nation.

The growth of the export sector of Bolivia in the second half of the nineteenth century, and especially after 1880, thus had both its positive and negative aspects in terms of the nation's political, social, and cultural life. But it had some disturbing effects on the national economy as well. Not only did the growth of the silver industry revive the urban centers, stimulate the hacienda economy, and reorganize the internal economic space of the society, it made the Bolivian economy more vulnerable to international economic forces. Both the importers of manufactured goods, who paid for their purchases with hard currency earned in mineral exports, and the government, which had become totally dependent on taxes on international trade, were now intimately involved with the fortunes of the export sector. This sector in turn became ever more vulnerable to fluctuations in international demand the more successful it became. Thus the government, the mine-owners, and the national elite were subject to international constraints which created problems of stability over which they had little control.

Bolivia, in an economist's terms, was a classic example of an open economy. Since the bulk of internal purchasing power came from the leading mining sector, it was extremely vulnerable to changes in prices of its primary exports. Moreover, even in the mining sector, until late in the twentieth century, it was an economy dominated by one metal. To 1900 this metal was silver, and from that period until very recently it has been tin. Thus world price changes had a direct and immediate impact on the local economy. Powerful regional elites could be eliminated overnight by abrupt changes in international prices, with a consequent disruption of the very foundations of the governing elite. Bolivians learned to live with this uncertainty and tried to respond as quickly as possible to new price incentives. But the limitations of natural resources guaranteed that their response had its limits and that long-term economic progress was not inevitable for the nation as a whole.

It was this uncertainty that explains much of the behavior of the mine-owners who were predominant political leaders in the post-1880 period. Faced by falling world prices and limits to their own capital, they seized control of the government and directed its undivided efforts at lowering the costs of transportation, the most expensive element in the mining process. This meant that the miners wanted a stable civilian government whose fiscal resources could be devoted to massive railroad construction. In this aim, the miners and their allies were successful, though in the end the total collapse of the world silver market would lead to their own downfall.

Formal political parties were necessary to the political system that the mining elite desired. These were created in the debates over the War of the Pacific. The mine-owners took a pacifist pro-Chilean position from the early days of the war and grouped themselves around two key figures, Mariano Baptista, a lawyer for the mine companies, and Aniceto Arce, the largest single mine-owner and producer in the nation. The anti-Chilean and anti-peace group gathered their forces behind the popular Colonel Eliodoro Camacho, leader of the anti-Daza revolt and a leading Liberal theoretician.

The testing of the viability of these parties occurred in the elections of 1884. General Narcisco Campero, who had directed the diminished Bolivian war effort after overthrowing Daza, completed his legal term in office, established a viable Congress, and even put into effect in 1880 the constitution written in 1878. Overseeing a completely free election, the Campero regime was able to provide the stability for the creation of two coherent parties. The eventual winner of the election, after the necessity of a congressional second count, was the maverick mine-owner Gregorio Pacheco, Bolivia's second leading silver producer. With Mariano Baptista as his vice-president, Pacheco initiated the era of what Bolivians called the age of the "Conservative Oligarchy," which lasted from 1884 to 1899. During this period the two parties fully defined themselves, while the government concentrated on achieving a settlement with Chile and promoting major railroad construction.

Although Pacheco promised to remain neutral in the elections of 1888, in fact the Conservative regime threw its support behind Aniceto Arce. As a result, the election of 1888 became a violent affair, with the embittered Liberals finally abstaining altogether. Thus there was a return to the use of violence in politics by the end of the 1880s. This resort to violence was made inevitable by the refusal of all subsequent governments to relinquish the presidency to the opposition party. Once in office and close to the only major source of income outside of mining and the haciendas, politicians refused to give up their spoils by any electoral or democratic means. Voting in all elections was open and readily controlled by central government appointees in all the local districts, so presidential elections and congressional seats were easily secured. Each governing party guaranteed its majority in Congress but did permit a substantial representation of all the opposition parties as an easily supportable escape valve which did not seriously threaten its own control over office. The presidency, however, was to be controlled at all costs, including the use of total fraud. This meant that throughout the period of both Conservative and Liberal eras political violence was endemic. But it should be stressed that this violence was usually dominated by civilians of a particular party and was quite clearly limited to an urban and elite environment and involved little bloodshed.

Given the fact that the democratic processes seemed to be in play at all times, violence also tended to be confined to periods following illegitimate electoral defeat when an opposition party, and most of the voting public, felt that the government had violated their rights. Revolts tended to be timed to changes in presidential periods, and while the tradition of *golpes* (*coups d'état*) remained a permanent part of the political landscape, they did not of necessity represent the breakdown of powerful civilian rule, the emergence of social anarchy, or the instability of political life. While later commentators on Bolivia were to count the number of revolts and assume total disruption, in fact, the period from 1880 to 1936 was one of remarkable continuity and stability despite the periodic resort to limited violence.

The regime of Aniceto Arce (1888-92) represented the most spectacular period of Conservative rule. Arce crushed a major Liberal uprising. He then carried through a massive road construction program and initiated the vital railroad link from the Chilean port of Antofagasta to the city of La Paz, thus giving Bolivia access to the sea by rail for the first time in its history. Arce also founded a military academy and systematically professionalized the army. He adopted the now common practice of allowing Liberals representation in Congress but denied them access to the presidency. The result was another fraudulent election in 1892, with Mariano Baptista, the ideologue of the Conservative Party, emerging as president.

Like his predecessors, Baptista (1892-96) concentrated on railroad construction. He also signed a preliminary peace treaty with Chile and concentrated on developing Bolivia's natural rubber resources in the Acre territories. In turn Baptista passed his government along to the last of the Conservative oligarchs, the mine-owner Sergio Fernandez Alonso (1896-1899). By this time, however, the power of the Conservative regime, which was firmly entrenched in southern silver-mining areas and the city of Sucre, was being progressively eroded by the collapse of silver prices on the world market. In turn the Liberals found their strength progressively increasing, as they became more intimately associated with the rising urban professional classes of La Paz and with non–silver-mining groups, above all the new tin miners, intent on displacing the older oligarchy.

The rise of tin production as the primary industry of Bolivia after 1900 had its origins in developments of the Conservative era. The great age of the modern silver-mining industry had seen Bolivia obtaining the latest in mining technology, from the use of power tools and electricity to the employment of modern engineers. At the same time, the silver magnates and their Conservative regimes had made modern communications their primary task and had constructed a vital rail network connecting the mine regions to the Pacific coast.

When silver collapsed on the international market, it was possible to transfer the technology and communications to other metals. In this case a fortuitous expansion of world demand for tin in canning and a hundred other new industrial uses, along with its exhaustion in the traditional European mines, allowed Bolivia to capitalize on its resources and quickly and effectively respond to international demand. Tin had been an important by-product of silver-mining from the earliest times. But the costs of shipping it in bulk to European smelters had always been prohibitive, primarily because of Bolivia's primitive communications systems. The availability of cheap railroad transportation for the first time in national history meant that it suddenly became profitable for Bolivia to ship this mineral. Equally, the fact that tin occurred in exactly the same mining areas as silver, and often in the very same mines, meant that there was relatively little dislocation in terms of traditional mining enclaves or transportation networks.

The transition from silver to tin was a relatively easy one for the

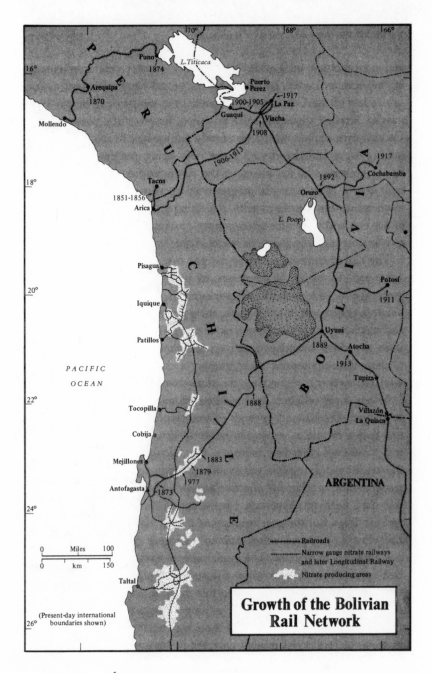

Growth of the Bolivian Rail Network

PERU

Puno
1874

L. Titicaca

Arequipa
1870

Puerto
Perez
1917
La Paz
1900-1905
Guaqui
Viacha
1908

Mollendo

1906-1913

Tacna

1851-1856
Arica

1892

Oruro

Cochabamba
1917

L. Poopó

Pisagua

Iquique

Potosí
1911

Patillos

Uyuni
1889
Atocha

PACIFIC
OCEAN

1913

Tupiza

Tocopilla

1888

Villazón
La Quiaca

Cobija

Mejillones
1883
1879
1977

ARGENTINA

Antofagasta
1873

0   Miles   100
0   km   150

CHILE

Railroads
Narrow gauge nitrate railways
and later Longitudinal Railway
Nitrate producing areas

Taltal

**Growth of the Bolivian
Rail Network**

(Present-day international
boundaries shown)

BOLIVIA

162

Bolivian economy and society to make. It was less easy for the traditional elite. First of all, the growth of tin mining had a boom-like
quality as production rose from quite minimal levels to massive exports
in a period of less than ten years. Moreover, while the general mining
zones were the same, there was a subtle but important shift of emphasis
to the north, with the mines in northern Potosí and southern Oruro
having the dominant role in production. Finally, the shift was so
sudden and the capital invested in fixed assets so heavy that many of
the traditional silver miners found it difficult to change over to tin.
The result of all this was that much of the traditional silver magnate
elite did not make the transition, a plethora of foreign companies entered the market, and a new group of Bolivian entrepreneurs emerged
for the first time on the national scene.

All these changes created an important rupture in the national
political scene. The old elite, entrenched in Potosí and its supporting
town of Sucre, found itself more and more incapable of suppressing
the growing popularity of the opposition Liberals. At the same time
the enormous growth of La Paz, which now became the key servicing
center for the new tin-mining industry, even further accentuated its
dominance in national economic and social life. This led to a combined Liberal and regionalist revolt in 1899, whereby the largely
Liberal elite of La Paz called for local federalist rule and the overthrow of the Conservatives.

The revolt of 1899 was in fact a rather costly and extensive military
operation which proved so difficult to win that the Liberals went
beyond the traditional rules and encouraged the Indian peasant
masses to participate. The result was the temporary intervention of
some Indian groups in national political life for the first time since
the early years of the republic. But once victory was achieved by the
Liberals not only was federalism forgotten, as La Paz became the de
facto capital of the nation, but the Indian troops were disarmed and
their leaders executed.

The new century thus saw the emergence of a new political party
and the creation of a new mining industry. In many ways the Liberal
regime which followed the Conservative one differed in few funda-

mental aspects. Both were committed to massive government subsidization of transport, heavy support for the mining industry, and
development and modernization of its urban centers. Both regimes
actively sought the destruction of the Indian communities and the
expansion of the hacienda system, while all governments proved to
be indifferent to the Church question, a prominent issue in most
other Latin American states.

During the Liberal era, the old patterns of political participation
persisted. While congressional elections would remain relatively free,
those for the presidency would be controlled, with a corresponding
resort to limited violence as the only means for "out" politicians to
obtain the executive office. An open press, civil liberties for whites
and mestizos, and a thriving intellectual life for the elite all were
maintained in the new Liberal era. But a new type of political leadership now emerged. Reflecting the complexities of the new mining
era, the tin-miners were far too involved in their own affairs to participate directly in national life. Meanwhile, the systematic support for
education and professionalization on the part of the Conservatives
finally had created a class of lawyers and *letrados* of sufficient number
and experience to run the affairs of the government.

Thus was born what later political analysts would call the *rosca*,
by which was meant a government of professional politicians operating primarily in the interests of the leading tin barons of the nation.
The economic power groups were now no longer required to intervene
directly in the political process to obtain their own ends. This proved
essential for the local tin leaders, since it allowed them fully to concentrate on the intense and competitive struggle for domination in
the Bolivian tin mines. Given the fact that there were no restrictions
on foreign investments in the mines and that Bolivia was open to all
types of entrepreneurs and engineers from abroad at the very beginning of its tin expansion, it is a surprise to note that Bolivians themselves emerged as the dominant mine-owners after three decades of
very intense competition. At the beginning, European, North American, and even Chilean capitalists competed with local Bolivian
capitalists for control of the tin-mine sector. Hundreds of companies

were established, many of them often working the same local mountain of tin. Yet despite the competition of all these powerful and well-endowed opponents, the local capitalists became the dominant group in control of the industry by the 1920s.

Of the three major leaders to emerge, the most powerful unquestionably was Simon I. Patiño. Born in the Cochabamba Valley in 1860, Patiño appears to have come from an artisan and part-cholo (or mestizo) background. He received a local secondary education and then apprenticed himself to various mining and mine-equipment importing firms in the 1880s and early 1890s when the silver industry still predominated. In 1894 he purchased his first share in a tin mine in Oruro, in the canton of Uncía on the border of the province of Potosí. By 1897 Patiño had purchased full control of the mine and in 1900 struck one of the richest tin veins ever found in Bolivia. By 1905 his La Salvadora mine had become the single largest tin mine in Bolivia, and Patiño had a full complement of foreign technicians and the latest in refining equipment. From this initial investment, Patiño rapidly expanded his holdings both vertically and horizontally. In 1910 he bought out his neighbor, the British-owned Uncía Mining Company, and in 1924 he completed his domination of the two mining centers of Uncía and Llallagua by buying the Chilean Llallagua Company and thus achieving his permanent position of controlling almost 50 percent of national production with a labor force of over 10,000 workers.

Meanwhile Patiño turned his attention to the vertical integration of his mining operations, and, in a move rare in Latin American capitalist circles, moved to control his European refiners. After joining forces with his North American consumers, he eventually took control over the world's largest smelter of Bolivian tin, Williams, Harvey & Co., Ltd., of Liverpool, in 1916. By the early 1920s, Patiño lived permanently abroad and could by then be more accurately described as a European capitalist, given his vast non-Bolivian holdings. Nevertheless, he remained Bolivia's dominant miner, its chief private banker, and finally its most powerful capitalist until his death in the 1940s.

Of the two other leading miners who emerged to divide evenly the other half of total production, one was also Bolivian, belonging to the old silver-mining family of the Aramayos, and the other was a European Jew by the name of Mauricio Hochschild. Both the Aramayo and Hochschild companies had heavy inputs of European capital, but both were—unlike the Patiño firms—largely run from Bolivia itself. While Hochschild had some investments in Chile, his primary residence virtually to the end of his career was in Bolivia, and this was his principal area of investment. For the Aramayo family as well, Bolivia was to be their primary area of activity. Thus by the 1930s, the big three miners who dominated tin production, and a good percent of the lead, zinc, wolfram, and other local mines, were based primarily in Bolivia, or, like the Patiño companies, wholly owned by Bolivian nationals. Given the totally open nature of the Bolivian mining industry to all foreign entrepreneurs from the middle of the nineteenth century onward, such national control was truly an unusual development in the history of Latin American mining.

The withdrawal of Patiño and the other new tin magnates from direct involvement in national affairs left Bolivian politics in the hands of an elite of rising urban professional upper-middle-class individuals and representatives of the provincial landed elite (men of modest landholdings and relatively few peasants, but with solid social backgrounds). Almost all of these men were trained in the law and, while committed to a liberal conception of parliamentary government and constitutional law, believed strongly in a caste system and rule by a white oligarchy.

This belief in caste was given support by the surprising stability of the social structure of Bolivia, despite all the recent and very rapid changes that had occurred. Thus in the census of 1900, only 13 percent of the population were listed as "white." Equally, while the census implied a major growth in urban population since 1846, this was based on a rather generous definition of urban as any community over 200 persons. The use of the more realistic definition of urban as towns over 20,000 population, however, shows how little significant change had occurred. Thus from 1846 to 1900, the percentage of the population living in such towns had increased from 6 percent to only 7 percent. Even La Paz, the largest urban center of the nation, had only grown to some 55,000 persons in 1900, or just 12,000 more than half a century before. Though new mines had created several new towns in southern Oruro and northern Potosí, the booming mining industry in 1900, with its 13,000 workers, still absorbed only 1 percent of the economically active population.

Thus despite the growth of a new export sector, the expansion of new elite white and cholo classes, and the massive breakdown of Indian land ownership in the rural areas, Bolivia remained surprisingly traditional in its social makeup. The Liberals therefore felt little compulsion to concern themselves with the serious class and caste problems which divided this multi-ethnic society.

The Liberals were even more aggressive against the free communities than their Conservative predecessors had been, and they even disarmed and destroyed the Indians who had supported them in the 1899 revolt. They also justified themselves to the same economic elites by continuing powerful government support for the mining sector. This involved advocacy of free trade, minimal taxation on mining and the landed and monied elites, and government subsidization of railroad construction. Even in terms of their political ideology, the Liberals showed themselves to be no more liberal than their predecessors. Like the Conservatives before them, this new breed of political leaders also refused to relinquish presidential office to opponents. Despite the tremendous growth of the national economy, the government still represented an important source of employment, with the president the major guarantor of that employment. Thus the traditional patterns of open parliamentary elections, fraudulent presidential elections, and limited civilian-led coups to replace long-term party rule continued to be the norm.

Once in office, the Liberals adopted virtually all the positions of the previously despised Conservatives. Federalist ideology was totally abandoned and a centralist regime fully established in La Paz. In their desperation to complete the railroad network and to modernize the cities, they willingly abandoned national territories and traditional international positions, a policy that left Bolivia totally deprived of its access to the sea and rather heavily indebted as well.

The first of these major international developments was the Acre dispute. In the heart of the Amazonian rubber boom area, the Acre territories adjoined the Brazilian border and were largely populated by Brazilian migrants. When the last Conservative regime succeeded in establishing a customs house on the Acre River at Puerto Alonso and collected an enormous sum on the rubber being shipped through to Brazil, the local tappers revolted. The Liberal regime sent in troops to the distant eastern lowlands to crush the revolt, but covert Brazilian support gave the rebels enough strength to overcome the Bolivians. The result was total defeat for Bolivian arms and the annexation of the Acre territory to Brazil in the Treaty of Petropolis in 1903 for the sum of 2.5 million pounds sterling.

While the Liberal government had made a concentrated stand on the Acre territory, it was much less aggressive on the Chilean front. Here it went well beyond the most extreme concessions ever proposed by its Conservative predecessors in an attempt to obtain funds and terminate a long-standing and politically sensitive issue which it felt was distracting national resources. Reversing their previous irredentist stand which demanded an unqualified return of the seized territory, the Liberals signed a formal peace treaty with Chile in 1904. Bolivia agreed to cede all seized littoral lands and gave up its demands for a Pacific port. In turn Chile agreed to construct a railroad from Arica to La Paz, provide a formal indemnification of £300,000, guarantee internal Bolivian railroad construction loans, and give up its special most-favored-nation arrangements on trade with Bolivia. Although the treaty formally resolved the Pacific littoral question, in fact, the issue has remained an unresolved question of Andean international relations from the 1880s to the present day.

But at that moment the Acre and Chilean accords gave the Liberals relative peace on the international front and extensive financial support to continue railroad construction. Internally, as well, it removed the major international issue of political dispute. The elimination of this divisive issue, the adoption of the basic economic program of the

Conservatives, and the decline of the Sucre elite resulted in the almost exclusive domination of the Liberals in national government. So strong was the liberal movement, in fact, that there would be no coup attempts from 1899 until 1920, a record in the history of the political evolution of the nation.

The first Liberal regime was led by José Manuel Pando (1899-1904), the great leader of the party in its years of opposition. While Pando kept to some of the positions of his earlier years, the men who followed were far more pragmatic and interested exclusively in power. These new men were dominated by Ismael Montes, the second president of the Liberal period, who would end by serving for two terms in office (1904-9, 1913-17). A lawyer by training, Montes represented the new breed of middle-class urban politicians. A forceful personality with a shrewd instinct for politics, he was able effectively to prevent the rise of an opposition party of "outs" until after World War I. In this effort he was aided by the tremendous boom in the economy brought about by the rising exportation of tin. This provided the funds for a major expansion of the state bureaucracy, which in turn he used to buy out all potential opposition.

Moreover, the national elite was also effectively compensated by the new Liberal era by a massive commitment to public-works construction. With a positive and rather sizable balance of trade surplus, Montes was able to secure private international bank funding for governmental loans. In 1906 came a huge United States private bank loan which enabled Bolivia to complete its international rail connections with spurs to the major interior cities of Cochabamba and Sucre as well as the international links to the mining centers of Potosí and Oruro. A new railroad was constructed to Guaqui on Lake Titicaca, thus linking up with the Peruvian rail network. There was also major urban construction, sanitation, and lighting projects, and a high pitch of economic activity until the crisis of 1913-14 on the eve of World War I.

Montes was thus able to dominate the selection of his successor, Eliodoro Villazón, and then to secure his own formal re-election in 1913. But the second Montes administration was not the unqualified triumph the first had been. Liberal administration attempts to establish a national bank had created bitter pressure from a key element of the elite. Next, the sudden pre–World War I crisis in international trade caused tin production and exports to decline by a third between 1913 and 1914. Finally, adverse weather conditions caused a severe agricultural crisis in that same period.

With money tight, and government revenues declining, the freewheeling Montes suddenly found himself with an intransigent opposition which he could not buy off. Moreover, having been in power too long, he was unwilling to use tact or subtlety to calm this growing opposition. The result was the almost inevitable splintering of the Liberal Party into two formally constituted groups. The new party which emerged out of the previously undivided Liberals was given the name of Republicans and formally established in 1914.

Thus Bolivia once again returned to a more normal two-party arrangement. But as both Montes and the founder of the new party, Daniel Salamanca, recognized, this new political grouping was a carbon copy of the Liberals. It drew its strength from the same classes; it unquestionably supported all demands of the mining establishment; and it was as racist and oligarchic as its opponents. Montes called them liberal "apostates," while Salamanca claimed his party's aim was only to guarantee free elections and the restrictions on presidential power. The final result of the return of effective two-party politics was a return to the policies of closed and fraudulent presidential elections and an ultimate resort to violence and coups on the part of the opposition.

The recovery of the post–World War I period enabled Montes to carry through his banking and financial reforms with little Republican opposition and even to win popular support among the some 80,000 voters in the republic in congressional and presidential elections. In 1917 he passed his government on to a more moderate successor, who proved unable to keep the Republicans under control. With strong support from disgruntled elements in the business community, the Republicans made considerable headway, and, when the last Liberal president, Gutiérrez Guerra, attempted to control the elections of

1920, the Republican Party rose in a successful revolt and ended Liberal rule.

The advent of Republican rule, which lasted until 1934, brought a subtle but important shift to the political system that had evolved in the post–Pacific War era. From simple two-party systems, the national political scene would begin to evolve toward more multi-party groupings. At the same time the standards of belief, based on nineteenth-century liberal ideology and supported by a strong element of racism, would slowly begin to change. Finally, the extraordinarily open nature of the national economy would mean that Bolivia was one of the first nations in the world to feel the full effects of the great crisis in the world economy known as the Great Depression.

The economic growth which had been the hallmark of both Conservative and Liberal governments had been initially confined to certain elite groups. By the second decade of the twentieth century, this growth was beginning to have important effects on the mestizo and Indian sectors, but often in a conflictive manner. The expansion of the haciendas led to increasing land conflict with the community Indians, which would lead to a series of major revolts in the 1920s; but even more important and more immediate for the elite was the organization of the first modern labor unions in Bolivia. Though organizational activities went back to the nineteenth century, Bolivia was several decades behind its neighbors in labor agitation and organization. It was not until 1912 that the first May Day celebration was held and not until 1916 and 1917 that even local urban labor confederations were established. Important national and/or urban strikes did not begin until 1920.

For the first time, the elite became aware in the decade of the 1920s of the existence of alternative demands and of potentially threatening groups outside the elite political arena. As political life became more complex in the Republican party era, it would lead to the emergence of minor parties which for the first time seriously discussed the problems and potentials of class conflict. Also the 1920s witnessed the first stirrings of European Marxist thought as it arrived to Bolivia, filtered through Argentine, Chilean, and Peruvian writers.

Almost immediately after seizing power, the Republican Party divided into two opposing branches, one led by the urban middle-class intellectual, Bautista Saavedra, and the other by the Cochabamba hacendado and politician, Daniel Salamanca. It was Saavedra and his followers who were able to seize the initiative and take control of the government and the party in 1921. But Salamanca and his forces established a new "Genuine Republican" Party and proceeded actively to agitate against the new regime.

The increasing political tension of the 1920s combined with the deepening political crises and the beginnings of the Great Depression to unleash political violence and social conflict more intense than anything experienced in the previous decades. Saavedra had hardly been installed in office when a massive Indian uprising in Jesús de Machaca in the Lake Titicaca district led to the killing of hundreds of Indians and dozens of local whites and cholos. Saavedra unhesitatingly used full force to suppress the revolt and attacked the community governments, or ayllus, as reactionary institutions that had to be forcibly suppressed. Thus he took a classic nineteenth-century Liberal position on the Indian question.

Saavedra, however, proved more open in his views on organized labor. He began to view it as an important area of potential support, as his own bases in the upper and middle classes were eroded by Genuine Republican and Liberal opposition. Denied the support of the traditional regional elites and the hacendado class, he sought to find new bases of support by initiating the first modern labor and social legislation in Bolivian history. He also expressed a willingness to support limited strike activity and unionization drives, a first for a national president. But faced by increasing strike activities, including serious agitation in the mines and the first general strike, which occurred in 1922, Saavedra found himself quickly withdrawing his tentative support. In fact, troops were used in a bloody suppression of miners at Uncía in late 1923, one of the first of many such mining massacres. Thus while his labor legislation and pro-labor speeches represented some awareness on the part of the white elite that class conflict existed in Bolivia, the constant retrenchment of the regime on this issue revealed that Saavedra held this position more as a result of political expediency than because he and his followers had advanced well beyond the beliefs of nineteenth-century liberal and positivist thought.

The 1920s were a period when other members of the elite began slowly to adopt non-traditional positions. In 1920 the first local socialist parties were established. By late 1921 a national Socialist Party was founded which, though a small group of intellectuals with minimal labor support, nevertheless began to discuss such basic issues as Indian servitude (*pongueaje*), the legal recognition of the Indian community governments, and the rights of labor and of women. While these ideas were new and revolutionary in the Bolivian context, they were already part of the well-established and more radical Marxist political tradition of all of Bolivia's neighbors, including Peru. The famous splintering of the Latin American Marxian socialist parties and the rise of the communist movements in South America in the 1920s, for example, found no echo in Bolivia. Bolivia did not produce its first even moderate Marxist party until the end of the 1920s, while its first formal communist party was established only in the 1950s.

Much of this early agitation was associated with the short but very intense depression which began the decade of the 1920s and resulted in a severe but temporary drop in mine production. Once production resumed by late 1922, labor agitation began to subside. Moreover, Saavedra found that the nascent organized labor movement, though finally establishing its first national federations and producing its first general strike, was too weak a support for his regime. The lower middle classes, finding themselves favored for the first time by mild social legislation, supported Saavedra. But, given his strong personality, it was inevitable that the Liberals and Genuine Republicans would join forces to oppose his regime, so he found it more and more difficult to govern.

The increasing loss of traditional elite support led Saavedra to consider rather traditional responses. After his first tentative moves toward labor and the lower middle classes, he turned toward foreign private capital markets for funds to promote major development projects, the source of popularity of previous governments. He negotiated a $US 33 million private banking loan in New York for railroad, public works, and *Banco de la Nación* financing. These were the classic concerns of Liberals and Conservatives before him. But debt servicing for Bolivia was already high, while the terms of the loan, which included direct United States control over Bolivian taxation services, were totally unacceptable to most Bolivians. There was little question, in fact, that Bolivian negotiators had been corrupted and that, despite its excellent credit rating, the nation had been forced to pay very high interest rates. The opposition to the so-called "Nicolaus" loan was immediate and intense.

To add to his problems, Saavedra in the arbitrary manner of Montes also tried to resolve the great debate surrounding the petroleum concessions on the Bolivian eastern lowlands region. In 1920 the Republicans had opened up the reserve areas to foreigners after Bolivian entrepreneurs proved incapable of developing productive wells. In 1920 and 1921 North American entrepreneurs secured concessions, but these smaller companies were really fronts for the Standard Oil Company of New Jersey, which in 1921 was permitted by the government to purchase these concessions, add new ones, and establish the Standard Oil Company of Bolivia. Given all the special treatment accorded to Standard Oil, and the intense opposition of the elite to Saavedra, it was inevitable that there would be an outcry.

Thus to all the usual issues of corruption, favoritism, and presidential domination, Salamanca and his more conservative followers added a totally new theme, that of economic nationalism. Opposition to exploitation of natural resources by foreign companies started in Bolivia virtually from the first concession ever granted in petroleum. While no outcry was ever raised over mining, and Guggenheim and other North American companies actively participated in the economy, petroleum became a special subject, and the attack against Standard Oil became part of the rhetoric of both the traditional right and the nascent left movements in Bolivia.

By the end of his term, Saavedra was desperately attempting to appease all factions. On the one hand he helped the mine-owners crush the Uncía strike in June 1923, with indiscriminate killing of workers and their families. On the other hand he carried out a major overhaul of the mining tax structure in late 1923 and succeeded in doubling the government's taxes on tin production. In a rage, Patiño in early 1924 removed his mining company headquarters from Bolivia to the United States, incorporated Patiño Mines and Enterprises in Delaware, and even lent the government £600,000 for railroad construction, in return for a guarantee from Saavedra not to raise taxes further for five years.

All of this was to no avail, and despite every attempt to control his successor and even prorogue his term, Saavedra was forced to turn his regime over to his own party candidate, Hernando Siles, whom he opposed. The subsequent Siles period was one of active political evolution and a continued splintering of the traditional parties. Faced by Saavedra's control of the Republican Party, Siles created his own Nationalist Party grouping. He supported the University Reform movement, a major innovation, and in 1928 radical students established the first FUB (National Federation of University Students of Bolivia). Both the socialists and the FUB, though still small groupings of intellectuals, were now suggesting radical transformations of society, with both calling for agrarian reform and the end of rural feudalism. They urged socialization of the natural resources and changes in the definition of private property and gave strong support to the nascent labor movement.

At the same time as the political scene was evolving into a more complex arena of conflicting class ideologies, the economic scene began to deteriorate to an alarming degree. In the period 1926-29, the government faced increased budgetary deficits and growing difficulties in meeting its international debt obligations. This was occurring just as the price of tin on the international market had peaked and had begun its long secular decline into the catastrophe of the Great Depression. In an attempt to meet this crisis, whose extent was as yet unknown, the government resorted to both traditional and some fairly radical measures. In 1927 and 1928, with the backing of specially created taxes, new United States private bank loans were secured. In the same year the government adopted the reforms proposed by the United States Kemmerer mission and finally established a government-controlled Central Bank to oversee all aspects of the national money supply. In addition, the temporary flare-up on the disputed Chaco border with Paraguay in late 1928 both presaged more bitter conflicts and gave Siles the excuse to use a formal state of siege to control his internal enemies. The border incident was a bloody affair, forcing Siles to call up the reserves and order an open reprisal. But he did not want a full-scale war to develop and negotiated an Act of Conciliation with Paraguay in early 1929.

The surge of patriotism, the imposition of states of siege, and the political and economic reforms carried out by Siles were having little effect on national politics. Siles proved to be too much in the traditional mold to permit the free play of democratic forces. His regime galvanized the Liberals, the Genuine Republicans, and the Saavedrista Republicans into a temporary united front. Meanwhile the deterioration of international tin prices was making itself felt. In 1929 Bolivia reached its all-time record output of 47,000 tons of tin exported but at a price that was below that of the early years of the decade. Whereas tin was quoted at $917 a ton in 1927, it had dropped to $794 a ton in 1929, and would eventually bottom out at $385 per ton in 1932. As tin prices declined, so, too, did government revenues, which were primarily taken from tin export taxes. By 1929, some 37 percent of the government budget was going for foreign debt servicing and another 20 percent for military expenditures, leaving little for bare government necessities, let alone for public works or national welfare.

Justifying his actions, as his predecessors had done, on the existence of a national crisis, Siles tried to continue in office beyond his presidential term. In mid-1930 he announced formal plans to prorogue his government by having parliament formally elect him for a new term. He then handed the government over to a military junta to oversee his formal re-election. But opposition to this move was universal. For the first time in national politics university students made their power felt by conducting major riots against the government. In response the army rose in rebellion, and the junta leadership was forced to flee. In the midst of the disorders there was even an invasion of Marxist radicals at the southern frontier town of Villazón. The Marxists attempted to lead a worker-peasant uprising, an action which found some echo in the urban labor movement. The result was the fall of Siles and his supporters and the first genuinely successful expression of more radical political activity on the national political front. Though the most traditional and conservative forces would ultimately gain victory over the 1930 revolt, it was nevertheless the first break in the unified political ideology of the white oligarchy and would eventually lead to an erosion of basic traditional beliefs.

After the 1930 popular revolt, an all-party alliance was created, and Daniel Salamanca eventually emerged as the presidential candidate of the coalition. A politician of the classic mold, Salamanca was even less attuned to the new developments on the student and labor fronts than either Saavedra or Siles. He was a rural landowner from Cochabamba, a famous parliamentary orator, and otherwise an extremely intemperate and unbending nineteenth-century-style liberal. His only immediate programs were moral government and free elections, meaningless slogans which he violated as rapidly as his predecessors had.

But the oligarchic republican government based on limited participation which had been established by the Conservatives in the 1880s was beginning to come apart by 1930. The Great Depression was descending with unparalleled severity on the open Bolivian economy. Prices dropped drastically, production plummeted, and government revenues declined precipitously. At the same time debt-servicing arrangements virtually destroyed the government's ability either to generate new unmortgaged taxes or to find funds for even the most minimal necessities. The subtle but by now clearly important shift in political ideology of the governing classes also began to be felt. The university student reform had brought radical Marxist thought into the homes of white elites for the first time in national politics. The labor movements began to get national attention with ever more severe strike activity, leading to military intervention in the mines and open warfare. Even the Indian peasantry had been unusually restive with two quite massive uprisings, the one at Jesús de Machaca in 1921 and one at Chayanta in Potosí in 1927.

In many ways the Depression would give a reprieve to the Salamanca government. Massive layoffs of workers forced many miners back into the countryside and into subsistence farming again, while the Depression wiped out most of the gains of the weakly organized labor movement. Indian peasants grew more passive as the great hacienda expansion age drew to a close with the end of heavy capital investments in rural landholdings. But the university youth would not quietly disappear, and the increasing impact of the Depression created a new awareness that Salamanca was incapable of responding to, except in total fear and repression. By the standards of the other countries of South America, Bolivian radicalism remained weak and relatively unsophisticated and a good generation or two behind developments in bordering countries. But the consistent refusal of Salamanca and his followers to offer a hearing to these ideas, unlike the Republicans of the 1920s, meant that the marginal radical and reformist groups would find themselves forced into an even more violent confrontation with the traditional political system. Nevertheless, these groups were still only a small sector of the elite society and might never have become the threat they did had not Bolivia undergone the greatest military disaster of its history under the leadership of Daniel Salamanca. The Chaco War was to provide the crucial disruptive force by which the traditional system of the 1880-1934 period would finally be destroyed.

Faced with an increasingly difficult international economic picture, the temporary Junta attempted to weld all the opposition parties into a united front. They succeeded in achieving unity between their overthrow of Siles in June 1930 and the following June. All parties agreed to run independently in the congressional elections but supported a unitary presidential slate with Salamanca as the presidential choice. But the increasingly severe economic crisis was beginning to have a profound impact on the nation and was leading to some fundamental realignments to which Salamanca would prove relatively indifferent.

Tin prices had begun a serious secular decline in 1927. By 1929 the stocks of unsold tin were also rising, which depressed prices even further. At this time Bolivia, with three other tin-producing regions—Nigeria, Malaya, and Indonesia—provided close to 80 percent of world production. Of the four, Bolivia had the lowest-grade ore, the highest transportation costs, and was therefore the highest-cost tin producer. It thus felt the shock waves first and also found it impossible to force the other major producers to cut production voluntarily, since at negative prices for Bolivians, the others could still obtain some profit margins. In July 1929, at the urging of Patiño, a voluntary Tin Producers Association was formed by the private companies working in the four major centers of production. They agreed to production cut-backs, which all three major Bolivian companies eagerly carried out in late 1929 and early 1930. But the non-Bolivian companies did not follow suit, so by mid-1930 the voluntary scheme was considered a failure.

With free market conditions intolerable and voluntary restrictions impossible to achieve, the producers decided in late 1930 to take the drastic measure of demanding government participation in the production control scheme. This was a major and abrupt change from the private mine-owners' belligerent stand against any kind of governmental intervention in private enterprise. For the first time, the Bolivian government would be assigned not only minimal taxing privileges but full control over production quotas, which would lead in the following decades to full marketing control over foreign sales. Clearly this was an act of desperation by which the main producers hoped to retain direct control over governmental decisions that affected them. But equally, it made possible the first really powerful intervention of the government in mining affairs. Moreover, while there would be rough agreements over quotas, the much reduced production schedules for all the firms meant that any one of them could easily and quickly increase production if their market quotas were changed by governmental decree. This suddenly introduced a special tension into the relationship between the big three and brought their competitive conflicts into the very halls of government. The big miners were now to pay considerably more direct attention to the local political scene than they had in some time, so they began to support differing factions in the elite itself.

Since there were only three major governments involved—Bolivia, the Netherlands, and Great Britain—it turned out that a forced quota production system could be successfully carried out, and on 1 March 1931 the International Tin Control Scheme went into effect, just a few days before the inauguration of the new Salamanca government. Bolivian production was drastically reduced, creating a massive internal economic crisis for the republic. Though the scheme of restricting production eventually reduced the world's unsold stock of tin and finally stabilized the price, it would not be before 1933 that Bolivian production would slowly begin to return to even moderate production levels.

All of these international changes and the resulting shock to the local economy were closely followed by the Bolivian elite. The Junta government experimented with public works schemes and fully supported all Patiño's production plans. It also cut budget outlays to the barest minimum and paid serious attention to the various national recovery projects being tried out elsewhere in the world. Of all the groups engaging in this debate about the national economy, the Liberals offered the most concrete proposals. Although their approach was an orthodox one, they suggested serious government intervention. But Salamanca seemed oblivious to the whole issue. Constantly asked what his economic ideas were, he replied evasively about the need for moral government. Such vacuous ideas might have been fine in times of growth with a stable social order but were meaningless in the contemporary context. As a result, his Genuine Republicans suffered total defeat in the congressional elections of 1931 and the Liberals had an absolute majority of votes. The rigid Salamanca suddenly found himself faced by a hostile Congress completely outside his control, with an economy he little understood, and a society suffering a severe malaise for which he could provide no solutions.

Almost immediately upon taking office, Salamanca proceeded to alienate most of the major groups in the society. While the Junta government had essentially continued the policies of the Saavedra and Siles periods of moderate reformism, with a strong interest in welfare as a result of the economic crisis, the Salamanca regime was a return to the more rigid orthodoxies of the past. He would also alienate the traditional elite parties by making his government a partisan one, despite the all-party support that had brought it to power.

His first cabinet in office, despite the domination by the Liberals in Congress and the calls for a government of conciliation to deal with the economic crisis, was an all Genuine Republican group. Next he announced to a rather startled public that the primary problem facing the country was not the economic crisis but radicalism and communism. While radical and communist thought and groups had finally established themselves in national life during the 1920s, they were still a fringe minority, even among the university youth and organized labor movements. This obsession with the "red" threat was something entirely new on the part of a traditional politician. Moreover, Salamanca radically shifted government policy from a moderate neutral stand on labor to one of open hostility. A national strike by the legal Telegraph Workers Union was not only opposed by Salamanca, but the union was dissolved, and a sympathetic general strike of the La Paz labor federation was also forcibly suppressed and its leaders jailed. Next the government paid government employees in promissory notes as a result of the budget deficit, and in late July Salamanca announced that Bolivia was defaulting on its external debt.

Thus during just one month in office, Salamanca alienated all the traditional parties, and above all the Liberals, with his partisan attacks and his extreme economic measures which most thought unnecessary. He also alienated the student, labor, and radical movements. At the same time despite his extreme retrenchment in normal government services, Salamanca proposed the most ambitious and expensive scheme for military penetration of the Chaco ever envisioned by a Bolivian president. Because large areas of the Chaco were still unexplored and unoccupied by either Bolivia or Paraguay, this new, more aggressive stance proposed by Salamanca for the Bolivian forces meant a major shift in national policy from a largely defensive to offensive position.

As the internal economic and political scene became ever tenser, Salamanca began to give more and more of his attention to the Chaco border question, which he saw as easily soluble with firm righteous stands, while the economic situation became ever more complex and seemingly insoluble.

On 1 July 1931 Salamanca used a typical border incident to break diplomatic relations with Paraguay, a move many felt was overly aggressive. Then, in his presidential address in August, Salamanca announced the continual decline in government revenues despite all the support to the tin scheme and other pro-industry measures. He stressed that virtually all government services had been cut, but then went on to announce an expansion of the military budget. He also proposed an open policy of total suppression of union or strike activity among the organized working classes of the nation.

Thus Salamanca had defined rather extreme positions at the same time as he had limited all his political options. This tense state of affairs might have continued indefinitely had Salamanca himself not deliberately taken his government on an even more provocative course as far as his Liberal opponents were concerned. In June Salamanca brought Demetrio Canelas, an Oruro party leader, into the Ministry of Finance. Canelas broke with the conservative policy of the previous months and pressed Salamanca on the need for more radical economic measures to combat the crisis. His primary proposal was for an inflationary monetary solution which was then being adopted by many countries of the world. He wanted Bolivia to get off the gold standard, adopt inconvertible paper money, and then to increase the money supply. The Liberals at first opposed these changes, especially as they controlled the Central Bank as well as Congress. But they were forced to accept them when Great Britain itself announced in September that it was going off the gold standard. As part of the sterling block, Bolivia was forced to do the same, so Canelas got his reforms. But prices immediately started rising, and the government position became extremely unpopular. In response, the Liberals put new pressure on the government, and, after a series of aggressive parliamentary interpellations of ministers, forced the Salamanca government to come to terms. Those terms included a formal bi-party pact and an agreement to give the Liberals veto power over all economic decisions.

Frustrated in his initiatives and independence in the economic sphere, Salamanca then attempted to implement his ideas on authoritarian government. Claiming that there was a communist menace that few other traditional party leaders seemed aware of, he proposed at the end of 1931 to enact a law of "Social Defense." This was a bill granting extraordinary powers to the president to deal with political opposition on the left and with the labor movement. The reaction to this proposal was intense. In January 1932 mass demonstrations by labor, the small leftist parties, the students, and the Saavedristas finally forced the government to withdraw the projected law from Congress. At the same time, Salamanca once more tried to outrun Liberal opposition on the economic front. Faced by government revenues anticipated to reach half of projected basic expenditures, he proposed to float an international loan. This was rejected by the Liberals, who not only obtained the formal ouster of the hated Canelas from the Ministry of Finance but finally in March 1932 forced Salamanca to accept three Liberal-appointed ministers in his cabinet.

Salamanca was now completely dependent upon the Liberals in all basic decisions affecting the economy. He also faced increasing radical opposition, which he in a large measure had created through his anti-strike and law of "Social Defense" activity. He thus became ever more embittered about the national political scene. But his impotency on the national front was not matched on the international one, as increasingly in the bitter days of 1932 he turned his energies to the Chaco. This was an issue that he could deal with, confident that the nation would follow him wherever he led them and secure that the Liberals and the radicals could not impede his field of action.

He built up the army systematically at the expense of every other government service. He also pushed the army into an ever more expansive exploration and settlement program in the Chaco. So clearly aggressive were Bolivia's intentions that throughout the early months of the year, radical groups began calling for an end to the war-like preparations. But on this issue there was a split between the fringe radicals and student groups and the more traditional parties. The Saavedristas, who now called themselves the Republican Socialist Party and who had joined the left against the Social Defense Act, fully supported Salamanca's Chaco adventure, while the Liberals also gave Salamanca undivided support in his buildup of the army.

Thus Salamanca found himself with strong traditional backing and decided to push this backing to the absolute limit. In May and June a major linkup between two army divisions led to a typical minor clash over an important watering spot in the Chaco. Bolivian troops ousted an already entrenched Paraguayan force. Later claiming that a pre-existent Paraguayan position did not exist, the Bolivian army refused to relinquish the new post and began a major and rapid buildup in the area to oppose the expected counter-attack by the Paraguayans. In the last days of June the expected counter-offensive occurred and was beaten back by the Bolivians. Up to this point, this incident was no different from dozens of others, and the number of troops involved was quite small and the conflict quite limited. Standard procedure now called for formal negotiation, but at this point Salamanca decided to break with precedent and push for all-out war. By late July full-scale warfare had begun.

This decision of Salamanca had a great deal to do with his bitter political frustrations in national politics and his perception that increasing economic crisis would lead to social anarchy. The fact that in May the International Tin Control organization adopted the radical procedure of prohibiting all tin production for the months of July and August and of reducing production thereafter to one-third of 1929 output meant that the most extreme cutbacks were proposed just on the eve of Salamanca's decisions concerning the Chaco. In response to the two-month closing and the extremely unbalanced trade situation which resulted, the government was forced to take complete control over all gold dealings of its citizens and also forced mine-owners to hand over 65 percent of their letters of exchange upon foreign currencies to the Central Bank. There is little question that this most extreme shutdown of the national export economy was of crucial importance in the decisions taken by the government in the following weeks.

There is no doubt, from all the documentation that has emerged since the war, that Salamanca and the Bolivian government deliberately escalated a typical border incident into a full-scale war to the surprise of even the Paraguayans. It is also evident that, when the final decisions were made, it was Salamanca who, against the written advice of his general staff, forced the conflict beyond any peaceful settlement into what would become Bolivia's most costly war in its republican history.

In popular belief, however, it was almost immediately accepted as truth that the Chaco War was the result of a basic conflict over oil lands between Standard Oil of New Jersey, with its support of Bolivian claims, and Royal Dutch Shell, which was entrenched in Paraguay. There is no doubt that toward the end of this long and bloody conflict, when victorious Paraguayan troops were reaching the end of the Chaco region and approaching the Andean foothills, oil became an important concern in their war aims. But until late 1935 the war was fought hundreds of miles from the nearest fields. Moreover, it was evident after the war that Standard Oil of New Jersey had illegally sold Bolivian oil to Argentina and thence to Paraguay, while claiming it could produce nothing for Bolivia from these same fields. The cause of the war, rather, must be found first in the complex political conflict within Bolivia and the strains caused by the Great Depression on a fragile political system; and its continuation can be understood only in terms of Argentine support for Paraguayan aims. The ability of Argentina to prevent peace moves until the end, along with continued Paraguayan successes, meant that once the war began Bolivia had little ability to stop its onslaught.

That the causes of the war were other than those claimed at the time does not in fact reduce the vital importance of the general belief in the Chaco War as an oil conflict. In the post-war period fundamental political and economic decisions, including the confiscation of Standard Oil in 1937 and the creation of a state oil monopoly company, were the direct result of this belief. Much of the bitterness of the post-war political scene, as well, was very much defined by this conception.

More important than the cause, however, were the consequences of the conflict. The Chaco War, in effect, destroyed the political system which had been in existence in Bolivia since 1880. The end of the war saw the collapse of both civilian government and the traditional political parties. Ideas which had previously been the coinage of only a small group of radical intellectuals now became the concern of much of the politically aware youth and ex-combatants. So distinctive was this change that Bolivians themselves would refer to the groups which came to maturity in the Chaco war as the "Chaco generation." The Indian question, the labor question, the land question, and the economic dependency on private miners became the new themes of national debate rather than the old issues of civil government, honest elections, and railroad construction. These discussions led to the creation of new parties and revolutionary movements in the late 1930s and 1940s and finally to the social revolution of 1952.

The Chaco War also marked an important turning point in the economic history of the nation. The Great Depression and the resulting Chaco conflict marked the end of the expansion and even the capitalization of the mining industry. Thereafter, production and productivity began to decline in an industry that saw virtually no change in its structure or patterns of investment until 1952. In the rural areas as well, the relative stagnation of the national economy brought an end to the great hacienda expansion boom, which had lasted from the 1880s until the late 1920s. By the end of this period landless peons had probably doubled, and the number of free community Indians was now considerably less than the number of peasants without land. Thus a fundamental restructuring of the rural economy had occurred in the period 1880-1932, but it ended before the complete destruction of the free communities and provided an endless source of conflict in the post-Chaco period as the haciendas went on the defensive.

All the growth which had occurred as a result of the great tin expansion had little impact in modernizing the society as a whole. It was still estimated that by 1940 over two-thirds of Bolivians were primarily outside the market economy, and even as late as 1950 the number of urban artisans in the national economy equalled the number of factory workers. Though two-thirds of the economically active population were engaged in agriculture, Bolivia was still a net importer of food-stuffs, including traditional highland root crops. Thus, while the tin boom did affect the third of the nation that was urban and Spanish-speaking, its multiplier effects had little impact on the rural population, except possibly to lower their standard of living as a result of the corresponding expansion of the latifundia system.

Bolivia entered the Chaco War as a highly traditional, underdeveloped, and export-dominated economy and emerged from that conflict with the same characteristics. But it changed from being one of the least mobilized societies in Latin America, in terms of radical ideology and union organization, to one of the most advanced. The war shattered the traditional belief systems and led to a fundamental rethinking of the nature of Bolivian society. The result of that change in largely elite thought was the creation of a revolutionary political movement that embraced some of the most radical ideas to emerge on the continent. The war would also create the climate for the development of one of the most powerful, independent, and radical labor movements in the Americas. From these perspectives, the Chaco War, like the War of the Pacific before it, would prove to be one of the major turning points in Bolivian historical development.

Chapter 7 • Disintegration of the Established Order, 1932-1952

The Chaco War began on 18 July 1932, when Salamanca announced to the startled nation that the Paraguayan forces had seized a Bolivian fort in the Chaco. That this fort was in reality a Paraguayan one that had been seized by the Bolivians at the end of May was quietly ignored. Salamanca ordered a major offensive that night and carried out a state of siege within Bolivia itself. At this point, the Bolivian General Staff refused to endorse Salamanca's war plans. It claimed that the army was unprepared for a major assault, and at the same time considered the escalation of the conflict to be out of all proportion to the incident. So intense was the debate between the general staff and the president that Salamanca was finally forced to acknowledge full responsibility for all his decisions relating to the initiation of the conflict in a formal written document. Having thus absolved itself from any responsibility for the assault and subsequent actions, the general staff, formally responding that it was suicidal and against the national interests, finally agreed to carry out Salamanca's decisions.

That Salamanca's gamble was a successful one is evident by the immediate support he received from the entire national political elite. Despite Paraguayan and international protests of the legitimacy of Bolivian claims, political and intellectual leaders supported Bolivia's position and claimed that it was Paraguay that was creating the bellicose situation. There were manifestos of support signed by everyone from Alcides Arguedas on the right to Franz Tamayo and Carlos Montenegro on the left. There were also major street demonstrations in all the urban centers of the nation as the economic crisis was momentarily forgotten. To guarantee unanimity, the government used a state of siege to round up labor and political radicals, either jailing or exiling such men as Ricardo Anaya, José Aguirre Gainsborg, and Porfirio Diaz Machicao, among others. Those of the left not jailed or exiled were immediately conscripted into the army and sent to the front lines. Thus in one quick gesture, Salamanca had seemingly exterminated the left that had so terrified him during his months of government. But this nationalistic euphoria was a short-lived affair. It was Salamanca himself, the modern Bolivian leader most fearful of radical revolution and most persistent in attacking the nascent radical left and labor movements, who became the prime causal agent in the creation of a powerful revolutionary tradition in national politics. For it was the conduct of Salamanca and his political followers in carrying the nation to war that was to destroy the entire edifice of traditional politics.

Despite Bolivia's mobilization and massive troop movements, the Paraguayans still assumed that they were dealing with a typical border incident. After retaking their fort in July, they returned to Washington and expected to continue negotiations on a non-aggression treaty. But Salamanca refused to budge, and three major forts of undisputed Paraguayan ownership were seized. These three forts—Boquerón, Corrales, and Toledo—were vital to Paraguay's defensive line. Their seizure necessitated a full-scale response, which the Bolivian general staff had recognized as inevitable and leading only to total war. But the rather quixotic Salamanca thought that by this one bold act he had destroyed all Paraguayan initiative and called a halt to military operations early in August. There now developed a bitter debate between

the generals and Salamanca as to what had really transpired on the
first contacts between the troops, who was to blame for the mobilization, and what were the ultimate war aims of the Bolivians. The language of accusation and recrimination was as violent as it would ever
become and clearly indicated an extreme pessimism about the whole
affair, which seemed to imply an ultimate and disastrous defeat for
Bolivian arms. And all this occurred in the first month of the war before Bolivia had lost a single major battle!

From such a beginning, the war quickly deteriorated into a corrupt,
bloody, and bottomless defeat and disaster for Bolivia. Realizing that
Salamanca meant to hold their forts indefinitely and at the same time
refuse to negotiate, the Paraguayans called out a general mobilization
and initiated a major counter-offensive. By September the Bolivian advance was totally stopped and the famous battle of Boquerón was begun. Some 600 Bolivian troops were successfully encircled by Paraguayan troops in their old fort. With only 1,500 troops in all on the
Chaco front, the Bolivians were unable to do anything about the en-
circlement. At the end of a month the troops were forced to surrender,
and a shocked nation received the news in the first days of October.

The effect of the fall of Boquerón was immediate and dramatic.
Already literate public opinion was subjected to wild rumors of Bolivian duplicity, was disturbed by the deliberate political use Salamanca
was making of the war, and was made increasingly uneasy by the
tense social situation as military conscription began to be felt in all
levels of society. The news of the Boquerón defeat thus led to major
rioting. On 4 October 20,000 anti-government rioters demanded the
resignation of Salamanca and the return of the German General Hans
Kundt, whom the Salamanca Republicans had overthrown in 1930.
Four days later Congress also formally demanded the return of Kundt
to lead the troops, as if this gesture would somehow restore the supposed prowess and ability to the Bolivian war machine. For their part
the military had had enough of the leadership of the civilian president,
and two major field officers, David Toro and Carlos Quintanilla, demanded his dismissal. Though the rebellion was eventually stopped,
the omnipotent power of Salamanca, which had lasted in its new form

all of four months, was over, and the beaten president was forced again to ask the Liberals to join him in a coalition government.

Before such a multi-party government could be formed, however, another Bolivian fortress was taken. By late October the Paraguayans had not only recaptured all their old forts but had now carried the offensive into Bolivian territory, outflanking and finally seizing the Bolivian fortress of Arze. The Arze battle was a total rout of Bolivian forces. The result of this major defeat was a breakdown in government and out-party negotiations. The Liberals and opposition Republicans attacked Salamanca, and he in turn encouraged mob violence against their newspapers. He also, in November, outlawed all unions and labor federations. But by December he had no more options left, and was forced to recall General Kundt from Europe to take over complete and effective control of the army, thus reducing his own role in the military to that of civilian adviser.

Though Kundt was an excellent organizer and rapidly rebuilt the shattered Bolivian army, he was a poor tactician and strategist. Having created a powerful force, he then spent six months wrecking it in a headlong assault on the impregnable Paraguayan fortress of Nanawa, in a campaign that lasted from January to July 1933. Not only did the Paraguayans hold this fortress, but they virtually destroyed the forces attacking them and then proceeded to outflank the Bolivians in other regions, inflecting a further series of defeats. By mid-year in 1933 the Paraguayans were not only destroying division after division but were making tremendous territorial inroads into the Bolivian-held part of the Chaco. By the end of the year Kundt was dismissed and General Enrique Peñaranda given charge of the army, with David Toro as his key adviser. But the change only deepened national pessimism. Under Kundt, 77,000 men had been mobilized, of whom 14,000 died in action, 10,000 were made prisoners, 6,000 deserted, and 32,000 evacuated because of sickness and wounds. This left 7,000 troops in the field, with 8,000 in rearguard support services—a pitiful and demoralized remnant of a once-powerful and well-equipped army.

Under Peñaranda a third army of some 55,000 men was organized, and for six months a relative stalemate occurred. But in August 1934 the

famous Paraguayan leader General Estigarribia finally found a weak
spot in Bolivian defenses and broke the Bolivian Chaco line. From this
point on, the Paraguayans made a mad dash to the Andean foothills,
and the war turned into an open struggle for oil, as the Paraguayans
were finally within striking distance of the Bolivian deposits. In the
four months from August to November the Paraguayans captured
more territory than they had ever claimed in their most extreme pre-
war demands.

By late November Salamanca had engineered the election of his
loyal supporter Franz Tamayo and was intent on completing his last
acts in office by destroying military opposition to himself. Specifically,
he traveled to the Chaco to force Peñaranda and Toro to give up control over the army. What occurred instead, was that on 25 November
1934, the army arrested Salamanca at their headquarters at Villa
Montes and forced him to resign. The government was then handed
over to the vice-president and Liberal Party leader Tejada Sorzano.

The immediate consequences of this military revolt were extremely
favorable for the Bolivian war effort. Tejada Sorzano was both an excellent administrator and an able politician. He quickly organized an
all-party cabinet, which even included Salamanca's supporters, got the
tin baron Aramayo to take over the Ministry of Finance, and then
gave unqualified support to the army command. Bolivia's war finances
were greatly strengthened, the internal conflicts on the home front
were ended, with even the attack on the far left being stopped, and a
united front was created. On the military side, Bolivia was now finally
close to its own supply lines, fighting in well-known and settled territories, and facing an enemy that was now dangerously over-extended
and badly underfinanced.

In the long term, however, the military golpe brought a basic turning point in national politics. The concept of civilian rule was now
broken, though few noticed it at the time in their hatred for Salamanca
and relief at his passing. But once having tasted power and found
justification for defense of their military honor—greatly stained by their
actions in the war—the colonels and generals proved totally reconciled
to the idea of constant intervention in governmental affairs and the

need for military control over the national political scene. Thus the coup of November 1934 marked the end of the era of civilian politics and the beginning of the end of the traditional party system.

With the fall of Salamanca the war slowly ground to a halt. The Paraguayans invaded Tarija and Santa Cruz and even seized some of the oil fields in early 1935. But without Villa Montes this advance could not be maintained, and a major battle for this southern Bolivian stronghold ensued. At this point there emerged Bolivia's most effective military leader of the war, Major Germán Busch, who took over the planning for the defense of the southern command area. Not only did he defeat the Paraguayans at Villa Montes, but he was able to mount a major counter-offensive which cleared all the Paraguayans from Tarija and Santa Cruz and led to the recapture of all of the oil centers previously seized.

At this point both sides proved ready for peace. Paraguayan resources were almost totally exhausted, and the defeat at Villa Montes meant that they could never take the Andean foothills region. At the same time, it was evident that continued warfare might cause some losses to their huge Chaco gains, as the new military leadership on the Bolivian side seemed to have revived Bolivian military abilities. For the Bolivians, the recapture of all the non-Chaco territories was enough of a victory. Though the government, unlike the Paraguayans, was well endowed with funding from a reviving mining industry and could have continued the war for some time, the entire nation wanted peace. The bitterness of the Salamanca years and the general belief that the war was fought for Standard Oil and was most likely initiated by Bolivia itself had created an hostility to the conflict which was endemic. A peace conference was organized in Buenos Aires in May 1935, and on 14 June of that year a formal peace treaty was signed.

Thus ended, almost to the month, three years of the most bitter conflict in Bolivia's history. Though Bolivia lost more valuable territory in its war against Chile in the nineteenth century, the fighting then had been minimal and the impact on the population itself slight. In the Chaco conflict, the losses were phenomenal. Over

65,000 were killed, deserted, or died in captivity, or roughly 25 percent of the combatants on the Bolivian side. These out of a total population of just about 2 million persons created war losses equal to what the European nations had suffered in World War I.

Moreover the very validity of national institutions had been deeply challenged by the war. The army itself had been organized by caste. The whites were the officers, the cholos the sub-officials, and the Indian peasants the troops. The only group to violate these divisions were the workers and radicals seized by Salamanca who were sent to the front lines. Thus the very caste system of the national society was fully maintained on the front lines, which created a severe gulf between commanders and troops and further encouraged the notorious corruption of white officers. For the few whites who did serve in the front line, the experience was a bitter one and committed many of them to a radical stance toward the racial divisions of their society. For the Indians it meant the continuation of the standard patterns of exploitation. Many troops deserted, and there were even several major front-line mutinies. But when the war ended the Aymara and Quechua troops, desperate to return home, went back to their farms and were reintegrated into the communities as quickly as possible.

But for the cholos and non-military whites, there was a different story. Many of these formerly committed individuals found themselves totally alienated from the traditional system. They had been appalled by the corruption and incompetence of the high command and shocked by the revelations of Bolivian duplicity in the war. To these youths of the "Chaco generation," their sacrifice had been in vain. They emerged from the war bitter at the army leadership that had led them into the disaster and frustrated with the political system that had created the whole Chaco imbroglio.

The most immediate release for this sense of bitterness and frustration was a great outpouring of social realist novels which began to appear in the first months of the war and continued to dominate national literature well into the next decade. Bitter proletarian novels became the Chaco genre, and in novel after novel, the cruelty of the

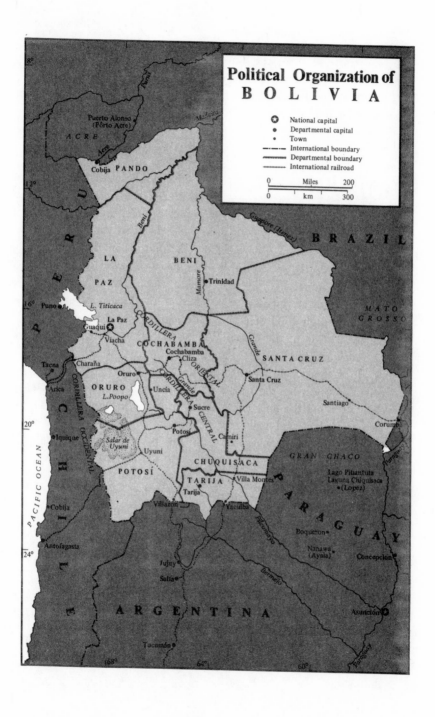

Political Organization of
BOLIVIA

✪ National capital
• Departmental capital
· Town
— · — · International boundary
———— Departmental boundary
········· International railroad

| 0 | Miles | 200 |
| 0 | km | 300 |

war, the waste of lives, the hunger and thirst, the incompetence, treason, and cowardice of the officer caste became common themes.

The Chaco novel did not arise phoenix-like out of the ashes of the Chaco defeat, but had its origins in the realistic and bitter novels of the generation of 1880. At the peak of Liberal peace and euphoria in the first decades of the century, such writers as Armando Chirveches, Alcides Arguedas, and Jaime Mendoza had published novels with themes of political corruption of elite politics and the exploitation and oppression of the mine-workers and the Indian peasants. Nor were such class themes the only ones explored by this generation, for Adela Zamudo in both poetry and the short story explained the problems of sexual discrimination. Building upon this heritage, the writers of the 1930s were able to express themselves in an idiom already well appreciated by the literate elite. The Chaco novel brought to them an intimate experience of the Chaco disaster. As much as any single form of political ideology or revolutionary propaganda, the realism of the Chaco War novel had a profound impact on the youth and intellectuals who made up the core of elite thought.

For all of their realistic portrayal, the Chaco novels offered few remedies for resolving the causes of the national disaster. But the novelists were not the only voices raised in bitter protest. The disaster also created a vital new radical political movement which did offer a host of challenging ideas to the national elite. Though Salamanca had done everything possible to destroy that movement, the very war he had created to justify his repression gave the left an important role to play. The pre-war radical left maintained a remarkably active front-line anti-war and anti–traditional-society propaganda, which in fact proved so successful that they were able to support desertion of troops and to become a major ideological force in the post-war era.

This radical reinterpretation of the Bolivian reality was a fundamental attack on the racist consensus of Bolivian society and on the oligarchic nature of its political and economic life. The war was attacked as the direct result of the multi-national corporations, specifically Standard Oil of New Jersey. It was felt to reflect the death pangs of the old order which, to defend its power, was forced to take the nation into an international conflict. For this group of radical thinkers, the *Indigenista* and Marxist ideology of the Peruvian Mariátegui was a fundamental takeoff for the reappraisal of Bolivian society. This conception of Andean reality held that the problem of the Indian was really a problem of exploitation and land; that the Spanish and their followers had robbed the Indians of their lands and attempted to destroy their culture in order to exploit them; that the passivity and backwardness of the Indians was in fact exclusively due to their exploitation. The only way to break this exploitation was to destroy the haciendas and return the lands to their Indian workers.

The radicals, among whom Tristan Marof stood out as the foremost Chaco-period thinker, also concentrated on the theme of the export economy. National development could not occur until the fruits of national wealth were fully exploited. This could not be done so long as private miners controlled the major source of national wealth, which was tin and the other minerals. All of the profits earned from the mines were shipped abroad or otherwise kept from promoting the national economy by these tin barons. Therefore the state had to take direct charge of the mines so as to retain the earnings generated by mining and use them to develop the nation.

Equally stressed was the distorted nature of the national state. It was held that the state itself was run by the *rosca*, a derogatory term which implied a group of politicians and lawyers who ran the state apparatus for the miners and hacendados. It was argued that the non-democratic oligarchic regimes by which Bolivia was governed were there by necessity, since this was the only way the economic mandarins could fully exploit the Bolivian nation. While Marof and others offered different solutions, all talked about worker, miner, and Indian peasant alliances whose ultimate aim would be "Tierras al Indio" and "Minas al Estado."

All of this propaganda on the left would provide the basic guidelines for organizing a thorough-going re-evaluation of Bolivian society. While few initially accepted all of the arguments proposed by the radical left, the enunciation of the primary problems of national society created the framework in which all future debate would occur. The theme of the nationalization of the mines was now firmly implanted in the political consciousness of the whites and cholos, and even the theme of the Indian and his just claims was now accepted as legitimate. That these themes found a responsive chord can be seen in the developments of post-Chaco War politics. It was seen as well in a subtle shift in the nature of post-war Indian uprisings, for, following the Chaco War, they became less and less classic caste wars and more and more social protest movements in which pan-Indian rights were the prime issue.

The increasing class consciousness on the part of Indian peasants was matched by a more radical Marxist commitment of both labor organizers and young radicals. So intense was the activity of desertion committees and anti-war groups that from their Argentine exile many of these movements finally coalesced into more permanent political movements. Thus in 1934, at a special Congress in Cordoba, Argentina, was born the first of the major post-war radical parties, the *Partido Obrero Revolucionario* (or Revolutionary Workers' Party), under the leadership of Tristan Marof and José Aguirre Gainsborg. Though a small grouping of radical exiles, this was a historic moment in the development of the Bolivian left, since it was the first party of the Chaco generation to be created, and in later decades it would form the vanguard of the revolutionary movement.

Although the POR was still a small group of radical intellectuals and would soon be riven by internal disputes over Trotskyism, its ideological impact was impressive. For this it had to thank Salamanca and the leadership who had initiated the war and led the country in three years of bitter conflict. The utter defeat of Bolivian arms, despite greater manpower, wealth, and resources, was a shock to most literate persons. But even worse was the much publicized corruption and incompetence of the officer class, which led to the wholesale destruction of troops through starvation, death, and capture. Finally, no Bolivian was left unaware, even before the end of the war, of the cause of the war and the role played by Salamanca in provoking the whole affair to save his government. In short, the literate public was bitter, frustrated, and angered by the war. There was surprisingly little hatred for the Paraguayans but much hostility shown by all Bolivians toward their own leaders. It was this public which at the end of the war demanded an accounting from all who had led them to this defeat. And when that accounting was not forthcoming, they sought to change radically the social, economic, and above all political order of the society in which they lived.

With the signing of peace in June 1935, all the political tensions came to fruition in the virtual collapse of the traditional party arrangements. While the army had asked Tejada Sorzano to prorogue his presidential term until the arrangement of a definitive peace, the older parties had opposed the moves, and the Saavedrista Republicans made a major bid for power, expecting to return to rule. But to the old groupings of Republicans, Liberals, and a small Siles grouping of Nationalists were now added a host of new parties all created on the eve of peace. These took on a plethora of exotic names and symbols, but what they represented fundamentally were all the youth and veterans who had formerly made up key supportive elements of the older parties. Suddenly the word "traditional" became an epithet for all the pre-war oligarchic parties, and everything from Italian corporatist to indigenista and Marxist ideologies became the currency of those who had formerly supported the old order. Blaming the recently deceased Salamanca for all the ills of the war, the Liberals and Republicans expected to go on as before, but that expectation was totally destroyed, for the base of consensus upon which the old parties had built their power base was gone.

At the same time as new movements arose, a bitter veterans' movement emerged as a powerful political force demanding basic accountings for the defeat. A vitally revived labor movement also demanded basic rights, and a nervous officer corps insisted on protection of their threatened caste. These three major power groups feared and opposed a return to traditional politics. The parties themselves could no longer mobilize the popular elite support to defuse these opponents, for that support had now fragmented into a host of brand new reformist, fascist, and radical groupings. Even among the traditional parties themselves, there were some important changes. While the Liberals held firm to classic positions and fully supported Tejada Sorzano, the old Siles Nationalist Party, the most reformist of the old groupings, was ripped apart in October at a national convention and formally dissolved, thus cutting any formal link between the new left and labor and the traditional politicians. The Saavedra Republicans announced a "socialist" program at approximately the same time and even changed their formal name to the Republican Socialist Party. But the socialist title brought little change to the group, and it was ignored by the post-war forces.

After the peace treaty, the able Tejada Sorzano government attempted to appease all of these new movements. It formally supported the veterans and their organizational drives. In October it initiated a formal court action against Standard Oil, actions which would ultimately lead to its confiscation. By the end of the year it was agreeing to general calls for a constitutional convention and even proposed on its own to set up new ministries of welfare and labor to initiate social reform legislation. But none of these gestures seemed to satisfy the reformist groups.

The fall of the government thus seemed inevitable. A reviving labor organization, tied to a tight labor market in a booming post-war economy, finally provided the catalyst for the overthrow of the regime. Finding powerful national support, even from the government, the returning labor radicals had succeeded in reorganizing all the old provincial confederations. In the face of a steep inflation which now hit the nation, the pent-up demand for wage adjustments overwhelmed the new groups. In May 1936, led by the radical printers union, a General Strike was declared. So powerful was the movement that Tejada Sorzano, fearing revolutionary violence, returned the police to their barracks and the general staff declared its neutrality and implicit support. The General Strike was a total success, and unionists even temporarily took over police powers in the cities. Demanding 100 percent wage increases, the workers declared the strike for an indefinite period. The obvious weakness of the central government in the face of this massive labor turnout was just the excuse that the restive officer corps needed to mature its plans, and on 17 May 1936 the old order was brought to an end when Colonels David Toro and Germán Busch declared a formal *golpe de estado* and took over the government.

The military coup of 1936 was to usher in an age of governments led by the younger Chaco War officers. It was also a period in which the military would come to reflect the divisions within national political life as a whole, shifting from moderate to radical and then all the way to conservative and traditional as the national political forces realigned themselves. For the young colonels who were to lead the Bolivian government in the next dozen years, it was a combination of identity with the "generation of the Chaco" and its demands for reform, as well as a clear fear of a reprisal which motivated their intervention. Veteran and congressional demands for war crimes tribunals proved a crucial motivating factor behind the army's own decision to intervene to defend its caste.

Initially, the colonels turned toward the ever-active David Toro to lead them, with Germán Busch being the power behind the throne. Much like Saavedra in his sensitivity to changing national currents, Toro sensed the mood of the nation and responded to it by declaring that his government would be one of "military socialism." As politically unsophisticated about Marxism as was Saavedra when he reentitled his party Republican Socialists, Toro meant by this "military socialism" essentially a populist and reformist administration to be led by the newly aware officer caste, which was somehow to atone for its Chaco disasters by bringing the nation a new social justice.

Immediately Toro made a gesture to labor by creating a Ministry of Labor for the first time in Bolivian history and appointing the head of the radical printers union as its incumbent. While this brought a small coterie of Marxist and anarcho-syndicalists into the government, the main civilian groups that came to be associated with the new regime were more closely tied to a modified fascist position.

The group that most clearly articulated the "national socialist" ideology was a small Socialist Party which had been created a few months before the Toro takeover. It was best represented by such political ideologues as Carlos Montenegro and Augusto Céspedes, both of whom would prove crucial in the formation of later mass movement nationalist parties. In the first months of the new regime this group began publishing *La Calle,* which became the organ for German fascist propaganda with a violent anti-Semitic position. The fact that one of the three tin barons, Hochschild, was Jewish, nicely provided the nationalists with a combined theme of attacking the mine-owners and also mouthing their thesis of an international conspiracy. The national socialists were influential enough at one point to get Toro to propose a formal corporate model for the national legislature and a forced unionization under state control. But the Labor Ministry radicals were adamant against these proposals and, while supporting labor's organizing needs, demanded that the government leave union control in the hands of the workers. Their opposition and Toro's own essential indifference were sufficient to terminate these plans.

While the new radical political groupings and the traditional parties constantly maneuvered to gain control over the direction of the Toro government, the restive officers became disenchanted with all the discussions, debates, and lack of unanimity among the civilians. The rather creative period of political ferment came to an abrupt end in late June when Busch announced the end of the military-civilian alliance, the exiling of the troublesome Saavedra, and the creation of an all-military regime. The powerless Toro was forced to accept these decisions and in the next few months governed with the aim both of pleasing Busch and the younger officers and of carrying out some moderate reforms which would generate national and popular support for his regime.

All this political and especially ideological ferment had created an unease not only among the naïve officers but also among the traditional elite. With the liberals unable to retain power, the Salamanca Republicans in disarray, and the Saavedra forces flirting with the new radical movements, the oligarchy felt called upon to reorganize its formal defenses. In May the tin miner Carlos Aramayo founded a new Centralist Party whose aim was to defend the interests of the elite. Although initially getting powerful support from the Miners Association, it would eventually collapse as a major force. But by its very creation it signaled to the older parties that their brief relaxation in the face of the post-Chaco fermentation was not to be tolerated. It was a clear oligarchic statement that politics as played under the old rules was insufficiently class-oriented and detracted from the basic role these parties should henceforth fulfill. While the radical movements might still be in their reformist and relatively ineffectual stage, their potential threat was clear, and the mine-owners wanted a more powerful response to this potential threat. The aim of the Centralists was to force the traditional parties to forget their old conflicts and to unite in a coherent coalition class-party group. This would be the aim of the mining elite from 1936 until 1952 as they sought to re-create the old stability through either legal or extra-legal maneuverings. The fact that the Centralist Party shortly disappeared from the scene, as coalition talks got under way among the Liberals and various Republicans, meant that the lesson had been learned by the traditional parties.

To satisfy the conflicting demands facing him, Toro in his usual way tried to compromise with all factions. He appeased the far right, by getting the radicals out of the Ministry of Labor, and responded to the reform groups by proposing a constitutional convention and a new national charter to articulate the reformist needs of the nation. But all these maneuvers still made Busch and his coterie of younger officers very nervous so that in the early days of 1937 Busch offered his resignation as a vote of no-confidence in the Toro regime. For all intents and purposes, this was a formal announcement of an impending golpe.

In response to the Busch threat, Toro sought to create a popular issue which would give him desperately needed support. Thus just ten days after the Busch pronouncement he speeded up the legal process against Standard Oil and on 13 March 1937 announced the formal confiscation of the Standard Oil Company of Bolivia. All of the holdings, equipment, and material of the company were automatically turned over to the newly formed state oil monopoly *Yaci-*

mientos Petroliferos Fiscales de Bolivia (YPFB) without compensation. This was a historic action both nationally and internationally. It was the first such confiscation of a major North American multinational company in Latin America and preceded the larger Mexican confiscations by a full year. At the same time it thrust the government directly into the market, making it a major producer of primary products. By this act, the Bolivian government deliberately broke with its more traditional laissez-faire position and began to take an active and positive role in the economy. The existence of minerals-purchasing banks in the nineteenth century and the active tin role forced on it by the tin schemes in the early 1930s were precedents. But this was to be the beginning of a definite trend, which by the 1950s would see something like half of the gross national product under control of state corporations.

Next, Toro began preparations for organizing a State Socialist Party and even received some tentative support from the newly established national trade union confederation. But all of this feverish activity did not quell Busch's growing feeling that Toro was not to be trusted and that he himself was now experienced enough in administration to govern the country in his own name and with the support of the junior officers.

In early July after fifteen months of some of the most chaotic but vital political activity in national history, the Toro regime came to an end when Busch announced that it no longer had the support of the army. Given the wide popularity enjoyed by the reformist Toro regime, it appeared to most observers that the unknown Busch would bring about the restoration of traditional party rule under stronger miner control. But in fact the Busch regime would prove to be a continuation of the period of reform and party reconstruction of the Toro era.

Though in his initial acts Busch seemed to show strong interest in reviving a coalition civilian government based on the traditional parties, in fact the opposite occurred. Despite repeated promises to support their return to power, Busch refused to allow the old parties to join the government. At the same time he continued to provide new legislation of a reformist and even radical nature and thus gave heart to the new reformist and radical parties. No one party was ever to be associated with the regime, and so the new party activity continued unabated, leading at the end of the decade to the establishment of powerful new national reformist parties. The traditional parties for their part found that the failure either to join the government or find voice in a normal parliament meant four bitter years of erosion, such that by 1940 they would be skeletons of their former selves.

It should be stressed that the reforms advocated and enacted by Toro and Busch were relatively mild welfare and pro-syndicalist proposals which involved no serious redirection of national resources or confiscation of private property except in the unique case of Standard Oil. In fact, the army, if anything, was more heavily subsidized in the post-war Toro-Busch era than it had been during the Chaco War itself. Though now reduced to a 5,000-man standing body, the military still absorbed 32 percent of the national budget in 1937. In addition, the more Busch moved toward the left, the more the leading generals of the older class of officers moved to the right, and the appointment of Carlos Quintanilla as head of the general staff involved a distinct loss of power for the radical younger officers.

While actual change under Toro and Busch was relatively slow and ameliorative, rather than rapid, structural, and radical, the era of military socialism laid the groundwork for more far-reaching change. Nowhere was this potential better expressed than in the new constitutional convention of 1938. Until the decision of Toro to call a constitutional convention, Bolivia had been governed under the constitution of 1880. This was the typical liberal constitution of the nineteenth century. In essence it provided for a relatively limited style of constitutional regime in which the rights of the individual were protected against the intervention of the State and the central government's powers were strictly limited.

This tendency to limit government intervention changed in Latin America with the Mexican Constitution of 1917. The revolutionary leaders of Mexico and the radical reformers in all the region now

demanded that the state take a positive role in the education and welfare of all citizens even if it reduced the property rights of the individual. Known as "social constitutionalism," this trend soon dominated
the political thought of radical Latin American theorists as they sought
to create blueprints for radical change and give a constitutional legitimacy to the new developments.

Such a change in constitutional theory was evident in all discussions of the immediate post-war period and became an important
common denominator among the new political forces appearing
among the Chaco War generation. In the elections for the Constitutional Convention of May 1938, the Busch regime finally came
around to supporting the new groups favored by Toro and even
permitted the veterans' movement and the central labor federation
to run their own slate of candidates. This, plus the weakened state
of the relatively disorganized older parties, meant that the composition of the 1938 Convention was extremely radical.

The result was that the old 1880 charter was dismantled and its
primary direction was changed according to the new pattern of social constitutionalism. The debates about the new provisions also
provided a national and legitimizing forum for the dissemination of
the most radical ideology current in the nation. While the more
radical proposals of agrarian reform, ayllu legitimation, and nationalization of the mines were ultimately rejected by the Convention, the
Constitution itself severely limited individual property rights. Property was no longer to be held an inalienable private right of individuals but instead was to be considered a social right whose
ultimate legitimacy was to be defined by its social utility. At the
same time, the State was to be made responsible for the economic
well-being of the individual, for the protection of women, children,
and the family, and for providing free and universal education. The
essential aim of the Convention in all of these articles was to commit the state to the full responsibility for the health, education, and
welfare of all its citizens. The classic liberal laissez-faire government
with a minimum of intervention was now replaced by the socialist

concept of an active state intervening in all areas of a citizen's private life in order to provide for the collective good.

Such active reformism left Busch rather bewildered. Shifting constantly from right to left, he seemed incapable of defining his own political position, just when the moderate leftist and even traditional parties were clearly defining their own positions in the post-war period. For the moderates and radicals, the Constitutional Convention provided a forum for both ideological education and the establishment of coherent political groupings. At the same time the right was also reorganizing its forces. The Liberals rejected their more reformist wing and gave their party over to the writer Alcides Arguedas, now a rather reactionary intellectual opposed to all the Chaco War reforms. Then in March 1938 the death of Saavedra ended the life of the last of the great pre-war caudillos and provided an impetus for all the Republican parties to rejoin in one united front. Almost immediately with the news of his death a series of agreements were worked out among the traditional parties known as the *Concordancia*. While this unity would come apart from time to time in the future, it was another step toward the end of independent traditional politics and henceforth the pre-war parties would more or less act as a consistent class defense grouping attempting to stem the onslaught of the new movements.

But none of these changes satisfied Busch, nor could he even make up his mind to accept the reforms of the 1938 Constitution. Despite the relative political calm on the national scene, the coherence of the new trends, and the relatively wide consensus they were enjoying, he still felt that the national debates were going nowhere. In April 1939 he declared that henceforth his government would be run as a dictatorship. By this act all political parties were prohibited from functioning, congressional elections were canceled, and the 1938 Constitution was suspended.

There now followed a flood of legislation of the Busch regime as expressed in a series of laws and codes, most of which were concerned with morality in government. But among these rather traditional and naïve acts, a new labor code was decreed in May 1939. Though having its gestation in the reforms proposed by the Ministry of Labor created under Toro, the final enactment of a modern labor code was a major piece of national legislation, and the *Codigo Busch,* as it was called, was considered—along with the Constitution of 1938 —the most lasting piece of governmental activity carried out under Busch.

Busch also fought back a rather bitter attack mounted by the tin barons against their dependence on the Central Bank for foreign sales. In 1936 Toro had established a Minerals Purchasing Bank to help small and medium-sized miners and to regularize mineral sales through government purchases. Even more important, he had required the big miners to turn over their foreign earnings to the Central Bank to be converted at special exchange rates into Bolivian currency. By maintaining a lower than open market exchange rate the government was thus able to quadruple its direct and indirect taxes from the mining industry. Busch not only defended the position of Toro on this but even further strengthened the requirement and lowered the special rates, thus increasing the government's share of profits from the mines to 25 percent of the value of total tin exports. Thus while the miners had hoped finally to return to a free market with Busch, his actions definitely ended their hopes, and from 1936 to 1952 the Central Bank, under radical and conservative regimes alike, maintained complete control over all foreign sales of Bolivian tin, manipulating the exchange rate to generate government income in the form of indirect taxes.

Despite all the concrete legislation carried out by the new regime, Busch seemed to remain totally dissatisfied with the political ambience. He was badly disturbed by the scandal over the sale of visas to Jews in Europe, despite his decision to provide such visas free for the European Jews to settle in the Chaco and eastern lowlands. He thought Hochschild was violating the rules on foreign exchange and had him arrested, and then was forced to release him a few days later. He kept organizing and then disbanding his own governmental party, only to renegotiate contacts with the traditional parties. And while he ruled by decree, hoping miraculously to change the destiny of Bolivia, a sentiment he often expressed in public, he also soon realized that most of his moderate reforms were having no dramatic impact.

From his last public speeches and acts it was evident that Busch was a driven and highly disturbed individual who seemed totally dissatisfied with anything that he carried out. In August 1939 he committed suicide and both stunned the nation and generated the kind of veneration and support he felt was lacking in his own lifetime. His suicide, plus the immediate change of politics which occurred upon his death, made Busch a true martyr to the revolutionary left. It also became a popular belief that the tin barons and their rosca of supporters had somehow killed the great Chaco War hero. While most scholars accept the evidence of a suicide, the death of Busch, like the role of Standard Oil in causing the Chaco War, became another powerful political myth in the armory of the radical and reformist left, adding legitimation to their demands for change by appeal to martyred heroes.

The death of Busch also brought an end to the charismatic leadership of the Chaco War officers and permitted the conservative oligarchy to terminate the experiment in military socialism. Working through the leadership of General Quintanilla, who headed the army under Busch, the right had successfully de-radicalized the army itself, removing key radical officers from power; and thus when Busch died the army was more than ready to turn the government over to the traditional parties. For many on the right, the death of Busch seemed to provide a golden opportunity to eliminate all the chaos and change which had occurred as a result of the post-war ferment.

The era of military socialism, however, had been a period of such profound change that a return to pre-war conditions was impossible to achieve. The period from 1936 to 1939 had been one of remarkable growth for the radical left, but even more so for the previously non-existent moderate left. It was a time of educating the Spanish half of Bolivia in contemporary radical and reformist ideology, a campaign which even reached some peasants and cholos. At times encouraged by Toro and Busch and at other times neglected and even persecuted, the left grew unchecked throughout the post-war years, especially among the middle class: the urban professionals, white-collar workers, university students, and literate white and cholo merchants and artisans. These were the very elements which previously had formed the hard core of support for the old political system. Shocked by the horrors of the Chaco disaster, these small but politically important classes rejected the traditional upper-class leadership and turned toward reformist ideologies to change the corrupt system.

For the radical left, previously a fringe group of intellectuals, the War and the Toro-Busch period were also a major period of growth. The vital groups of labor and university students, the heart of all radical leftist movements in Latin America, achieved new political power and at the same time became committed in the post-1935 period to a radical Marxist position. Moreover, having penetrated these groups, the radical left even began to have a hearing among the middle class as well.

All of this ferment meant that the traditional parties suddenly found themselves without their usual popular base of support. The economic elite of the nation, finding its traditional allies without power and faced by a sudden new militancy from the previously marginal left, demanded a defense for their class interests and an all-party coalition system to strengthen the very weakened position of the Liberals and Republicans.

Thus, the era of military socialism marked the end of the traditional political system that had been created after 1880 and saw the transition from a classic intra-class republican regime, with limited participation, to one based on class politics, with a major struggle developing over the participation of the lower classes in national political life. Though the moderate and far left were still unorganized and few stable parties had yet been created, the right found it impossible to stop their development. In the post-Busch period the struggle would become sharp and bitter as each side turned away from the civilian political structure and resorted to outright violence to support its ideological and class positions.

Upon the death of Busch, however, it appeared to the conservatives that the situation might be restored without destroying the old system. They immediately put pressure on Quintanilla to move toward open elections and a return to civilian rule. While Quintanilla clearly had ambitions to run his own government, he faced total opposition to a continuation in office. On the one hand the junior officers gave their loyalties to General Bilbao Rioja, a hero of the war period and a seemingly loyal supporter of the Busch-Toro line. On the other hand the Concordancia parties demanded an end to non-constitutional rule. Quintanilla finally decided after a month in office to proclaim the 1938 Constitution the legal charter and then called for elections for the presidency and a new Congress in March 1940. He removed the threat of Bilbao Rioja, now supported also by the left and veterans' movements, by exiling him in October, thus ending the alliance between the Chaco officers and the new left groups. It appeared as if the left was leaderless and the right could succeed to office in the traditional manner.

But the elections of 1940 were to prove a shock to the elite and were to reveal just how effective the post-war changes had been. While all the traditional parties gathered around the banner of General Peñaranda as their official candidate for the presidency and supported a unity slate of Liberals and Republicans for the congressional elections, the far left began to organize a systematic campaign behind the banner of a Cochabamba professor of law and sociology, José Antonio Arze. Arze was a member of the small fringe of radical Marxists who not only had opposed the Chaco War but also had fought the reformism of Toro and had been exiled by him in 1936. From his exile in Chile Arze had organized a Marxian socialist coalition of groups called the *Frente de Izquierda Boliviana* (or Bolivian Leftist Front). While the Frente had powerful labor and radical support, it never effectively organized itself into a coherent party. Nevertheless, Arze and his followers decided to oppose Peñaranda, and on his return from exile in February 1940 he presented his formal candidacy.

It was remarkable that Arze was able to obtain 10,000 votes out of the 58,000 cast in the election, though he was an unknown national figure, without formal party organization and with virtually no newspaper support. Furthermore, the reformists, or nationalists, who had been such an important element in the Toro-Busch regimes all supported the politically neutral and moderate Peñaranda, thus isolating the radicals even among the Chaco generation group. Yet despite all these obstacles, Arze was able successfully to convince 10,000 voters of the old regime—that is, the literate and urban whites and cholos—that a revolutionary Marxist program was the only viable one for Bolivia. The shock of the Arze candidacy destroyed the complacency of the right and put an end to its hopes to return to the pre-1932 system.

That complacency was even further disturbed in the congressional elections. The traditional parties found their worst fears realized as the left, in both its moderate and radical wings, took control of the new Congress, the first such representative body to meet in the post-war period.

The Peñaranda era of the early 1940s, rather than being a return to earlier norms, thus proved to be an important period of national definition and new political organization. Essentially a liberal politician, Peñaranda both was concerned with returning the country to the traditional parliamentary system and wished to support the allied powers in the great international conflict then being carried out in Europe. By these two efforts he provided the forum for debate and the national and international issues by which the left could organize and define its various positions and thus create more coherent and stable parties out of the several trends of radical and reformist thought which had risen in the previous decade.

The single most important group to emerge in the new Congress was the moderate-left, middle-class intellectuals who formed part of the Toro and Busch administrations and were influenced by fascist ideology. These so-called national socialists had supported Peñaranda's candidacy for the presidency but were bitter over his growing warmth to the United States. This pro-Allies policy also meant a conversion of the Bolivian tin industry into an ally and dependent of the United

States war industries, further angering these economic nationalists. Admirers of Germany and Italy on the international scene, the national socialists were committed within Bolivia to the nationalization of basic industries, above all the tin mines. Given their positions, it was in their interest both nationally and internationally to foster a powerful and radical mine labor movement. Under the direction of Carlos Montenegro, Augusto Céspedes—both then in charge of the newspaper *La Calle*—and Víctor Paz Estenssoro, who headed their congressional wing, a new party began to emerge in the Peñaranda era which finally took the name of the *Movimiento Nacionalista Revolucionario* (or Nationalist Revolutionary Movement).

To the left of the MNR there emerged a formal party from Arze's followers in the old FIB. Led by Antonio Arze and Ricardo Anaya, these Marxist intellectuals formally established a radical party called the *Partido de la Izquierda Revolucionario* (or the Party of the Revolutionary Left) in the middle of 1940. Calling for the nationalization of the means of production and the liberation of the Indians, the PIR also took a very strong pro-Soviet position on international affairs. Though still not officially a communist party, the PIR was extremely sympathetic to the cause of the Allies because of the policy of Russia.

The MNR and PIR emerged along with the Trotskyite POR as the three parties of the left that opposed the grouping of traditional parties variously known as the Concordancia or Democratic Alliance. All three believed in the nationalization of the means of production, and above all of the tin mines. All three believed in supporting the nascent labor movement, especially among the miners. But beyond this point there were fundamental differences. Both the POR and PIR went much further than the MNR and spoke of the Indian problem, demanding an end to personal service obligations and the latifundias. They also demanded that peasants be organized into coalitions with workers and the middle class to form a revolutionary vanguard. In this concern for the Indian peasantry the MNR program was silent if not essentially hostile, reflecting its white middle-class origins.

In the debate over international issues, which for the first time began to take on an importance in national politics, the POR remained indifferent to the great world conflict and was able to concentrate exclusively on national issues. The MNR and PIR, however, quickly divided over the international issues, with the MNR taking a frankly pro-fascist position and the PIR a pro-Allied one. Given the context of Bolivian mining politics, this meant that the MNR, like the POR, was in a far more independent position in relation to national politics than the PIR, which was always concerned that Bolivian mine production continue to support the Allied cause. This stand, and appeals from the right for an anti-fascist alliance, would seriously hamper its possibilities to maneuver.

At the beginning of the Peñaranda period, it appeared that the PIR was the dominant party of the left, with the MNR a distant second, and the POR a fringe minority. Since the left had a powerful voice in Congress, the labor movement readily responded to the changed climate among the elite. Feverish unionization activity occurred among the miners, with constant walkouts and strike activity, while all labor groups pushed for increased wages and better working conditions. The workers found major support for these efforts in Congress, and men like Víctor Paz Estenssoro became exponents of syndicalization rights. Though the traditional parties bitterly opposed the support of labor and the left's attack on the administration, Peñaranda refused to accept their advice to censure the three left parties. The parliament of the 1940s became the most radical and free in Bolivia up to this time.

Though liberal on political questions, the Peñaranda government took conservative stands on economic and labor issues. Desperately interested in obtaining the newly available United States government loans and technical assistance and long-term commitments for tin sales at reasonable prices, the Bolivians were faced by the implacable opposition of Standard Oil. Demanding compensation and/or a return of their facilities, Standard Oil, in a rather typical pattern, was able to control United States foreign policy toward Bolivia. Despite the long-term concern of the United States State Department in cutting off the close ties between Bolivia and Germany—which included everything from military missions and support for the national air lines (*Lloyd Aereo Boliviano*) to the subsidization of the MNR paper *La Calle*—and its unquestioned need to obtain mineral contracts, the State Department for a long time seemed incapable of overcoming the demands of the multi-national oil companies.

The need for Bolivian cooperation became so vital that by late 1941, however, the United States was indirectly applying lend-lease formulas to Bolivia, sending technical missions and finally arranging government-controlled long-term mineral purchasing agreements. In this context the Standard Oil Company finally agreed to negotiate. The eventual settlement involved "compensation" for Standard Oil for the confiscation, in terms of the Bolivians purchasing all the surveys and oil maps still in the possession of the multi-national company. In fact this was a victory for Bolivian diplomacy, since its confiscation was not challenged and even the legality of its position was accepted. But it provoked a storm of protest from the left and the nation as a whole, which still held Standard Oil responsible for the Chaco War.

So violent did the protests become that the government accepted falsified documents supplied by the United States, which accused the MNR of a fascist plot paid for by the Germans and so cracked down on the party. *La Calle* was closed, the German minister expelled, and the issue diverted from the Standard Oil settlement toward the issue of a fascist pro-Axis plot. The MNR deputies in Congress were not exiled, and the ensuing debate was a passionate one. It revealed that the PIR and other radical groups essentially distrusted the fascism of the MNR, even though they believed that the putsch attempt was probably a United States fabrication. While supporting the reformist and nationalist elements in the MNR program, they bitterly opposed the other aspects of the MNR ideology.

Much of the debate over international positions, however, was resolved for the various parties by external events. In December 1941 the United States entered World War II, and in January 1942 Bolivia decided to join the Allied forces formally and broke relations with both Germany and Japan. While the MNR retained its fascist sympathies, it was now no longer as closely associated with Germany, since that link was formally broken. This enabled the party to concentrate more fully on the national scene, which was becoming a hotbed of strike and union activity and to moderate its hostility toward the far-left parties.

That all of this radical agitation was having its impact was evident in two major events during the later part of the Peñaranda period. The first was the congressional elections of 1942 and the second the successful organization of a national mine workers union in the context of a major mine massacre. In both instances the power and militancy of the left and the increasing desperation of the traditional parties were evident.

In the congressional elections of May 1942, the traditional parties were able to gain only 14,163 votes, as opposed to 23,401 votes for all the new non-traditional groupings and parties. Thus the trend which had begun with the elections to the Constitutional Convention of 1938 continued through the presidential elections of 1940 and the congressional elections of 1940 and 1942. The erosion of support from the literate and largely white electorate for the traditional parties could not be stopped. In every election up to the vital presidential election of 1951, the essentially middle- and upper-class white electorate, by ever-increasing majorities, showed its opposition to the pre-war system of politics and moved further toward a more radical position which ultimately would see the destruction of the society that had created and fostered their growth.

With the progressive radicalization of the middle-class whites, there came a more profound radicalization of the laboring classes, and especially of their most powerful and revolutionary vanguard, the mine workers. As early as 1940 the various local mine unions had attempted to organize a national confederation of mine workers. Despite government attempts to break these organizations under pretext of the war effort, the miners' unions received powerful congressional support from all the left parties. In November and December 1942 a series of major mine strikes took place in Oruro and Potosí for higher wages and recognition. The longest and most bitter of these local strikes involved the Catavi mines owned by Patiño. In late December troops opened fire on the miners and their families, and hundreds of unarmed workers were slaughtered. The Catavi massacre became a major and powerful rallying cry of the left and of the mine-workers and the crucial event which welded the two groups together into a powerful vanguard. Though peasant and worker massacres by troops were not unusual occurrences in Bolivian history, either before or after 1942, the Catavi massacre took place at a crucial time in the organizational development of the left and labor, and so it became the single most famous *cause célèbre* in the pre-revolutionary period.

The government decided to make the Marxist PIR the scapegoat for the massacre and closed its newspapers and imprisoned its leaders. But it was the MNR which most capitalized on what was still an apolitical mine-workers' movement. Under the leadership of Víctor Paz Estenssoro, the party mounted a major congressional attack on the Peñaranda government in support of the miners, and coincidentally on the whole relationship between the mine-owners, the government, and the United States.

In the ensuing debates, the government eventually beat down a censure move but in so doing destroyed the coalitions that remained between the moderates and the increasingly radical left. The old moderate socialists grouping left over from the Toro and Busch period was destroyed in the debates over Catavi, and even many traditional politicians deserted their parties. The result was that the government found itself with the support of only the most reactionary Liberals and Republicans. The potential support of the PIR, which because of Russia's entrance into the war on the Allied side was now more sympathetic to the government's concerns over the unimpaired flow of minerals to the United States, was rejected by the Peñaranda regime. Thus the PIR was forced by the government itself to join the MNR and POR in opposition.

By the end of 1943 it was clear that the regime had lost control over the political scene. It had also begun to lose control over the army. Several small revolts had been attempted, and news began to circulate of secret military lodges. The most important of these clubs was the RADEPA, which had been organized in the Paraguayan prisoner-of-war camps among the junior officers. With the overthrow of Bilbao Rioja and the radicals just after the death of Busch, RADEPA emerged as the single most politically aware group in the army and the inheritors of the title of military socialism. But unlike their predecessors, this group and its various offshoots were far more inclined toward the fascist line than the reformist-socialist one. In late December 1943 these officers finally allied themselves with the MNR and carried out a successful coup against Peñaranda, thus bringing into power the first MNR government in Bolivian history.

The new regime which emerged was a military junta led by the totally unknown Major Gualberto Villarroel, who was neither a war hero nor a major figure in the military-socialist era. Nevertheless, his position within the RADEPA was vital, and he was totally committed to the vague reformist and fascist model that the group espoused. Accepting three members of the MNR in his cabinet, Villarroel attempted to ally his minority officer group with the new radical movements.

In organizing the new government, the MNR put up Paz Estenssoro as its leader: the extreme fascist wing was represented by Carlos Montenegro and Augusto Céspedes. However much the junta felt sympathies for the Axis cause, by 1944 the realities of the situation required them to moderate their expectations. When the United States and the majority of Latin American governments refused to recognize the junta, the regime was forced first to divest itself of the more extreme MNR leaders and then to call for their complete removal by the early months of 1944. But this temporary break with the MNR in no way destroyed the ties between the two groups, and the ideological line of the regime became defined by MNR concerns.

These concerns involved an attempt to bring the Indian masses into national politics and support the mine-workers' movement, especially the labor wing of the POR. The MNR worked closely with the mine leader and *porista*, Juan Lechín. This support, along with assistance from the railroad workers, finally led to the organization of a national miners federation, some 60,000 strong, at Huanuni in June 1944. The *Federación Sindical de Trabajadores Mineros de Bolivia* (or Federated Union of Mine Workers of Bolivia) immediately took over the leadership of the labor movement as its most powerful national union and gave important support to the MNR and the junta, despite labor opposition to the regime and traditional support for the PIR.

In terms of the Indians, the regime finally assembled over 1,000 Indian caciques from both the Quechua- and Aymara-speaking peasantry in the first national Indian Congress in La Paz in May 1945. At this convention Villarroel both promised a major drive toward providing educational facilities in the free communities, a drive which was in fact to have some impact, and for the first time issued a decree that abolished the hated labor service obligations of the Indians known as pongueaje. A truly revolutionary act and one detrimental to the foundations of the entire latifundia system, this decree was never put into force. Nevertheless, it provided a minimum position for the Indian radicals, and the Congress itself gave many of the traditional Indian leaders their first cross-community contracts, thus paving the way for important mobilization of peasant ideology against the hacienda regime.

In a final area, the regime both supported the worst tendencies of the MNR and also let its own fascist ideology be fully expressed. In the area of democratic rights and civil liberties, the Villarroel regime would prove to be one of the most vicious in national history. When the PIR took a major portion of the votes in the constitutional convention elections of 1944, the government simply assassinated its leaders and jailed its followers. In turn, a short-lived revolt in Oruro in late 1945 gave it the excuse it needed to pick up leading traditional politicians and execute them. This resort to violence against middle-class intellectuals and politicians was new to Bolivian politics and deeply divided the nation, rendering most of the reform activities of the regime useless as most members of the elite viewed the regime as one of gangsterism and fascism.

Ultimately it was the use of police violence and the regime's hos-

tility to the Marxist and the traditional political leaders that finally
destroyed it and temporarily reduced the MNR to a distinctly minor
power in the national scene.

Throughout 1944 and 1945 the continued repression of both far
left and far right finally forced the two groups into an anti-fascist
democratic coalition. By early 1946 this coalition had control of most
of the non-miner labor movement, the university students, and most
of the national political elite. Despite continued government repression, the coalition gained ground and in June and July 1946, when a
teachers' strike was held, they were able to mobilize popular and
student opinion. On 14 July 1946 a popular protest march turned into
a popular revolt. Thus, without the defection of any army or police
officials, the civilians carried out an overthrow of the regime. In the
violence of the moment, Villarroel himself was dragged from the
presidential palace and hanged from a lamp post in the central plaza.

It would thus seem that the MNR and the RADEPA had been
fully discredited and that the future lay with the PIR, which in
fact was the key radical element in the popular July revolt. But
within three years of the revolt and exiling of the MNR leadership,
the MNR again emerged as the most popular party on the left and
the single most powerful political movement in the nation. This
extraordinary reversal of fortune owed as much to the astuteness of
the MNR as to the gross incompetence of the PIR leadership. For
what the MNR quickly realized, and the PIR forgot, was that the
Chaco generation still lived and that the demands for change were as
vibrant and as powerful as ever. It was to prove to their credit that the
MNR learned from its disastrous experience with the military fascists
and was able to re-emerge in the period of the so-called "sexenio," the
six years from 1946 to 1952, as a radical and popular party of change.
To carry out this change, it determined to rid itself once and for all
of its fascist elements. In this it was helped by Lechín and his miners,
who were committed to revolutionary transformation and demanded
that the party support their program. At the same time Paz Estenssoro
and such new leaders as Hernán Siles Zuazo concentrated on re-
establishing their solid middle-class base, with a strong program of

economic stabilization on the one hand and economic nationalization on the other. So successful would they become that in the subsequent revolutionary mythology the murder of Villarroel by the popular crowds in July 1946 would be converted into a major reactionary act and Villarroel would become another martyr, along with Busch and the miners of Catavi, in the revolutionary pantheon of the nation.

In all these developments, the actions of the PIR were crucial, for in the overthrow of the MNR and Villarroel the PIR decided that only full cooperation with the traditional parties could serve their cause, and in this they committed a fundamental mistake. For just as the MNR did not forget the changes wrought by the Chaco conflict, neither did the traditional parties. Wedded to their now nakedly class-defense position, the Concordancia of traditional parties was intent on destroying the new political forces unleashed by the various reformist and radical regimes. They were thus delighted both to use the PIR to cover their own actions and to have it blamed for all their anti-labor moves, especially those directed against the threatening mine workers. The traditional parties, once securing power, were determined to stop all the changes which had occurred and attempted to return to the pre-war system. But this was a quixotic hope. They would end by destroying not only the PIR but also themselves. At the conclusion of the sexenio, the traditional politicians could no longer contain these new movements, so they were forced to abandon constitutional government entirely and rely on naked military power as the only defense against popular demands for change.

Just how revolutionary those demands were became clear in the months after the revolt. At the fourth national miners' Congress at Pulacayo in November 1946, the FSTMB adopted the thesis of the permanent revolution and called for a violent armed struggle for the working class. The so-called Thesis of Pulacayo was a bitter and revolutionary document which rejected all reformist and ameliorist positions. Although it accepted the July revolt as a popular one, it challenged the anti-fascism of the Democratic Alliance parties and spoke of the true fascism of the oligarchy. It demanded a worker-peasant alliance and a government under worker control. Even in its very specific demands, usually the moderate part of worker declarations, the FSTMB took an extreme position. It called for the immediate arming of workers, for worker participation in management, and for the promotion of revolutionary as opposed to economic strikes. This in fact was the most powerful statement of the POR wing of the miners, and it not only committed the miners to revolutionary action, but also forced the MNR, which had sought to control the mine-workers' movement, to adopt a far more revolutionary stand.

In response to the radicalization of the miners, the government decided on a policy of repression and used the PIR ministers to direct the attacks on the workers. The PIR for its part, once having tasted power under the temporary post-Villarroel government, refused to relinquish it when the Republicans won the election of 1947 and continued in a coalition cabinet. This was to prove a fatal mistake, for the Republicans under Enrique Hertzog and Mamerto Urriolagotia were the most reactionary wing of the traditional parties and were determined to destroy the FSTMB and all radicalism in the labor movement. In early 1947 it was a PIR Minister of Labor who ordered the troops into the mines, and, with the bloody suppression of a strike in Catavi, the PIR was destroyed as the representative party of the left.

At the same time the MNR never lost its middle-class following, even though most of the leaders, including Víctor Paz Estenssoro, were in exile. In the 1947 elections they had been reduced to their minimum popular support but still gained 13,000 votes as opposed to the 44,000 of the victorious Republicans. Then, as the PIR was destroyed and the traditional parties showed increasing hostility even to the moderate post-war reformism of the Toro-Busch and Villarroel model, the MNR succeeded in picking up even more votes. By the mid-term congressional elections of May 1949 they emerged as the second most powerful party after the Republicans, despite strong government opposition. So unexpected was their comeback that Hertzog resigned the presidency and turned the government over to his vice-president Urriolagotia.

Despite all these signs of long-term structural change in the political arena, the Republicans refused to change course and the PIR refused to leave the government. Shortly after the congressional elections, more strikes began at Catavi, leading to the exiling of Lechin, Mario Torres, and the other leaders of the FSTMB. News of their exile led to an armed workers' uprising in Catavi and to a massive army intervention in the mines. By this act, it appeared that the army had completely purged itself of all reformist elements and totally committed itself to the repressive policies of the Republican regime. Fearing a worker and MNR revolutionary movement, they united themselves as never before behind their conservative upper-officer caste.

But now the post–World War II decline in international prices for tin triggered a severe fiscal crisis in government. Prices began to rise rapidly on the domestic market. The Republican government could not effectively deal with the economic stagnation and inflation, so it lost its following even among previously supportive groups. Thus key elements of the elite showed themselves indifferent to the final showdown between the government and the MNR. As for the MNR, the violent suppression of the workers and the use of fraud to reduce the electoral victories of the party led the MNR to commit itself fully to an armed overthrow of the regime. In September 1949 the MNR under Siles Zuazo organized a civilian revolt and for two months fought the army in all the provincial cities, even setting up a temporary headquarters in Santa Cruz. Although the revolt was crushed with much bloodshed, it marked an important change in the style of national politics. First of all, it was an entirely civilian operation. The army maintained absolute unity against the rebels and fully supported the regime. Despite the former close alliance between the MNR and the army, the officer corps stood firm against the party and fought it to defeat. The revolt was unique as well in its coalition of worker and middle-class support, for the miners totally committed themselves to the revolt. All of these actions further forced the party away from what remained of its fascist wing and toward Lechin and his ex-Trotskyite followers. It also indicated to the party that, despite all its old ties, it would have to make the revolution by destroying the army itself.

Though the regime again exiled the MNR leadership and otherwise attempted to destroy the party, the MNR's strength only increased from day to day. An indication of its increasing dominance over the worker movement came in May 1950, when the factory workers of La Paz turned a strike into another MNR-labor movement armed insurrection. Planes and artillery were used on the workers' quarters of La Paz to destroy the revolt. But the significance of the event was in the MNR's takeover of the urban labor movement, hitherto a stronghold of the PIR. Now the party had the support of virtually all of organized labor, whatever its local political complexion, as well as most of the middle class.

That the PIR was finished was evident by late 1949. Although the more radical members finally forced the party out of the government after the congressional elections, they could not make it take a more revolutionary stand. In early 1950 the youth group of the party deserted its ranks and formed an official Bolivian Communist Party, while the PIR dwindled into insignificance. Meanwhile the MNR made one last attempt at gaining power by democratic means. In the May 1951 presidential elections it ran a slate of Víctor Paz Estenssoro, who still remained in exile, and Hernán Siles Zuazo. To the dismay of the right, the MNR won the election with a straight majority, gaining 39,000 votes out of 54,000 cast. The Republicans gained only 13,000, and the PIR ended with just 5,000 votes, even less than the Liberals.

Before the MNR could take the presidency, however, the army decided to intervene and prevent it from coming to power. In the days after the election, Urriolagotia resigned and illegally handed over the presidency to the chief of the general staff, who in turn appointed General Hugo Ballivián president. The new government immediately annulled the elections and outlawed the MNR as a communist organization, the new rhetoric reflecting the developing Cold War in the international context. But the military found only the Republicans and a small right-wing pro-clerical fascist party, the *Falange Socialista Boliviano,* willing to give it support. Moreover, even the generals realized the inevitable outcome of the coming struggle, and many leading officers decided to take diplomatic positions abroad at this crucial movement in the conflict.

To all observers it became evident that the MNR would now attempt to take by force what it had been denied at the polls. Never loath to use violence, the MNR went into full-scale military opposition, convinced that only a policy of civil war would give them the government. The officer corps, despite all their attempts at subverting the army, remained totally loyal to the junta. Thus Paz and the more conservative leaders of the party finally agreed that an arming of all civilians and the commitment to a popular armed uprising were the only solution. Even in the civil war of 1949 the party had not opened the armories to the public but had used only its own members in the fighting, fearing that a total civil war would lead to the destruction of all order in Bolivia. But now they were committed to that position as the only one which could lead to victory.

In this context of intense plotting and much violence, the regime suddenly found itself in the midst of a complex international conflict over the sale of tin to the United States, which led to a severe depression in the national economy. In late 1951 the government supported the tin miners' complaints about the low price offered by the United States government for the long-term purchase of tin. The result was an agreement to stop sales and consequently to stop production for a few months to force the United States to come to terms. While this tactic would eventually prove successful, it only exacerbated the political and economic tensions in the country.

After numerous attempts, the final revolt got under way on 9 April 1952. In three days of intensive fighting, during which the armories were opened to the public and the miners marched on La Paz, the army was finally defeated. At the cost of much destruction and the loss of over 600 lives, the MNR returned to power. But the 1952 party was a vastly different one from the pro-fascist group overthrown in 1946. It was now a party of radical middle-class elements and revolutionary workers and represented a new type of radical populist movement. It had also come to power at the cost of the traditional political parties and the main institutions of order and authority, the army and the police. By accepting the workers' participation and ideology and by arming the populace, it had committed itself to a totally destructive stance in relation to the old order, and despite its traditionally limiting reformist ideology it was now committed to a revolutionary outcome.

Having achieved power against the united opposition of the army and the traditional parties, the MNR leaders felt under no obligation to offer a moderate program or compromise with any traditional institution, political or military. Soon not only the urban white and cholo classes but also the rural Indian masses were in possession of arms, and the army and the national police force were completely disorganized. The aims of the party were known to all, the arms were in the hands of a militant populace, and the exiled leaders returning from abroad were not to be restrained. Thus began Latin America's most dynamic social and economic revolution since the Mexican Revolution of 1910.

Chapter 8 • The National Revolution, 1952-1964

To understand the revolution that took place in the months after April 1952, it is essential to understand the nature of Bolivian society and economy at mid-century. Though still retaining all the classic characteristics of an under-developed economy and society, Bolivia had experienced marked changes in its social composition. Between 1900 and 1952 the urban population (those living in cities or towns of 5,000 or more) had risen from 14.3 percent to 22.8 percent of the national population. Moreover, in each of the departments of the country, the major urban centers had grown faster than the population as a whole. The level of literacy and the number of children attending school also increased in the same period, especially after the heavy inputs into education carried out by the post-Chaco regimes. Thus between 1900 and 1950 literates rose from 17 percent of the population to 31 percent, while the pre-university student population went from some 23,000 to 139,000, or from 1.3 to 4.6 percent of the total population. At the top, however, much less change had occurred, and while the number of university students by 1951 had reached

12,000, only 132 persons in the entire country had graduated with post-secondary degrees in that year.

But if one were to characterize Bolivia in 1950, it would still be as a predominantly rural society, the majority of whose population was only marginally integrated into the national economy. Of all economically active persons registered in the census of 1950, fully 72 percent were engaged in agriculture and allied industries. Yet this work force only produced some 33 percent of the gross national product, a discrepancy which clearly indicates the serious economic retardation of this sector.

The cause for economic backwardness in agriculture is not hard to discover. Through the constant expansion of the hacienda system at the end of the nineteenth and beginning of the twentieth century, land distribution had become one of the most unjust and uneconomic in Latin America. The 6 percent of the landowners who owned 1,000 hectares or more of land controlled fully 92 percent of all cultivated land in the republic. Moreover, these large estates themselves were under-utilized, with the average estate of 1,000 or more hectares cultivating but 1.5 percent of its lands. At the opposite extreme were the 60 percent of the landowners who owned 5 hectares or less, true minifundias, which accounted for just 0.2 percent of all the land and were forced on average to put 54 percent of their lands into cultivation.

Bolivia represented a classic Latin American latifundia system. The extreme inequality in the division of lands was essential in the control of rural labor. Given their overwhelming dominance, the landowners successfully controlled access to all the best lands in all the zones of the republic. They thus obtained their labor force by offering lands in exchange for labor. In return for free labor on the domain of the estate, landless Indian laborers were given use of usufruct lands of the landowners. The Indians were required to supply seeds, tools, and in some cases even animals for this work, which left the owner with few capital inputs to supply. The Indians were even required to transport the final crop.

This system did not involve debt peonage or other means of force, and Indians tended to move in and out of the latifundia with no re-

strictions, but the increasing pressures on land in the free community
area, especially after the last great age of hacienda expansion, com-
pelled the peasants to adapt themselves to the system. While the urban centers were expanding, they were not doing so fast enough to
absorb the growing rural population. The subdivisions of plots in the
free communities was rapidly reaching crisis proportions, so more and
more sons were forced to work either on the haciendas to obtain land
to feed themselves and their families or as a cheap labor force in the
mines and towns.

To add to the Indians' work obligations on the hacienda, the hacendado also required personal service to himself, his family, and his
overseers. *Pongueaje* (personal service obligation) had been part of
the work requirements of estate Indians since colonial times. But it
did not make these obligations any less onerous. The one thing universally hated by all Indian peasants was the *pongo* service. It required attendance on the hacendado family even in a distant urban
residence and took up large amounts of time and effort, all at the
peasant's own cost.

With labor inexpensive, with seeds and even tools sometimes free
or at minimal cost, and with protected agricultural markets, the incentives for hacendados to invest capital in their holdings were minimal.
In fact, absentee ownership was the dominant form in all the rural
areas, and the overwhelming majority of hacendados lived in urban
centers and had urban professions. The result of this system was the
use of rudimentary technology and poor quality seed with consequently extremely low yields of foodstuffs. Thus the agricultural sector was so backward that it was unable to meet the needs of the expanding population in the urban centers and of the nation as a whole.
Whereas 10 percent of the imports in the 1920s was food, the figure
was 19 percent in the 1950-52 period, and a good proportion of the
imported food was traditional Andean root crops which were produced only in Bolivia and Peru. Inefficient, unproductive, and unjust,
the Bolivian agricultural system not only failed to satisfy even traditional food demands, it kept a large percentage of the national work
force out of the market by holding down their income in exploitive

work and service obligations. This in turn restricted the market for manufactures to the small urban minority and the relatively few active agricultural centers such as the Cochabamba Valley.

Given the limited nature of this internal market, it is not surprising to find that Bolivia had only a very small industrial sector, which in 1950 accounted for but 4 percent of the economically active population. Industry essentially consisted of some textile factories and food-processing plants. Moreover, by 1950 it was estimated that there had been little change in the capital structure of this sector and that the majority of the factories were over-aged and under-productive by world standards.

The same pattern of lack of new capital inputs which affected agriculture and industry was even more evident in mining. From the late 1930s onward there was apparently little new investment in the mining sector, just when most of the mines began to run out of richer veins. Thus aging plants and declining quality of minerals inexorably forced the costs of mining up to levels that were becoming uneconomic and non-competitive except in periods of wartime shortage on the world markets. By 1950 Bolivia was the highest-cost producer of tin on the world market, and in some years the industry was barely covering its costs. The margins of profit were extremely thin, making the industry even more sensitive to very minor fluctuations in world prices. Moreover, even when prices took a sudden upturn, the low quality of ore available and the low productivity of the mines meant that Bolivia found it extremely difficult to increase production. By 1952 it was still the case that the best year of tin output was 1929, when the nation had exported 47,000 tons of tin. In fact that figure remains a record until the present day.

Thus while the social structure was slowly changing and the political system disintegrating, the economy was experiencing a stagnation and a relative decapitalization in key sectors. It would thus prove relatively easy to undertake the changes which the MNR would carry out as a result of the revolution of 1952. The haciendas, owned as they were by a largely absentee class, and with little capital invested, could be seized without major opposition. Moreover, given peasant mobiliza-

tion, they could not be held without full support from the police powers of the State. The takeover of the aging mining sector by the state
also would not be vigorously opposed by the tin barons so long as ade-
quate compensation could be provided. In short, the strength of the
economic elite was relatively drained at the time of the revolution,
much as their political power had been weakened.

The new MNR leaders found themselves in total political control of
the nation at a time when the elite was economically weak and incapable of opposing fundamental social and economic reforms. The long
and bitter opposition of the oligarchy to their coming to power in the
sexenio had ended by wiping out significant civilian political opposition to the MNR and had even put the army in such a position that
it was willing to destroy itself rather than see the MNR come to victory. The three days of fighting between the civilians and miners on
one side and the army on the other had seen the collapse of the military. This was the truly shocking event of April 1952, for in one moment the entire police power of the State was overwhelmed. The
wholesale distribution of arms to the populace at large, the creation
of urban and rural militias, and the neutralization of the national police changed Bolivian political, economic, and social reality beyond
even the wildest expectations of the MNR leadership.

For Bolivia, a typical racist state in which the Indian non–Spanish-
speaking peasantry was held in control by a small white Spanish-
speaking elite, political power was ultimately based on violence rather
than consensus. Among the third of the population who were part of
the national Spanish culture and who practiced "politics," there was a
relatively developed consensus. But only force could cement a union
between them and the Indian masses. Once that force was neutralized
and the peasants obtained arms, the whole system would become un-
raveled. Moreover, once the class-conscious workers also received arms,
the ability to retain traditional systems even in the urban areas became
a difficult task.

Thus, no matter how limited the aims of the more moderate leadership may have been even in April 1952, the reality of the collapse of
the state and the arming of the popular masses and their leaders meant

that a massive social revolution would be the end result. The "reluctant revolutionaries," as some have called them, were thus slowly and inexorably forced to propose a total reorganization of Bolivian society.

At the beginning, of course, the regime made several dramatic gestures which would create further pressures for reform at an even more basic level. One of the first acts of the new regime was to establish universal suffrage by eliminating the literacy requirements. In one stroke, the Indian peasant masses were enfranchised, and the voting population jumped from some 200,000 to just under 1 million persons. Next the army was reduced to a bare minimum. The national army college was temporarily closed and some 500 officers purged from the ranks. While the army itself was given the task of its own reorganization, it was so reduced in power and number that many persons believed for a time that it had ceased to exist. Moreover, the MNR civilian militias soon were better armed than the police and the army and took over all the internal duties that these two forces usually managed.

The MNR also set about reorganizing its forces so as to strengthen its own power base. The regime fully supported the miners when they set up a new national labor federation, the COB (Bolivian Workers Central), in the late days of April. While the COB proclaimed itself politically neutral and allowed the POR, PIR, and the new PCB to have representation, it in fact became a powerful ally of the regime and ended up by naming three labor ministers to the new cabinet. Lechín, who was head of the FSTMB, also became head of the COB and in turn was given the Ministry of Mines and Petroleum. Moreover, whatever the political conservativism of the hard-core MNR leaders, the COB and FSTMB represented the radical revolutionary wing, and they were not slow in enunciating a total revolutionary program. One of the COB's first acts was to issue a set of demands which included nationalization of the mines without compensation, liquidation of the army and its replacement by the militias, and a full-scale Agrarian Reform decree abolishing the latifundia system and all forms of work obligations.

In the next few months the MNR leadership under President Víctor Paz Estenssoro and Hernán Siles Zuazo slowly began to respond to the political and para-military pressure of the workers but tried to restrain their reforms as much as possible. It took until July for the regime to declare the export and sale of all minerals a state monopoly, which would now be handled by the Banco Minero founded by Busch. Though a logical step according even to pre-reform patterns, it had taken several months of intensive debate to get even this far. But those in the party who wished to stop at this point were faced by increasing worker demands for uncompensated confiscation.

So powerful did this pressure become that the leadership finally agreed to full-scale nationalization. In early October the government set up a semi-autonomous state enterprise to run any state-owned mines, which was given the name of *Corporacíon Minera de Bolivia* (COMIBOL). Then on 31 October they nationalized the big three companies of Patiño, Hochschild, and Aramayo. By this act they turned over some two-thirds of the tin-mining industry to COMIBOL and state control.

While the labor radicals had demanded confiscation without indemnification, the MNR was concerned about elaborating such a revolutionary principle and also wished to allay the fears of the United States government. Since the MNR had done everything to smooth those relations, including ending the tin boycott on largely United States government terms, it did not wish to antagonize a potentially dangerous ally. Given that the Cold War was in full development and that the United States was actively intervening in Guatemala to suppress a radical government, the MNR hoped to avoid the label of a communist-inspired regime. Since the United States had in fact initially mistaken the MNR for a fascist and Peronist-oriented party, recalling its old role under Villarroel, it had initially been rather indifferent if not mildly supportive of the new regime. Thus, not only did the regime promise compensation but it made no gestures toward nationalizing any other mines, including the several medium-sized non–tin-producing mines owned by American companies.

Internally, the regime was forced to accept COB and FSTMB direction. The workers obtained two out of the seven seats on the

Board of COMIBOL, and worker representatives in all the mines were given veto power in COMIBOL decisions which affected workers. In short, the regime set up what was generally called worker "co-government" in the mine administration. This system of organization shifted important power toward the workers, who pushed both for increased hiring and for the establishment of well-subsidized *pulperías,* or company stores.

Meanwhile in the last half of 1952 and the beginning of 1953 rural society began to collapse, despite all the efforts of the regime to control the situation. With the army ineffectual, arms quickly reaching the countryside, and young political radicals spreading the word, a systematic peasant attack on the entire latifundia system had developed. In many ways similar to the peasant movement known as the "Great Fear" in the French Revolution, the period from late 1952 until early 1953 saw the destruction of work records in the rural areas, the killing and/or expulsion of overseers and landowners, and the forcible seizure of land. Meanwhile the peasants, using traditional community organizations, began to organize peasant *sindicatos* with the encouragement of the COB, to receive arms, and to create formal militia organizations. Although the countryside had been relatively indifferent and little affected by the great conflicts of April 1952, it was the scene of tremendous violence and destruction by the end of that year.

However reluctant the new regime may have been to attack the hacienda problem seriously, the massive mobilization of the peasants, now the majority of the electorate, and the systematic destruction of the land tenure system forced the regime to act. In January 1953 it established a broad-based Agrarian Reform Commission which included members of the POR and PIR as well as MNR functionaries, and by 3 August a radical Agrarian Reform decree was enacted. The decree tried to salvage whatever modern capital-intensive sector remained in the rural area. It provided formal compensation for the landlords in the form of twenty-five-year indemnification bonds and granted the ex-hacienda lands to the Indian workers through their sindicatos and comunidades, with the proviso that such lands could not be individually sold. While compensation was demanded from the Indians for the lands they seized, in fact, all the qualifications imposed by the commission became dead letters.

In the predominantly Indian areas, almost all the lands were seized, and the Indians quickly stopped paying compensation, with the lands, in effect, being confiscated. The only exceptions were the relatively unpopulated Santa Cruz region and such southern medium-sized hacienda regions as Monteagudo, which had some modest capital-intensive agriculture and no resident Indian populations, and the small-holding vineyard region of the Cinti Valley. Everywhere else, the hacienda was abolished, the hacendado class destroyed, and a new class of communal peasant landowners established.

At the same time, largely through the efforts of the COB, the communities were organized into sindicatos, and a COB representative even sat as the first Minister of Peasant Affairs. But this tutelage of the Indian organizations by urban labor and mine-workers soon ended, and peasant leaders emerged as major powers in the rural areas. Although there were numerous competing groups and regional associations among the Indians, the most important centers of peasant political leadership became the community of Achacachi in the Lake Titicaca district and the pueblo of Ucureña in the Cochabamba Valley. The former became the center of Aymara peasant organization and the latter of the Quechua speakers. While often working at odds with each other, and constantly being suborned by the regimes in power, the peasants nevertheless retained total control over their own sindicatos and have been vital sources of national political strength from 1952 until the present day.

With the elimination of the hated hacendados and many of their cholo middlemen, and the granting of land titles, the Indians became a relatively conservative political force in the nation and actually grew indifferent if not hostile to their former urban worker colleagues. The appeasement of their land hunger turned the Indians inward so that for the next two generations the primary concern of the communities and their sindicatos was the delivery of modern facilities of health and education and the guaranteeing of their land titles. Otherwise they were receptive to reformist and even conservative policies in the urban centers.

The genius of Paz Estenssoro was to realize the importance of this totally new and quite conservative force on the national scene. As his power declined among his former supporters in the middle class, and his dependence on the radical COB and workers' groups grew, he realized that he would have to create an entirely new power base for the center and right wings of his party among the peasantry. So successful was this drive that for the next quarter-century the peasantry became the bastion of the conservative elements of the central government. And once created, this alliance would survive the initial destruction of the MNR and even the return of rightist military regimes.

Just as the left was growing and new peasant power was developing, the MNR found itself losing its most basic and traditional center of support, the urban middle class. The collapse of the state, the subsequent nationalization of the mines and destruction of the hacienda system, and the massive shift of government resources into social welfare programs all created havoc in the national economy and in government income. The takeover of the mines drained massive sums from the state coffers, and agrarian reform reduced agricultural deliveries to the cities drastically, thus necessitating massive food imports to prevent starvation. The only way to resolve all of these problems was to increase national currency. The result was one of the world's most spectacular records of inflation from 1952 to 1956. In that time the cost of living increased twentyfold, with annual inflation rates of over 900 percent.

By this decision to finance the revolution through the dramatic devaluation of national currency, the MNR in effect was making the middle classes pay for part of the revolution. Fixed rents were wiped out, and urban real estate values disappeared overnight. Suddenly the middle class found its most fundamental interests attacked. The elimination of a large part of their incomes created immediate hostility to

the regime. Formerly the heart of the party and its staunchest supporters, the urban middle class deserted the MNR on a major scale.
Rejecting the PIR and PCB as viable alternatives, they shifted their
allegiance to the previously minor Bolivian Falangista Party.

A conservative Catholic party with fascist leanings, the FSB was established in Chilean exile at the Catholic University in Santiago in
the 1930s. Like the POR a relatively minor party in its early phases,
the FSB had powerful Church support and was committed to a moderate nationalist position. But given its appeals, it competed with the
center and right groups who were supporting the MNR in the pre-
1952 period, while its clerical leaning alienated the majority of followers, given the weak position of the Church in national society. But
when the MNR attacked the income of the middle class after 1952
and in effect forcibly shifted its savings toward the more popular
classes, the clericalism of the FSB was forgotten and it emerged as
the most powerful party in the urban centers. The new strength of the
FSB was revealed in the mid-term elections in the first Paz regime and
even more so in the presidential elections of 1956, in which the FSB
effectively dominated the cities, seizing most of the MNR's traditional
pre-1952 supporters.

But by this time the coalition of urban radicals, party stalwarts and
government officials, and the peasantry had emerged as the major coalition of the MNR. Thanks to the workers and the peasants, they
were able to accept their loss of the old electorate and still emerge with
landslide victories at the polls. But despite its losses to the right and
its dependence on the left, the MNR refused to go all out toward a
socialist revolution. It constantly stressed its legitimacy and relationship to the old order and, while nationalizing the big three mine companies, did everything in its power to attract new foreign capital and
to protect private property. In the Agrarian Reform it did sacrifice
property in a major way, but it still attempted to retain the Santa Cruz
area as a prime zone for the expansion of private investment. Finally,
while the creation of COMIBOL and YPFB made the government
the single largest producer in the national economy and created a

"state capitalism" model for the economy, the government development corporation, CBF, expended large sums in providing working capital for the private industrial sector.

The seeming divergence between right and left policies in the Paz Estenssoro government was resolved toward a largely right bias by the last years of his first government. Faced with a bankrupt economy, an inability of the regime even to feed its people, and a lack of capital to undertake all the ambitious welfare and reform programs proposed, the party decided to throw its weight toward its right wing and seek financial assistance from the United States. As early as June 1953, under intense United States pressure and the refusal of Patiño's Williams Harvey Company smelters in England to refine its tin, the government agreed to compensate Patiño, Hochschild, and Aramayo. The following month the United States signed a minerals purchasing agreement and also announced both a doubling of the previous aid program and the immediate shipment of 5 million dollars' worth of food under Public Law 480.

Bolivia was the first Latin American country to receive such a food exports grant. By the end of a decade of massive aid Bolivia had achieved the extraordinary distinction of having obtained 100 million dollars in United States aid, making it at that time the largest single recipient of United States foreign aid in Latin America and the highest per capita in the world. So dependent upon this aid did Bolivia become that, by 1958, one-third of its budget was paid for directly by United States funds.

For the United States, the Bolivian aid decision was an extremely paradoxical one, since it occurred under the very conservative and Cold War regime of Secretary of State John Foster Dulles and President Dwight Eisenhower. Hostile to all revolutionary regimes, the United States Republican administration would seem to have been the regime least likely to be receptive to Bolivian requests for aid. But the recent emergence of radical regimes in Guatemala and Guyana had created an unusual fear in the United States of losing control over the Western Hemisphere, and it was convinced that Bolivia would quickly follow suit. Faced with the first challenge in the Cold War to its absolute hegemony over its Latin American sphere of influence, the Eisenhower administration felt that supporting the MNR "fascists" was the only way to prevent the revolution from falling into communist hands.

Along with these larger international concerns, there was also the fact that the conflict over tin purchases by the United States Reconstruction Finance Corporation had actually weakened the military regime and had aided the rebellion of the MNR, which stimulated a sense of guilt in the administration. Moreover, Bolivia had actually been a model region for the first of the major Latin American aid programs, and its modest Point-Four aid under Truman had achieved major results. Thus there existed within the local United States embassy an important group of experts who favored continued aid to Bolivia and accepted the Paz Estenssoro line that he and his regime were the only factors preventing a communist takeover. Finally, given the small amount of United States investment in the Bolivian mining companies and/or in agricultural lands, none of the confiscation decrees had seriously affected United States companies, so that the State Department was under no pressure to oppose the regime.

The massive aid which poured into Bolivia did prove to be vital in providing economic security and growth in Bolivia. Public Law 480 food shipments gave Bolivia the crucial foodstuffs needed to pass through the period of severe agricultural dislocation occasioned by the Agrarian Reform. This aid undoubtedly gave the government the equanimity to deal with the peasants that it might otherwise not have had if there was real starvation in the cities. It also provided funds to establish a modern road system so vital to the integration of the national society. United States aid was also crucial in the development of the whole Santa Cruz region, which is so important to the Bolivian economy. Massive inputs of capital into health and education were also instrumental in developing Bolivia's backward social services into a more modern system. Finally, the very crucial funding of direct government operations, along with the food programs, provided the social peace which might not have existed had the regime gone unaided. Given the money needed to keep the regime afloat and the population fed and clothed, the absence of that funding would surely have led to a more bloody social history than Bolivia experienced after 1952.

But this aid was not without its price, for the United States government, despite all belief to the contrary, refused to divorce its policies from that of private United States companies operating overseas. This meant that along with its unceasing demands for the reduction of the power of COB and the end to worker co-government in the mines, the State Department also demanded a change in the political economy of Bolivia as it affected United States investments. Such concessions included everything from repayment on defaulted bonds from the 1920s to new investment and petroleum codes favorable to United States interests.

Thus, while the United States poured aid into every part of the Bolivian economy, it resisted all efforts by the Bolivians to fund YPFB, despite its recent success in developing new petroleum production. It was made clear to Bolivia that new investments in petroleum would only come with a new petroleum code that permitted direct United States private investments once again in Bolivian oil. Thus in October 1953 a new petroleum code was drawn up with United States technical assistance, and by the end of the decade some ten United States companies were operating in Bolivia, the most important now being Gulf Oil Company, which began operations in 1955. Moreover, when Brazil's state-owned oil company *Petrobras* proposed to the Bolivian government that it be granted concessions under both pre-existent treaties as well as the new quite liberal code, the Bolivian government refused all overtures.

Next came direct United States pressure to resume payment on private North American loans from the 1920s upon which Bolivia had defaulted in 1931. These 56 million dollars' worth of loans had already been declared fraudulent by the Roosevelt administration in 1943 and had never been an issue in relations between the two governments. Yet now the State Department demanded full and complete payment, plus interest on these now quite speculative bonds. The result of this pressure was that Bolivia was forced to resume payments in 1957.

It was evident that the United States was willing to put enormous pressure on the Bolivians to satisfy private United States economic interests. Given the heavy United States support of the regime and the fact that most North American demands involved potential investments or support in the Cold War, MNR decisions to accept dictates in these areas did not substantially affect the revolution itself. But the decision to force Bolivia to accept monetary stabilization was another matter entirely, for the decision to cut its spending and stop printing currency would have a dramatic impact on the political, economic, and social policies of the regime.

To understand the willingness of the Bolivians to accept the mid-1950s International Monetary Fund's aid program which required total stabilization, one has to go back to the internal struggles within the MNR regime itself. From the beginning the MNR had emerged with two rough groupings, a center-right and middle-class wing represented by Siles Zuazo and a left and labor coalition led by Lechín and the COB. While favoring one side or the other, Paz essentially played the role of neutral leader above the factions. The far right of the party had been destroyed in an early abortive coup attempt, so most of the moderates had finally accepted the various reforms. But the moderates still put pressure on the regime to maintain its middle-class base. It was also the moderate wing of the party that demanded a modernization of the economy, even at the expense of some of the social aims of the revolution. Given the completion of the initial destructive phase of the revolution and the continued sluggishness of the national economy, it was probably inevitable that the moderate conservative elements would, with strong support from the right, come to dominate.

However the two groups split ideologically, there was no question that the two sides worked closely together. Thus when Paz stepped down, it was agreed that Siles would run for the presidency and that Lechín would seek the third presidential term when Siles stepped down. To seal the agreement, Siles accepted the Labor Minister in charge of peasant affairs, Ñuflo Chavez Ortiz, as his vice-presidential running mate.

In the June elections of 1956, it was evident that the MNR had little trouble mobilizing its powerful peasant and worker coalition so that it obtained a comfortable majority with some 790,000 votes. But the erosion of the middle classes was also evident in the 130,000 votes, largely urban and white, which the FSB captured, making it the second largest party.

It was an attempt to recapture this extremely hostile and restive middle-class base, as well as to further its ideas of development, that the Siles regime decided to accept the dictates of the IMF. Moreover, given the increasingly difficult situation of the national economy and the total inability of the regime to survive without direct United States subsidies, it was inevitable that some concessions had to be made. This was especially necessary, as the United States now stopped supporting the tin industry through minerals purchase arrangements, and international prices continued to decline, thus reducing government maneuverability even further.

At this point the regime had only three options: generate the capital it needed by completely socializing the economy, which it was ideologically unwilling to do; continue with the inflationary program until a total collapse occurred and/or a Falangista revolt ended the regime; or accept the United States terms and extract the largest aid possible for doing so at the minimum cost to its social programs. It opted for the last solution.

Under Siles the United States worked out its "Stabilization Plan" by late 1956, and Bolivia accepted it under IMF auspices in January 1957. The plan required that Bolivia balance its budget, end the food subsidization of the miners, hold down wage increases, create a single exchange rate, and adopt a host of other measures restricting government initiative and expenditures. Even by the usual IMF standards, the Bolivian plan was an extreme one, envisioning the creation of a stable currency with almost zero inflationary growth within the space of one or two years.

There is no question that the harsh IMF plan was relatively successful. The currency was stabilized, deficits in government spending were cut, and COMIBOL achieved a more balanced budget. By the early 1960s, in fact, Bolivia was finally able to give up direct United

States budget subsidies. Also a great deal of foreign private, and above all government, capital now entered Bolivia in the form of loans and investments. Productivity in the mines did increase, and the economic stability needed for internal savings and investment finally began to be achieved.

But the costs were high. The United States insisted that the program be carried out regardless of political consequences. Eventually the left was forced into strong opposition to the Siles regime. Vice-president Ñuflo Chavez resigned, and Lechín led a series of major mining strikes. Siles tried to mediate between the MNR left and the United States, but falling world tin prices and unrelenting United States pressure kept forcing his hand. After many bitter strikes, the subsidized pulperías in the mines were closed; but by then a serious rift had developed within the party. Also, the United States now felt confident that it could isolate and destroy Juan Lechín, who became in the eyes of the United States the arch enemy.

Just as Siles never used force against the miners and achieved almost all the concessions from COB through hunger strikes of his own and threats of resignation, he never seriously rejected the left of the party. Holding that stabilization and retrenchment were the only policies which could guarantee the victories of the left and suppress the rising right wing and the Falange, he nevertheless accepted the idea that Lechín and the COB would succeed him in 1960. But continuing United States pressure, now influenced by a series of Cold War liberals who were United States ambassadors under the Democratic regimes, still opposed Lechín and the left. Hoping to diminish this hostility and to prepare the way for the left, Lechín and Siles agreed on a compromise platform for the third presidential term. Paz was again to lead the party, and Lechín would be his vice-president. Hoping that he could influence North American opinion by proving his moderation, the new vice-president in the second Paz term tried to show his total acceptance of the United States. He traveled to Washington and even went to Formosa to meet with Nationalist leaders and thus symbolically accept the worst Cold War positions of the United States. He also agreed to end worker co-government in the mines when it became the price for the arrangement of a major infusion of German and United States government investments in COMIBOL in the so-called "Triangular Plan."

But despite these concessions, Lechín could not dispel United States hostility, which went back to the earliest days of the revolution. And it was this United States intransigence that Paz Estenssoro decided to use to destroy his dependence on the left of the party. While Siles had opposed the left on policy grounds but supported its legitimacy and right to power in the party, Paz Estenssoro showed himself implacably opposed to the continued power of COB and the mineworkers in his regime. It was unremitting North American hostility toward Lechín and the left which gave Paz the crucial support he needed to attempt a full-scale reorganization of the party and a prolongation of his government in office. The planning for an attack on Lechín was evident in the policies of the second Paz administration of 1960-64.

But the temporary weakening of Lechín did not break the power of the left. Paz began to rearm the army heavily, justifying this constantly to the United States as a means of preventing communist subversion. Moreover the United States army now infiltrated the Bolivian command structure, and most officers in the Bolivian armed forces received advanced training outside of Bolivia at a United States military base.

"Internal subversion" became a major theme of United States training for the army and counter-insurgency a basic policy. Moreover, the regime prevented the militias from rearming and did everything possible to shift the balance of military power back to the army and away from the civilian and worker militias. Thinking that this policy was eminently viable and that Paz could carry it through to completion, the United States fully supported Paz's bid for a third term. But at this point Siles and Lechín joined forces and broke with the party, thus temporarily destroying the MNR. Finding himself with only the army and the peasants as his major supporters, Paz put up a leading general, René Barrientos, as his candidate for vice-president.

The election of 1964, given Paz's control over the now passive peasantry, was assured. But with the left and center of the MNR in total rebellion, the Falange still an implacable enemy, and his dependence on the military complete, it was inevitable that the army would be encouraged to overthrow him. Thus in November 1964, a few short months after the presidential elections, the army ousted Paz in a relatively bloodless coup and put the government in the hands of a junta headed by the vice-president General Barrientos. Thus the army was back in national politics, and it would remain the dominant force in the national government from 1964 until today.

Chapter 9 • The Military Interregnum, 1964-1982

The overthrow of Victor Paz Estenssoro and the temporary disintegration of the MNR brought to an end the first phase of the National Revolution of 1952. For the next eighteen years various groups and institutions within the national society would struggle to dominate and direct the forces which had been unleashed in the period of the National Revolution. The army, the peasants, organized labor and both traditional and newly emerging political parties, all sought to direct the new social and economic order. In this long, bitter, and violent struggle there emerged a more sophisticated political system and a more complex society, but at a high cost to all.

Though leaders of the MNR opposition initially assumed that the overthrow of Paz Estenssoro was a temporary transition leading to the continued domination of the old National Revolutionary leadership, the reality was that a new political era had emerged in 1964. Younger military officers who had come to power under the MNR were to create a new political system based on a complex alliance with the peasants, and in hostility to democratic politics and organized labor. Many of these military officers had fought against Che Guevarra and had slowly come to espouse aspects of an ideology which for a variety of reasons justified the legitimacy of military authoritarian governments as the only solution to modernization—an ideology prevalent in this era in the military establishments of neighboring South American countries. Many of these regimes would also find support among the newer elements of the wealthiest classes and newly powerful regional elites which saw the military as more likely to favor their interests than the old MNR.

But the institutional change, often chaotic personnel advancements and ideological conflict within the army itself, as contrasted to more traditional and firmly hierarchical military organizations in Chile, Argentina and Brazil, created an officer class that was far more unpredictable than many others in Latin America. Thus the era of military regimes was one of marked and radical shifts of viewpoint, abrupt changes of regime, and constant emergence of new and unexpected personalities. But despite all the very rapid and often seemingly random changes, there existed a series of basic arrangements that were only rarely modified. These coalitions were based on the army's acceptance of the basic social and economic reforms of the National Revolution and above all a firm commitment to Agrarian Reform and mobilization of the peasantry. It was their recognition and active acceptance of the peasantry which would mark these new military regimes as semi-populist ones essentially based on an often unexpressed, but nevertheless fully functioning, alliance of peasants and the military. All these features were clearly expressed in the first of these military regimes, that of René Barrientos, which established most of the basic norms that would dominate the military governments in the years to come.

Though the COB, Lechín, and Siles initially supported the Barrientos government, the new regime quickly showed its implacable hostility to organized labor and the left. It was also indifferent, if not hostile, to leftist supporters and sought its urban support in a new governmental party coalition from among the Christian Democrats and elements of the Falange.

The Barrientos regime gave unstinting support only to the revolutionary reforms that affected the peasants, such as Agrarian Reform and universal suffrage. One of the first acts of the new regime—one supported by every subsequent regime of the left and right—was to declare its unswerving support for Agrarian Reform and for further distribution of land titles. Full assistance was also given for welfare programs, rural education, and the peasant sindicatos, which both retained their arms and received protection. In fact, the Barrientos regime became the most popular one after Paz in the countryside. A native speaker of Quechua, Barrientos, who made a major effort to support and dominate the peasant unions, was known for his largess in buying individual aid and general peasant support. The result was an urban anti-labor and conservative military regime allied with the Indian peasantry. It was, in short, a powerful coalition that only the rampant corruption and instability of the army itself rendered unworkable.

Almost immediately upon taking office, the army, both for political and what it claimed were economic reasons, launched a major attack on the unions. The Barrientos regime argued that the miners' FSTMB and the central federation, the COB, had to be destroyed if COMIBOL was to become a profitable and well-managed state enterprise. In the first few years of his government, Barrientos in fact succeeded in dismantling the FSTMB, firing some 6,000 miners and suppressing all strike activity. Finally it even carried out a major massacre of miners on the night of San Juan in June 1967 at the Catavi-Siglo XX mines. By his activities, Barrientos temporarily succeeded in decapitating the union movement, but he did not really eradicate its potential power. Bolivian labor had become radicalized in the 1940s and successfully resisted the repeated interventions and suppressions which a succession of military regimes attempted after 1964. Nevertheless, the almost constant use of troops at the mines succeeded in isolating and temporarily controlling the once-all-powerful labor movement for the first time since 1952.

Meanwhile, the pro-foreign capitalist policy of the new military regime, along with the long-term reforms initiated by the MNR, was finally beginning to revitalize the national economy. A combination of rising tin prices on the international market, heavy inputs of foreign capital, and forced retrenchment of the work force and wages created the first profit for COMIBOL in 1966. Thereafter began a long-term trend in production and prices that was to make COMIBOL an important source of government revenue. Basic changes now occurred in the private mine sector as well. Fully encouraged by all the MNR governments through special subsidization and other assistance, the medium and small mine sectors also increased production, with the middle-rank mines becoming especially important and rising to about a third of total output in the tin sector by the end of the decade. Thus not only was COMIBOL itself expanding but the entire industry was becoming more complex, with a new group of middle-size mine-owners emerging as a powerful force in the private sector.

This policy of active encouragement to the private sector, while part of the original MNR programs, was even further stressed by the Barrientos regime. In 1965 a liberalized investment code for foreign capital had been issued: United States Steel was allowed to rent the Matilda zinc mine from COMIBOL, while Gulf was given further concessions to complete its oil export pipeline from Santa Cruz and Tarija to the altiplano and thence to the Pacific coast.

While suppressing labor and left groups, Barrientos was actively encouraging the new economic elite emerging in the mines and urban sectors. In the 1966 presidential election, Barrientos was able to put together a powerful coalition party of peasants, the new wealthy groups, the conservative Falange politicians, and members of the government bureaucracy. Despite his landslide victory and the seeming disintegration of the formal left opposition, however, worker hostility toward the regime did not abate, and for the first time since 1952 the La Paz government began to experience a problem with armed rebellion.

While many small, largely intellectual urban-based guerrilla groups began to operate during the Barrientos period, the most important instance of rebellion came from a source totally external to the national scene. In March 1956, Argentine revolutionary Che Guevara arrived in Bolivia. Establishing a base camp in the province of Santa Cruz, Che was apparently more interested in setting up a central guerrilla headquarters for operations in Argentina and Brazil than in affecting Bolivia itself. Although he was in touch with the Bolivian Communist Party, he made no serious attempt to contact or work with the miners. Yet at this very moment the mining camps were centers of siege by the army, and violence and conflict were an almost daily occurrence. Rather, Che seemed intent upon quietly establishing an extremely isolated training center for his small band in preparation for other adventures.

But in March 1967, almost a year after his arrival, Che and his group at Nancahuazu had their first clash with the Bolivian army, which was hunting them. Receiving massive support from the United States Army, Barrientos and his Chief of Staff, General Ovando, put all their resources into crushing Che. By April, Regis Debray, the French journalist accompanying Che, had been captured, and by October the rebels had been taken and Che executed.

Thus Barrientos was easily able to survive both the formal and the armed opposition of the left and yet retain a vast popular support among the peasantry and the middle class. There is little question that when he died in an air accident in April 1969 Barrientos was still in full control of the national political situation. Despite the tremendous corruption of the regime, the defection of his close friend and Interior Minister, Colonel Arguedas, and other problems, Barrientos proved to be such a consummate politician that he could surely have obtained a second term in open elections.

However astute and able Barrientos may have been, the military caste which supported him was incapable of maintaining his ideological and political position. Even with their return to power under Barrientos, the officer class remained divided and corrupt. Despite the common background and experience of most officers, their political tastes differed widely, so that there was no guarantee that their past histories would prove any guide to their future political positions.

All of this became evident in the regimes that replaced Barrientos. From 1969 until 1982, one military regime after another would emerge, with their politics stretching all the way from extreme left through reformist to reactionary right. Government policies depended completely on the personalities and ideas of the individual officers who seized power and in no way reflected a coherent position of the army itself. Whereas in most of the major states of South America in this period the army was presenting a corporate personality and common policy toward the civilian world, in Bolivia this did not occur.

With the death of Barrientos, his vice-president, the civilian and conservative leader Siles Salinas, took power. But he lasted only a few months and was replaced by General Ovando, Barrientos's partner in the 1965 coup and head of the general staff. Taking power in September 1969, Ovando proved to be more in the mold of the moderate reformist MNR tradition and, in fact, tried slowly to push the regime toward a *modus vivendi* with the left. In October 1969 he nationalized the Gulf Oil Company of Bolivia, and by early 1970 had once again legalized COB and the FSTMB and permitted Lechín to return to power. Finally, the troops were withdrawn from the mines for the first time since 1964. To all of this liberalization, he also added an important element of reform as he gathered together a group of old PIR and socialist-type civilian politicians and encouraged them to continue with the reforms of the early MNR period.

In the end, however, Ovando could neither mobilize the popular support of Barrientos nor organize a coherent political party system to support his regime. At the same time, the army had become restless since Ovando had been in power as chief of the general staff and/or as president for some eight years. Frustrated ambitions of the military thus played their part. Also, while the organized labor movement was grateful for the liberalization, it was neutral toward Ovando and would not support his regime.

The result was the military decision in October 1970 to replace Ovando with General Juan José Torres, his former chief of staff. Thus began one of the most extraordinary governments in Bolivian history, for from October 1790 to August 1971, when he was overthrown, Torres would prove to be the most radical and left-leaning general ever to have governed Bolivia.

Though he had been a Falangista in his youth, had been active in the campaign against Che, and had fully supported the army's actions in the period up to his own takeover, Torres emerged as an idealistic left politician who wanted to extend Ovando's "democratic opening" to include even more radical mobilization of workers and left politicians.

One of his first acts upon taking office was to attempt a major shift in the international relations of Bolivia. He did this by finally accepting Russian and Eastern European financial aid for COMIBOL. Such support had been offered several times in the past, but the MNR and previous military governments had procrastinated in accepting it under pressure from the United States. Torres signed contracts for the construction of a tin smelter, thereby liberating Bolivia for the first time from its dependence on European and North American smelters to process its ores. In the end the Russians were to provide almost as much financial assistance to COMIBOL as the United States, each giving in the neighborhood of a quarter of a billion dollars.

Torres matched his new policy of accepting Russian aid with a systematic attack on United States support. He annulled a special COMIBOL contract with a United States mining company for extracting tin from Catavi wastes and then in April rescinded the contract with U.S. Steel for running the Matilda Zinc mine. While this type of anti-United States company sentiment was not without its precedents, Torres went one step further and formally expelled the Peace Corps on the grounds that it was fomenting abortion policies among the peasantry. Though this move was supported by both the far right and the far left, it produced a strong negative reaction from the United States, which now found itself almost totally estranged from Bolivia, for the first time since 1952.

The fact that Torres could take his opposition to this extreme largely reflected the changed conditions of the Bolivian economy. By the end of the decade of the 1960s and the beginning years of the 1970s, Bolivia was finally beginning to reap the economic benefits of all the economic and social investments carried out by the MNR from 1952 onwards. The development of a modern road system, the tremendous economic growth of the Santa Cruz region, the heavy investments in YPFB and in COMIBOL, and finally the culmination of the long-term trend of rising mineral prices on the international market were combining to produce major growth in the national economy. Added to this were spectacular advances in literacy and public education and the freeing of human resources through the abolition of all the pre-1952 restrictions on the rural population, which thus provided a major payoff in the increased value of human capital in the country. The Bolivian government became far less dependent on direct United States assistance to maintain the level of government investments or even to provide expanded development funding. Between international financial sources and the beginnings of a heavy private investment in minerals developments and commercial agriculture, Bolivia found itself relatively free of its former exclusive dependence on North American largess.

In the national sphere Torres also made a systematic attempt both to create new political movements out of the chaos of the post-1964 collapse of the MNR and to obtain the direct support of the labor movement. But in this area he was only to obtain partial success, for labor feared uniting its fortunes with the destinies of a military leader, and it suffered from its own basic disunity. Torn by the divisions of the Communist Party into Moscovite and Chinese wings, and the subdivision of the PIR into numerous factions, the COB, Lechín, and his supporters failed to unite on policies and actually feared the increasing radicalization of their erstwhile middle-class radical allies. At the same time their experiences under Barrientos made them wary of, if not totally alienated from, the peasant sindicatos and confederations. In early 1970 the COB did establish a political assembly, which sought to bring some unity to the old MNR left and all the various Marxist parties.

As a result of this activity, a so-called Popular Assembly was founded in June 1970 for the purpose of replacing the old parliament. But this Assembly neither obtained the legitimacy of a popular vote nor did it formally retain the powers of a Bolivian legislature, despite the fact that it was housed in the Congress building. Ultimately made up of some 218 delegates, the Assembly counted only 23 representatives of the peasant confederations, as against 123 delegates from the labor unions, of which the FSTMB alone had 38. It also contained all the major left groupings, including a new party which had just been formed out of the left wing of the Christian Democratic movement and the university sector of the old MNR. This was the *Movimiento de la Izquierda*

Revolucionaria (or Left Revolutionary Movement), which, along with
the left wing of the old MNR under Lechín and Siles, would eventually become the nucleus for a powerful left coalition.

But just as Torres was unable to unite the labor support for his
regime, so the radical left and labor were unable to secure the full cooperation of the relatively unstable Torres. Thus, while the Assembly
spent a good deal of time frightening the right and the center with
symbolic acts of defiance, it could not get any new systematic legislation passed. Moreover, the government refused to supply arms to the
workers or in any way challenge the power and supremacy of the army
as an institution.

The agitation of the Popular Assembly led to a powerful mobilization of the civilian center and right behind a military coup attempt. In
January 1970, Colonel Hugo Banzer, then head of the *Colegio Militar*,
attempted such an overthrow, but the army remained loyal, so he was
exiled. Nevertheless, neither the left nor labor seemed to take this
action seriously enough. In the subsequent months the Assembly supported a worker takeover of the conservative national newspaper *El
Diario* and also refused to challenge seizures of small mines and some
Santa Cruz haciendas by workers and peasants supported by the pro-
Chinese Communist Party. All of this activity produced such resentment that, when Banzer again entered the country in August 1971, the
left was unable to stop the golpe. Supported by Paz Estenssoro's old
right and center MNR party and by the FSB, Banzer received major
financing and support from a Santa Cruz regional elite that was particularly disturbed by the threats of extending agrarian reform to the
new zones of commercial agriculture.

The overthrow of Torres was not without resistance. Though Torres
refused to open up the arsenals to the workers, students and workers did
oppose the military, while loyalist troops also attempted to defend the
president. The result was that the Banzer coup of 1971 was the bloodiest
overthrow since the April 1952 rebellion.

The Banzer government and its seven years of rule were to prove an
important turning point in national development. The trends which
had been developing in terms of long-term changes in the international

price structure for minerals were finally having a profound impact on the national economy. Between 1970 and 1974, for example, the current value of Bolivian exports almost tripled (from $226 million to $650 million). Given the preceding twenty years of investment and structural change and the development of basic infrastructures, this new wealth was easily absorbed, and thus a true economic boom occurred within the nation. Not only were there major investments in medium-sized mining and the expansion of non-tin mineral exports, but the Santa Cruz region now yielded significant surplus production and, for the first time in Bolivian history, the nation became an exporter of agricultural products, above all sugar and cotton. Urban construction boomed, and there was even some development in the manufacturing sector.

At the same time, the twenty years of significant investments in education were finally having an impact. Now a group of technical experts arose within the government and its autonomous production agencies that gave the regime a new source of power and expertise. Added to the appearance of this powerful new professional and service sector, was a new vitality shown by the traditional middle class, as well as the rise of new regional elites. In this respect, the sudden growth of the city of Santa Cruz is striking, for it moved from fourth-largest city in the republic in the 1940s to second in the 1970s, and became as well a modern advanced urban metropolis connected to the rest of Bolivia by all-weather paved roads and tied to the outside world by daily international flights. The expansion of Santa Cruz brought a profound change to national and regional power groups. Given the enormous investments in oil and agriculture in the Santa Cruz region and the growth of its population, it was inevitable that the largely white and cholo populations would demand a greater voice in national decision-making. This led to increasing pressure on the part of Santa Cruz for La Paz governments sensitive to its needs and supportive of its power pretensions. For the first time in national history there existed an important source of economic and political power outside the traditional intramountain and valley regions, the old heartland of the pre-Columbian and post-Conquest populations.

With the growth of new regional power groups and the strengthening of the traditional middle classes by new modern sectors, there was a relative decline of traditional peasant power. The Banzer regime was consistent with its predecessors in pushing Agrarian Reform and encouraging active lowland colonization. It granted more land and benefited more peasant families than any previous regime, military or civilian. Thus of the 31 million hectares granted to the 434,000 landless peasant families between 1953 and 1980, some 81 percent of the land went to 62 percent of all families in the military interregnum period from 1964 to 1980, with the Banzer regime alone granting over half the total lands and benefiting half of all the landless families. But despite this strengthening of a fundamental aspect of the military-peasant pact, Banzer was the first of the generals deliberately to reduce the importance of the peasants in national political life. Though the Banzer government in other respects continued many of the policies of the Barrientos regime, it showed a marked change in this one important area. Ultimately the peasants were neither united in their relative passivity nor eternally grateful for the granting of land titles. The tremendous growth of population in the rural areas and the consequent fragmentation of holdings, plus the emergence of a new class consciousness of peasants as farm producers for urban markets, were beginning to have an effect on the rural populations. No longer content with titles, they now wanted credit and price supports and other government assistance in improving their leverage in the marketplace. Nor was it an accident that the first peasant-military confrontation and massacre since 1952, which occurred in the Cochabamba Valley in January 1974, concerned peasant protests over government-maintained food prices.

Finally, the Banzer administration would also reflect the long-term changes in South American political developments. The Brazilian model became an example to the Bolivian military. There developed under Banzer the idea that democratic rule ultimately led to social chaos, as more popular elements were allowed to participate in natural politics: only through "depoliticizing" these masses and "re-educating" them along more submissive lines could a strong and proper government emerge. The new military ideology held that the political participation of popular forces under democratic rule was dangerous to the proper growth of a modern capitalist economy. Only through careful tutelage and "controlled" participation could rapid "modernization" occur in a "peaceful" environment. Thus the role of the military was seen as one of protection of the upper class and their middle-class allies, within non-democratic regimes. Military intervention was no longer seen as a temporary affair, but rather as a long-term alternative to open politics. This was the model first fully developed by the Brazilian armed forces, and later applied with varying success in Bolivia, Chile, and Argentina.

Initially, however, the regime seemed to follow the model of a conservative populist government elaborated by Barrientos. Since the focus of the golpe had been the conservative Santa Cruz region, and since the old Paz Estenssoro wing of the MNR and the Falange had supported him, it appeared inevitable that the government would move to the right. In fact this is what it did almost immediately upon taking office. The COB and the FSTMB were again declared illegal, and all of the parties to the left of the traditional MNR were formally denied recognition. This resulted in the jailing of many persons and the exiling of the leadership of the MIR, PRIN—which was then the name of the old Siles-Lechín wing of the MNR—as well as the deliberate use of assassination and torture.

There were also some expected important modifications on the international front. As far as world politics was concerned, Banzer immediately moved to resolve the conflict with the United States that had erupted under Torres. A new and much more liberalized investment code was enacted, and considerable aid was again sought, and obtained, for the building of army matériel and personnel. But the new relationship with Russia and Eastern Europe had become too important for even the Banzer regime to reject, and so the socialist states continued to provide long-term aid for the development of tin and other smelters.

It was in fact on more local international affairs that the regime made some fundamental shifts. While the debate over a right to a Bolivian port on the Pacific continued to cause conflict with Chile, despite the similarity of the regimes, the Banzer government made an abrupt shift in the traditional alliance with Argentina in favor of a new and close relationship with Brazil. Reflecting long-term Santa Cruz interests in opening up their economy and products to Brazilian markets, the Banzer regime signed an important series of international economic decrees which favored Brazilian participation over Argentina in the development of Bolivia's natural resources, above all with the gas and iron ore resources of the Santa Cruz region. Of all the international actions of his government, the new Banzer policy toward Brazil most angered the traditional politicians of the altiplano.

Thus, aside from some subtle shifts in international relations and the startling increase in violence and torture, the Banzer regime at first seemed to differ little from the Barrientos model. While hostile to the peasantry, for example, the Banzer regime in fact distributed more land and gave out more titles than any other administration since the pre-1964 regimes. Moreover, Banzer followed the Barrientos model as well in creating a national political party and forced his two allies, the Falange and the Paz Estenssoro wing of the MNR, formally to ally themselves with his "Frente" before participating in the government.

This attempt at creating a populist right-wing military government would ultimately prove uninviting to Banzer and, by late 1974, he announced an abrupt shift in his entire regime by carrying out an "auto-golpe," as it was called, and establishing an all-military non-party government based on support of the technocrats and non-aligned ex-politicians. Dismissing the MNR from his regime and then exiling Paz Estenssoro, he announced that all parties, even those of the center and the right, were henceforth abolished and that the army would now rule without any democratic concessions whatsoever.

The decision to break sharply with tradition was clearly based on two important developments, one international and the other local. The first and most important factor was the overthrow of the Allende administration in Chile in September 1973 and the coming to power of the Pinochet regime. By this act, the Chileans were now seen as following the Brazilian model and even extending it. It was also clear to Banzer that the model of a non-democratic authoritarian and anti-party regime was becoming the norm in the region.

The second factor was the extraordinary growth that was suddenly affecting the national economy. In 1973 and 1974 alone the price of tin on the world market almost doubled, which in turn resulted in a doubling of the total value of national exports and the creation of the largest trade surplus in national history. Along with this abrupt growth of the value of total exports, there also came very important shifts within the relative values of these exports which promised long-term benefits as well. Rising oil prices suddenly turned Bolivia's relatively small oil output into a bonanza export, which in 1974 accounted for 25 percent of the total value of exports. Of more long-term significance, since oil exports ceased by the end of the decade, was the beginning of the export of the very abundant supplies of natural gas, which began to leave Bolivia for the first time in 1972 and by 1974 accounted for 4 percent of all exports, a figure which would rise steadily throughout the decade. And finally, and probably most important, the first exports of smelted and processed tin started in 1971; by 1974 they accounted for 9 percent of the value of all exports. All this meant that traditional tin ore exports and other unrefined minerals had dropped from approximately 80 to 90 percent of the total value of exports in the decade of the 1960s to an average of just under 50 percent by the middle years of the 1970s.

There were also important changes in the mix of exports in the non-mining, petroleum, and refining industries. The first exports of agricultural products had begun in 1970, with sugar and then cotton, and grew substantially in the following years, accounting for 6 percent of the total value of exports by 1974. While this was still a relatively small item in the total of goods being exported, it was the second-fastest-growing export in the country in the years 1970 to 1976, at an annual average growth rate of 49 percent, just behind the phenomenal growth of natural gas exports, which were increasing at 50 percent per annum.

The boom of 1974 seemed to represent long-term change in the nature of Bolivian exports and economic growth, not just the classic short-term boom cycle resulting from the sudden shifts of international prices, which would so dramatically affect this classically "open" economy. Santa Cruz was now permanently exporting its agricultural produce and, when sugar prices fell, the shift to cotton showed that a basic infrastructure now existed which could survive shifts in world demand. At the same time, it was evident to all that Bolivia's natural gas exports to its neighbors, primarily Argentina and Brazil, represented an almost unlimited market that would expand steadily in the coming years. Finally, long-term price growth for non-tin minerals and the export of finished tin metal seemed to imply a long-term and quite prosperous economic future for the country.

Even considering its long-range trade, Bolivia no longer found itself dependent on any one trading partner as it had in the past. The Latin American Free Trade Area now took a third of its exports, Europe another 20 percent, and the United States only a third, with the Asian nations taking the rest. Moreover, the mix of imports was also quite varied, with the LAFTA countries and Asia taking on greater importance and Western Europe and the United States lesser weight. These fundamental changes occurred only in the early 1970s, for as late as the mid-1960s the United States and Western Europe between them were accounting for between 90 percent and 95 percent of the value of all exports and between 70 percent and 75 percent of all imports. By the middle and late 1970s these figures were down to between 55 percent to 60 percent of exports and 45 percent to 50 percent of imports respectively.

The extraordinary increase in the favorable balance of trade led to heavy imports of goods, both capital and consumer, and to increased private foreign loans. As a result, there occurred an incredibly high debt-servicing which very quickly wiped out the account's surplus. But it also led to an extraordinary building boom. The major cities of La Paz and Santa Cruz, above all, became dotted with modern skyscrapers, and the whole urban architecture of these two vital cities changed. The entire airport system was overhauled and jet airports extended to several more interior cities, with an international airport being constructed in Santa Cruz. Even more crucially, the paved road network was extended from La Paz to Oruro and to the Lake. A paved road broke through the Chapare frontier in the province of Cochabamba, thus opening up the modern illegal trade in cocaine. Chapare, which had produced no more than 5 percent to 10 percent of total coca production in the nation prior to the new road, was producing over 70 percent of the national crop by the end of the decade, almost all of this production going into international trade.

Thus new wealth was being generated in the nation, and a more powerful middle and upper class, more tied to modern economic pursuits, was developing. Through the efforts of the Andean Pact and LAFTA agreements, in which Bolivia received special consideration, there was even some modest but important growth in the national manufacturing sector. It was these new industrialists, the middle-sized mine-owners benefiting from sharply rising world minerals prices and the new commercial agricultural elite of Santa Cruz, with their demands for stability and security, whom Banzer hoped to satisfy when he established his dictatorial regime in late 1974.

The new authoritarian regime would not last even the hoped-for six years Banzer had promised when he announced his auto-golpe in November 1974. Banzer could not control the social forces unleashed by the new economic boom nor could he seem to unify the military behind his rule. In October 1972 he had carried forth a devaluation of the peso by 40 percent, the first devaluation since the 1956 stabilization act, and the resultant inflation of prices and the clamp-down on wages through force proved to be only stopgap measures. Despite the maintenance of troops at the mine heads and intervention in all the unions, along with the supposed liquidation of the FSTMB and COB, strike activity and worker violence continued. By early 1976 there were national strikes, and Banzer had to close the universities to prevent the spread of anti-government activity. Then a two-month miners' strike, despite its illegality and the government show of force, demonstrated the inability of the regime to stop the unions except by use of violence.

Not only was the regime unable to suppress the illegal but quite powerful labor movement, but it also lost most of the middle-class nationalist vote when it finally admitted total defeat on the Chilean negotiations for an outlet to the sea. Despite Banzer's desperate attempts to extract a solution at any cost, including even the proposal to exchange Bolivian territory for a port, nothing could be extracted from Pinochet, and by the end of 1976 all negotiations were abandoned. The total failure of Banzer's foreign policy in relation to Chile and Brazil thus alienated from him a large part of conservative support along with an important section of the military. Finally, and probably most important of all, the new economic elite to which Banzer had made such important appeals just did not wish to continue to support the military in power. While the middle class and upper class had provided the civilian base for such military regimes in the rest of Latin America, these classes in Bolivia were more willing to trust their power in the democratic arena than to continue with a regime like Banzer's. With corruption and restlessness in the military at very high levels, and with officers representing every possible political line, the civilian elite could not trust the outcome of an anti-Banzer coup, since there was no way of knowing if the next leader would be a Torres, a Barrientos, or a Banzer. Having seen the rather ineffectual role played by the radicals in Torres's Popular Assembly and realizing that there existed a powerful moderate vote both in the urban and rural areas, the elite felt their needs could be better defended through civilian party rule.

By the end of 1976 the pressure from within and without the regime was building and the election of Jimmy Carter as United States president seemed to promise an important change in United States support for the regime. By early 1977 Banzer announced that he would soon liberalize the anti-syndical and anti-party decrees and he formally promised to hold presidential elections in 1980. But this timetable was too slow for the opponents of the regime, so by the end of the year Banzer announced that elections would be held in 1978, two years earlier than planned. In November, just three years after their promulgation, all the authoritarian decrees were removed. So hostile had the army become to him that Banzer was even forced to announce that he would not become a candidate.

But even this was not enough, for demands were soon made for a total amnesty for the 348 syndical and political leaders in exile. When Banzer refused, there began in late December 1977 a hunger strike by wives of mine union leaders in the Cathedral of La Paz. The Church fully supported the move, and by early January over 1,000 persons had joined the hunger strike from all over the country. The strikers demanded not only total amnesty but complete syndical freedom as well. This was a truly extraordinary development in national politics and indicated the depths of the popular hostility to the regime. So overwhelming was the strike that Banzer was forced to capitulate and was even made to sign a formal agreement with the human rights groups supporting the movement.

Almost immediately the returning workers seized the unions from the government appointees who had controlled them, and within days the FSTMB and the COB were re-created with virtually the same leadership that had existed prior to the 1971 coup. Strikes, labor agitation, and feverish political activity developed throughout the country, with the result that Banzer was forced to give up any pretense of attempting to maintain himself in office and/or run for the presidency. The army leadership gave full support to his chosen successor, General Pereda Asbun, and the regime expected to move toward a controlled civilian government on the basis of the usual peasant support for the central government. Despite the one use of violence against the peasants in January 1974, the Banzer regime had spent a great deal of time, money, and effort in retaining its peasant supporters and had become one of the most active regimes in terms of land distribution.

Opposing the army and its candidate was Hernán Siles Zuazo and a new grouping of left and center political parties. Leaving the Paz-dominated MNR party in 1972, Siles had established his own MNRI, or left MNR, in Chilean exile. The MNRI banded together with the new MIR and other groups to form a loose electoral coalition called the UDP (Democratic and Popular Unity) just before the July elections. To the shock of the military the election showed that the peasants were no longer voting as a bloc. So many peasants supported the popular Siles slate, along with the masses in the cities, that the regime found the election going against them. At this point Pereda carried out a coup, declared the elections invalid, and proposed to run the government for another year before calling new elections.

The Pereda government lasted only a few months as the junior officers showed that they had finally had enough incompetence from the senior generals. In November came a successful military revolt, and the new junta under General David Padilla not only proposed free elections but announced that the government would not present a formal candidate or support any of the civilian contenders. It was evident to Padilla and his supporters that the popular hatred for Banzer was so intense that the military would have to give complete freedom to the civilians or face the potentially violent opposition of the parties, many of which were not adverse to attacking the officer corps, as had been done in 1952.

Thus began one of the most politically creative periods in recent Bolivian history. In the space of four years and in three presidential elections, the older patterns of national voting shifted in important ways, ushering in a new and more complex political system in Bolivia which predominates until today. Instead of one massive popular party based on peasant support, the new social and economic complexities of the 1960s and 1970s had finally found expression in the political arena as well. Starting in 1978 and continuing to the present day, there emerged a host of competing parties which were supported by complex combinations of urban and rural voters. Bolivia had in fact produced a modern electorate.

This new diversity in the national electorate reflected not only the changing economic scene but the changing social one as well. The social and economic reforms of the post-1952 era were continuing to have a profound impact on the entire population. As the 1976 census revealed, Bolivia had finally felt the full effects of the introduction of modern social welfare in terms of health and education. The introduction of minimal medical care to virtually the entire population meant that the death rates in Bolivia had finally dropped and stabilized at lower levels. This meant that the birth rates, which remained high (at approximately 44 per thousand), would begin to have a profound effect. Thus, despite an overall mortality rate of 18 per thousand and an extraordinarily high infant mortality rate of 202 per thousand live births in the late 1970s, Bolivia after 1950 had a population growth of 2.6 percent per annum, with the total population increasing naturally from 2.7 million persons in 1950 to 4.6 million by 1976.

Moreover, this growing population was far more urban and far better educated than had been preceding generations. Whereas in 1950 the total of persons living in towns and cities of any size was just 34 percent, by 1976 this figure had risen to 50 percent (with 42 percent of the population living in cities of 2,000 persons or more). Only 31 percent of the school-age population or above were considered literate in 1950. By 1976 the figure had climbed to 67 percent, with over 80 percent of the children in the 10-to-14 age category now listed as attending school. Finally, the percentage of Spanish speakers had risen to such an extent that by 1976 it was finally to become the majority language of Bolivia for the first time in republican history. Of the 4.6 million persons listed, 1.6 million were now considered monolingual speakers of Spanish and another 1.7 million were bilingual in the language, representing together 72 percent of the population. Monolingual Indian speakers, despite the growth of the rural population at unprecedented rates, had now declined. Quechua monolinguals had fallen from 988,000 to 612,000, and Aymaras from 664,000 to 310,000 between 1950 and 1976. While the percentage of Spanish-speaking monolinguals had changed little between the two censuses, there had been a tremendous growth in bilinguals, which was clear evidence of the impact of the schools on the rural areas. Not only had the cholo population expanded enormously, as these figures imply, but even more important, rural Indian peasants were now using Spanish on a large scale along with their traditional Indian languages.

Thus the Bolivian electorate of 1979 was better educated, more literate, and more Spanish-speaking than any other population in Bolivian history. Both Víctor Paz Estenssoro and his revived MNR, as well as Siles and his UDP alliance, found support among the peasants and the workers. Moreover, the new professional classes established new parties and alliances to express their particular needs. Suddenly the new and older parties found themselves in a balanced series of groupings on the right, the center, and the left. Even Banzer succeeded in organizing his own party with some important regional support.

These very complex political divisions explain why the elections of July 1979 saw Siles and Paz Estenssoro leading the major groupings, and why another old politician from the MNR days, Walter Guevara Arze, would emerge as the compromise candidate, once the two leaders fought out the election to a draw. Until the new and younger leaders could determine their strengths in open elections, they preferred to support the heroes of an earlier age. The election of 1979 was therefore truly extraordinary. One of the most honest elections in national history, it brought over 1.6 million Bolivians to the polls, with most of the alliances and parties showing strengths in all regions, and with Santa Cruz in fact ending in the anti-Banzer camp.

Though the victor of the election by a small margin was Paz Estenssoro and his rejuvenated MNR party, no candidate in fact had a majority. Moreover, the hostility was so intense against Banzer that no other group would ally with him in the new Congress. To forestall a bitter fight, Congress eventually decided to rerun the elections the following year and appointed Walter Guevara Arze, president of the Senate and an old friend of both Siles and Paz Estenssoro, as the caretaker president until the new elections.

The first civilian regime since 1964, the administration of Walter Guevara Arze lasted only a few months and was temporarily overthrown by a military junta in November 1979. But the political opposition within the nation was so intense, with violence and general strikes leaving over 200 dead, that the military could not control the situation and was forced out of office within a few weeks. A compromise civilian, Lydia Gueiler Tejada, was put into office. She was the first woman president in national history and one of the few in all of American history. The selection of Gueiler also demonstrated the tremendous popular support for the return of a civilian regime. No party in November 1979 supported the coup, while the few civilians who joined the temporary military junta, mostly coming out of the old MNR, were later totally rejected by the voters. The accusation that Víctor Paz Estenssoro had supported the coup attempt was sufficient to break the electoral deadlock that had occurred in the previous two elections, and in a third national election in as many years Hernán Siles Zuazo and the UDP achieved a plurality victory in June 1980.

The temporary return to civilian rule under Gueiler cost too many concessions, however, to the hardline military officers led by General Luis Garcia Meza. They refused to allow Siles to assume office, so that in July 1980 the army seized the government, despite opposition from all civilian parties and groups. But the return to an early Banzer-style authoritarian military regime had destroyed neither the powerful unions nor the civilian party system. Though declared illegal as in times past, these organizations continued to maintain a powerful following among the civilian population. Throughout the two years of junta domination, there was massive civil opposition, which included everything from illegal strikes and marches to hunger demonstrations, which destroyed any possible civilian base for these regimes. The level of corruption in the army achieved new heights with its direct involvement in the newly emerging international cocaine trade. Finally the authoritarianism of the officer class reached the point where they carried out the assassination of nine leaders of the MIR in La Paz in January 1981 and organized para-military death squads along the model of contemporary Argentina. So extreme had the situation become that the Meza government, which lasted until August 1981, and those temporary juntas which followed it, employed internationally known fascists such as the Italian Pier Luigi Pagliari and the German Klaus Barbier of World War II fame.

Consistent civilian opposition, the highly publicized and internationally condemned corruption of the army, and the unresolved economic problems of the late 1970s came to haunt the junta governments and finally destroyed even their support among the officer corps. These economic problems derived from the dependence of the nation on the profitability and performance of autonomous government agencies. After seven years of Banzer rule these administrations were in total chaos. Though Bolivian exports had risen from $200 million at the beginning of the Banzer regime to over $700 million by the end, and government investment in development projects had reached an extraordinary 48 percent of the national budget, the bulk of these funds had been badly misspent. Above all, the three major autonomous agencies— YPFB, COMIBOL, and SNAF (the national smelting agency)—had overbuilt capacities and underfinanced new explorations. The result was that by the late 1970s the country was over-supplied with refineries and smelters and faced declining production of petroleum and tin because of insufficient exploitation. At the same time the public debt generated by these firms was staggering, and the resulting financing of the debt for the public sector was taking an extraordinarily high 30 percent of foreign exchange earnings by 1980. Finally the economy began to suffer a serious long-term crisis with the combination of declining international prices and falling primary exports. Beginning in 1978 the Real Gross Domestic Product (PIB), which had been growing throughout the decade, now actually declined. Whereas in the early years of the decade growth rates were as high as 6 percent per annum, by 1976-77 they dropped to 3 percent, and by 1977-78 there was no growth whatsoever. In the following year there was negative growth, the first time that this had occurred since the late 1950s. This crisis in national production continued uninterrupted into the next decade, with the worst annual decline (of −6.6%) occurring between 1982 and 1983. Bolivia was entering into one of its longest depressions in national history, a crisis which would last into the decade of the 1990s. In the context of this political and economic crisis, the violent and exploitative military regimes became an anachronism the country could ill afford. Nor could a violent military, however repressive, control so mobilized a society.

Chapter 10 • The End of an Era and a Difficult Transition

The forced resignation of the last military junta in September 1982 and the decision to recall the Congress which was elected in 1980, finally brought an end to the era of military authoritarian regimes. This reconstituted Congress immediately elected Hernán Siles Zuazo to the presidency in August 1982. In one stroke the old political system was revived. On the left was Siles Zuazo, the leader of the reconstituted progressive wing of the MNR, who was allied with traditional labor leaders of the central confederation, the COB, newer peasant leaders, various parties of the left, and the important MIR group of radical intellectuals led by Jaime Paz Zamora, who became his vice president. To the right and center were the parties which had run in the original 1979 and 1980 elections, all now well-developed political forces which would dominate the national political scene for the next decade. In the center was the historic MNR–led by Víctor Paz Estenssoro– which incorporated both the older center and right of the party as well as younger leaders who had emerged in the period of the National Revolution. There was also a strong group of older Indian leaders

269

who, though now independent of the MNR itself, still gave strong support to Paz Estenssoro. Finally there was the ADN (Acción Democrática Nacionalista), the party which was founded by Banzer at the end of his military rule, and which he then expanded in April 1979 to include elements of the old Falange as well as the reconstituted PIR. To the surprise of many, this party proved more forceful than expected and not only legitimated Hugo Banzer as a powerful civilian leader but gathered together under his banner the new economic elites, such as the private mining entrepreneurs and large-scale farmers of Santa Cruz, as well as many of the highly trained technocrats who had emerged in the twenty-five years since the National Revolution. Though tied to the army, Banzer managed to remain distanced from the military juntas of the 1979-82 period and consistently threw his support behind the democratic processes, thus becoming a pillar of the civilian political system.

The military interregnum thus only delayed the emergence of a younger civilian political leadership and gave one last chance for the old leaders to rule until such time as the new generation could finally evolve during the normal processes of political participation. While the leadership in the first part of the 1980s was from the 1950s, by the second part of the decade a new circle of younger politicians finally emerged and began to take over the national political scene. Much of this transition would occur in the context of the worst economic crisis Bolivia was to experience in the twentieth century.

With surprising decisiveness, Siles moved to dismantle the ferocious para-military apparatus which the last military juntas had constructed with the aid of Argentine officials and foreign fascists. In rapid order the Gestapo leader Klaus Barbier was exported to France and the terrorist Pier Luigi Pagliari turned over to the Italian government. Argentines were expelled and the government moved quickly and effectively to remove the more authoritarian leaders from the army. Thus the initial national and world reaction to the government was quite enthusiastic.

But the economy inherited by the Siles Zuazo regime in August of 1982 was in tatters and the situation would only worsen in the rest of the decade. Although an able opposition leader with a reputation for probity, Siles was an incompetent administrator and poor political negotiator. Within months of his election he alienated the MIR and his other major supporters, and proved incapable of controlling a seriously failing economy. It was these combined factors which would destroy the credibility of his regime—though not the legitimacy of civilian rule.

The end of the OPEC price inflation in the late 1970s and the decline of mineral and petroleum production combined with the state mismanagement of the junta period to create a bankrupt public sector and a deeply depressed private economy. Just between 1980 and 1984 the value of agricultural output declined by 11 percent and the value of exports by 25 percent. Agricultural production itself was badly affected by a severe drought in 1983. The foreign debt contracted in the days of high world mineral prices and low interest payments reached some $3 billion by 1983, which, while low by Latin American standards, was high for Bolivia. This sum represented 80 percent of the total Gross Domestic Product and in 1984 the servicing of this debt was equivalent to 36 percent of the value of all exports. Even more significantly, tin production went into a severe and seemingly permanent decline for the first time in the twentieth century. Although annual production was still averaging above 30,000 metric tons in the 1970s, and in the upper 20,000 tonnage range in the first four years of the decade, in 1984 it dropped below 20,000 and kept declining. In 1983, for the first time, hydrocarbons—and above all natural gas—replaced tin as Bolivia's primary export, and in that same year Bolivia was passed by Brazil as Latin America's largest tin producer and was down to just 6 percent of world production. By the last years of the decade production fell below 10,000 tons per annum, or half of Brazil's rising alluvial tin production, and in 1986 private mine owners (grouped into "Mineria Mediana" and "Mineria Chica" categories based on size of production) for the first time outproduced COMIBOL. The era of tin in Bolivian history could be said to have officially ended by the second half of the 1980s.

Although international demand for cocaine would begin to generate an important parallel market for Bolivian exports, even this highly profitable export could not compensate for the general decline in the mining economy and the disappearance of foreign loan funds. At the same time, the government proved incapable of controlling costs as state revenues went into a severe decline. The inevitable solution for the Siles government was to print more money. Between 1980 and 1984 the total stock of money in circulation increased by over 1,000 percent. Prices in such a situation followed quickly, and by May of 1984 Bolivia was officially entering hyperinflation with rates of price increases of over 50 percent per month. Whereas growth in the decade of the 1970s had averaged 4.7 percent per annum and inflation just 15.9 percent, in the decade of the 1980s growth was averaging −2.3 percent and inflation 1,969.4 percent per annum. Inflation jumped to three digits in 1983, and to an incredible annual 2,177 percent in 1984. In the first six months of 1985 it rose to 8,170 percent on a per annum basis.

In such a context of total fiscal crisis, it was inevitable that Siles Zuazo would soon find himself with little popular support and most of his political allies deserting the government. In January 1983, Paz Zamora resigned the vice-presidency, and his powerful MIR withdrew from the government. Siles also lost the support of Lechín, the COB, and many of his old allies from the MNR. Despite self-imposed hunger strikes recalling his successful 1957 tactic and even a temporary abduction by the military—which was stopped by mass civilian opposition—Siles was unable to govern effectively or force through any serious stabilization policies. Given this impasse, Siles, who began his presidency in 1982, was persuaded that he should abandon the presidency early on the grounds that his mandate really dated from 1980. Under intense political pressure to leave and with this face-saving legality provided, he agreed to hold presidential elections in July 1985.

The election of 1985 provided an opportunity for the older parties, particularly the so-called historic MNR and the ADN to establish their presence as powerful entities. But it also gave many of the newer groups, which had formed part of the democratic and left alliance behind Siles, the opportunity to emerge as independent entities. On

the established left, the MIR of Paz Zamora and the Partido Social-
ista-1 of Marcelo Quiroga Santa Cruz, founded in the 1970s, stood
apart as the two most important parties. Even more significant in terms
of future developments, however, was the appearance of the Movimiento Revolucionario Tupac Katari, which represented a straight
Indian rights party and would gain 2 percent of the popular vote.
Indian leadership had been alienated by the COB for many years and
associated in the mind of the left with the military-peasant alliance, but
in fact an autonomous new Indian leadership had been emerging. As
early as the late 1960s younger independent leaders arose among the
traditional rural *sindicatos,* especially among the previously more
quiescent Aymaras. The 1974 Cochabamba blockade and subsequent
peasant massacre by the military had given an impetus to these new
men. In 1976 the Tupac Katari movement was organized among
Aymara peasant leaders in the La Paz region. By the end of the 1970s
the movement took over most of the official government peasant unions
and organized its own CSUTCB (Unified Syndical Confederation of
Peasant Workers of Bolivia). What began as a cultural movement
quickly took on political and syndical aspects, and by 1981 the Kataristas had seized control of the Aymara peasant unions and had gotten
representation in the COB. In that year, for the first time, the COB
appointed an Indian peasant leader and a member of this movement,
Genaro Flores, as one of its leaders. This coming of age of Aymara
peasant leaders reflected not only a new political sophistication and
autonomy among the previously dependent peasant groups but also a
broadening of the traditionally urban and mine-oriented Bolivian labor
movement to incorporate more effectively the mass of rural workers.
Finally, the Indians now presented to white society a series of demands relating to their perceived unequal treatment from the state in
terms of agricultural prices, provisions for credit, education and health.
They also proposed a series of revindications in relation to the nature
of Bolivian ethnicity and the more basic racial definitions of national
society.

The election of 1985 brought 1.4 million voters to the polls, with
Banzer gaining a plurality of the votes (29%) just beating out Víctor

Paz Estenssoro. Despite his electoral victory, Banzer did not control Congress, which was dominated by the center-left parties. These parties decided to ally themselves with the MNR, as they still recoiled from the anti-democratic origins of Banzer and his ADN. Thus Congress chose 77-year-old Victor Paz Estenssoro for his fourth term in the presidency, and he came to power on the 6th of August of 1985. While his previous administration of the early 1960s had basically laid the foundations for the military-peasant alliance, and his role in the military *golpe* of the early 1980s was rather sordid, Paz Estenssoro remained a powerful figure among the peasant masses who associated his name with the still vividly supported Agrarian Reform of 1953.

To the surprise of both enemies and friends, this seeming relic of a past era proved to be the most dynamic and able civilian politician to rule in the last two decades. Abandoning traditional positions, accepting radical reforms, ruthless and quick in his political responses, he soon dominated national life in a manner which recalled his very first presidential term. Without question his single most impressive act was his so-called New Economic Plan of 29 August 1985. Adopting many of the proposals of the ADN, and even arranging an informal pact with them, Paz Estenssoro imposed an economic program which was both traditional in its structure and unusual in its context. While contemporary Argentine and Brazilian governments faced with the same problems of a runaway inflation and an international debt crisis were still applying to their local economies what their economists would come to call a 'heterodox shock," Paz Estenssoro turned toward a traditional "orthodox shock" treatment. Currency devaluations, floating exchange rates, freed public sector prices, new taxes and more effective collections, and a severe cutback on government expenditures were the policies adopted. The national economy immediately went into a deep recession, but annual inflation was reduced overnight to a two-digit level.

Thus to the surprise of all, Paz Estenssoro would adopt the principles of economic liberalism and reject the economic nationalist and state capitalist ideology which he himself had been fundamental in implanting in twentieth-century Bolivia. The reasons for this rejection were twofold. First was the impact of hyper-inflation for the second time in modern Bolivian history, a crisis that virtually destroyed the functioning of the national economy; and second the total collapse of the expensive state mining system which had been constructed on the basis of a tin industry which was rapidly going out of existence. These two irreducible events in a society more developed and more complex than the one Paz Estenssoro inherited some thirty-three years before meant that a radical solution had to be adopted. With the help of external experts, Paz Estenssoro in a matter of a few months carried out a classical orthodox economic shock the likes of which were a textbook model of conservative economic policy.

By the terms of decree #21060 on 29 August 1985, the national currency was devalued; a uniform and free floating exchange rate established; all price and wage controls eliminated; public sector prices substantially raised; government expenditures severely restricted; real wages of government employees reduced. Payments on Bolivia's foreign debt were temporarily halted—the only heterodox action of the program. With prices rising and investments halted, the economy went into a severe recession. An attempted general strike was stopped by a state of siege, and the general popularity of the end to hyper-inflation gave Paz Estenssoro the support he needed to force through the reform. Along with the fiscal shock came major tax reforms which went back to many of the recommendations of the Harvard University tax advisory group known as the Musgrave Commission of the 1970s. A value-added tax was soon imposed, and the state coffers once again began to accumulate surplus funds. Paz Estenssoro also successfully undertook one of the most difficult tasks in such a state capitalist system: the systematic attack on the state bureaucracy. With gas replacing tin as the primary export as early as 1983, with world tin prices falling to extremely low levels and local costs continuing to rise, production fell to its lowest point in the twentieth century, the very purpose of COMIBOL made little sense. Paz Estenssoro began the dismantling of this once powerful state agency that was fiercely supported by the mine workers union (the FSTMB) and the COB. The reform of COMIBOL, meant the emasculation of the labor organizations. Be-

tween 1985 and 1987 COMIBOL was reduced from 30,000 workers
to only 7,000. Even YPFB was forced to dismiss 4,000 workers and
was reduced to a work force of 5,000 in the same period. All this led to
a major decline in the power of COB and organized labor in general,
which no longer was able to play the powerful political and economic
role it had assumed in Bolivian society since the 1940s. One indication
of these changes was the retirement of Juan Lechín as head of the
FSTMB in 1986 and his removal from power in the COB in the following year. For the first time since 1944, one of the three great leaders
of the MNR held no office in the organized labor movement. The
much weakened FSTMB was taken over by Trotskyite leaders, and
the COB secretariat taken over by the traditional Communist Party
(PCB). At the same time, the peasant central confederation, the
CSUTCB, dominated by the peasant sindicalist katarista movement
led by Genaro Flores, now became the single most important group
within the COB.

The continuing crisis of the world tin market helped Paz Estenssoro
greatly at this moment of conflict with the organized miners. In October of 1985 the International Tin Council, a 32-nation-supported
organization which purchased tin for price support purposes, went
bankrupt and the international tin market collapsed. For almost half
a year no tin was traded on the London minerals market and even the
world's leading tin producer, Malaysia, was forced to close 100 tin
mines and lay off 4,000 workers. By world standards Bolivia was the
highest-cost producer of one of the lowest grade ores. Given these high
ore costs and the inefficiencies of the Bolivian smelters, which finally
went into production in the early 1970s, Bolivian refined tin—just like
its unprocessed ores—could find no market. The result was that this
costly to construct allied industry was almost totally abandoned by the
late 1980s. No matter what the government might have done, Bolivia
was now incapable of selling its tin products on an overstocked world
market. Thus the hunger marches, general strikes, road blockages and
protests brought little support for the miners from any other element
in the society. When Paz Estenssoro broke up their demonstrations
and jailed their leaders there was little serious opposition.

But the political and fiscal success of the so-called New Economic Plan was achieved at the cost of economic growth and the increase of social misery. Unemployment soared to over 20 percent and the traditional mining centers of Oruro and Potosí went into severe economic decline. But just as in the 1950s United States aid was fundamental in alleviating the worst aspects of the government austerity plan, the rise of an illegal and parallel coca economy provided Bolivia with some crucial resources to lessen the impact of this harsh shock treatment. Although coca leaf production was native to Bolivia and was a major domestic crop produced in the Yungas valleys of the Department of La Paz from pre-colonial times, it slowly emerged as a major export crop in the 1970s with the rising world demand for cocaine—its principal derivative—and with the opening up of new coca-producing lands in the tropical eastern lowlands.

The construction of the first modern roads in the 1950s to the amazonian foothills region of the Chapare, a lowland tropical district in the eastern end of the province of Cochabamba, brought highland peasant migrants in large numbers to these undeveloped lands, and coca was one of the traditional crops produced. With higher alkaloid content than Yungas-produced leaf, the Chapare product was not highly prized for local consumption by the Andean Indian populations, and initially the Cochabamba migrants who farmed the area were not major coca producers. But the Chapare leaf proved ideal for producing cocaine. The changing drug consumption fashions of the populations of the advanced world economies, and above all that of the United States, moved toward cocaine as the drug of choice in the 1970s. This proved to be a boon for Bolivian producers, who accounted for more than a third of world production. With Chapare leaf more highly desired on the international than on the national market, and with its location far from traditional urban centers, the Chapare region from the mid 1970s became the dominant center for coca leaf supplies being used for illegal cocaine exports. Not only was coca native to the region, and a highly labor intensive product, but it was overwhelmingly produced on small farms, with an estimated two-thirds of production coming from plots of six hectares or less. These peasant-owned plots were grouped into colonies and large peasant unions which were an effective voice for the small landowners. Thus for the first time in modern Bolivian history, a primary export product was dominated by small peasant producers. Given the labor intensive nature of the crop and the powerful peasant syndical movement, international traders were content to leave the cultivation of the leaf in the hands of small farmers and confined themselves to processing and marketing the output of peasant producers. Though eventually Bolivian merchants would produce cocaine base (or paste) from the peasant-produced leaf by the mid-1980s, final crystallization and commercialization of the product on the world market remained in the hands of Colombian middlemen. Although the Chapare and the neighboring region of the Beni and the cities of Santa Cruz and Cochabamba became the centers of the export trade, the Yungas continued to produce coca leaf for its traditional internal Indian consumer markets.

Though there are obviously problems with estimating the size and importance of this "clandestine" economy, which forms part of the so-called informal or unregistered market, it is evident that even by conservative calculations, coca exports were as important as, if not more important, than, all legal exports by the mid-1980s. In 1984 it was roughly estimated that cocaine exports were worth over twice the $724 million of legal exports. Though alternative estimates for the following year amounted to only half this figure, this was still a sum equal to the value of total exports. Physical output followed rising exports. Whereas only 12,000 hectares were devoted to coca-leaf production in 1976, by 1985 the area of cultivation had grown to over 66,000 hectares; output in this same period went from just under 15,000 tons to some 153,000 tons, with the Chapare region alone producing over 100,000 tons in 1986 on some 40,000 to 45,000 hectares. By this time a minimally estimated quarter of a million farmers were cultivating the crop. Without question, coca-leaf production has become the single most important agricultural crop, though even in the Chapare, coca peasant farmers also grew food crops.

But cocaine exports are facing international controls of an ever more stringent nature. Producers in Peru and other areas are increasing production at the expense of Bolivia's market share. Falling world prices for cocaine have also led to lower profits, and finally the changing tastes of North American and European consumers suggest that the market for coca is an unstable one with less growth potential in the future.

There is also a debate in Bolivia about the relative benefits retained from coca exports. There is no question, however, that the government has done everything possible to encourage reinvestment in the national economy. These cocaine profits have provided Bolivia with the only major source of economic growth in the last decade. Natural gas, the next most important Bolivian export, has been going to debt-ridden Argentina, which has often failed to pay for its Bolivian imports. Although alternative minerals, soybeans, and non-traditional agricultural exports have been developed, the Bolivian economy has yet to find a viable mix of exports with which to return to a period of growth.

This being the case, it is no accident that despite the boom of the 1970s and the continued investments in social welfare and education, Bolivia in the 1980s and early 1990s remains, along with Haiti, one of the poorest countries in the hemisphere. Though heavy state investments have brought health facilities and education to the mass of the population for the first time, the continuing poor performance of the economy in the face of high population growth has meant that the indices of health and welfare remain among the lowest in the Americas. The orthodox shock of 1985 and the continuing decline of the formal economy have further eroded the welfare of the population. The immediate effect of the New Economic Plan of August 1985 was a rise in unemployment to 20 percent of the registered urban work force. But as of 1984 only 20 percent of the population was covered by social security benefits. Though expelled miners and unemployed urban workers were often absorbed into the rural economy, a factor which modified somewhat the impact of this orthodox shock and low level of benefits, the popular classes still have suffered harshly as a result of the declining national economy.

While infant mortality dropped from some 200 deaths per 1,000 live births in the 1960s to the level of some 100 deaths in the late

1980s, this much lower rate is still one of the highest of any American country. Equally, life expectancy at birth over the past three decades has only risen some five years, or from the mid-forties to fifty years of age. But this is still some twenty years below that of the more advanced Latin American societies. The cause for this continuing crisis in health is primarily economic, as various studies of nutritional consumption show that the Bolivian population is probably the most undernourished in the hemisphere. It was estimated in the late 1980s that over three-quarters of the national population lived in a condition of poverty and earned incomes below the national minimum wage.

The rapid growth of the national population has also meant that government investments in social services and education have not had as dramatic an impact as would be expected. In the census of 1988 the population stood at 6.4 million persons, having grown at a rate of over 2 percent per annum in the previous decades. This growth means that Bolivia contains one of the world's youngest populations, with the mean age of its citizens being eighteen years of age. While birth rates are finally beginning to decline in line with the previously sharp drop in overall death rates, Bolivia still has one of the fastest growing populations in the world.

Moreover, Bolivia is still, in the late twentieth century, a primarily agricultural and rural society. Despite a generous definition of urban population (urban being defined as towns of 2,000 persons or more) only 51 percent of Bolivians were listed as urban in the census of 1988, though it should be recognized that over half that number were found in just the four largest cities (La Paz, Santa Cruz, Cochabamba, and El Alto). Of the economically active population, the biggest group by far (or 43% of the work force) was still engaged in agriculture. Moreover this rural work force remains predominantly peasant. In 1950 something like 75 percent of the foodstuffs sold in Bolivian markets were grown by peasants and only 5 percent by agro-industry (the rest being imported). Thirty-one years later, peasants still produced 63 percent of food sold in Bolivia, compared with only 15 percent for agro-industry, despite all the national and foreign investments in the latter. It was also calculated that two-thirds of the persons living below

the poverty line were peasants. This rural population has least benefited by government investments in welfare. On almost every index,
the rural and semi-rural population of Bolivia suffers severely relative
to the urban sector. Thus only 30 percent of rural houses have piped-in
running water, compared with 89 percent of urban houses. Almost
half of urban homes have internal sanitation facilities, but only 3
percent of the rural ones do. Only 27 percent of rural homes have electricity, whereas it is almost universal in urban areas. These figures are
suggestive of the enormous problems that still remain for almost half
of the national population.

Only in education has there been a significant change as a result of
heavy government investment. Some 74 percent of the population
over the age of five years was considered literate in the census of 1988,
a rise from 67 percent in 1976, and just 31 percent in 1950. Despite
the growth of Spanish literacy and the decline of Indian monolingual
speakers, however, monolingual Spanish speakers are still a minority
of the population and have grown in relative importance very slowly
in the last three decades. Monolingual speakers in Spanish were just
36 percent of the population in 1950; thirty-eight years later they still
were only 44 percent of the population. Nevertheless the impact of
education is shown in the very dramatic decline in the number of
monolingual Quechua and Aymara speakers, who were 1.5 million
persons in 1950 but numbered only 384,000 in 1988, or just 8 percent
of the total as compared with over half the population in the earlier
census.

The great change has been among previously Indian monolingual
speakers who now speak Spanish as well. Bilingual Indian-Spanish
speakers in the census of 1988 make up the same percentage as monolingual Spanish ones, having risen even since the census of 1976,
when they were only 36 percent of the total. All this is a reflection both
of the increasing education of even the rural population and of the
increasing choloization of Bolivian society. Although monolingual
Aymara and Quechua speakers are disappearing, they are not being
replaced by monolingual Spanish speakers. Rather, the traditional
Indian languages are surviving with a surprising vigor despite the lack

of any systematic bilingual education. With economic power shifting toward the cholo population as the economy continues to decline, there has been a revival of pride in the traditional languages, to such an extent that radio, the primary medium in Bolivia (with half the rural homes containing radios—as opposed to only 3 percent of all homes in the country containing televisions), is now effectively bilingual and Indian language programs are commercially viable.

In the last decade the political power of the cholo population has also been finding expression, not only in traditional and radical parties but even with the transformation of a quintessinal cholo town into the country's fourth largest city. In 1988 the working-class suburb of El Alto on the outskirts of La Paz was finally incorporated as an independent city, whose administration was taken over by the new cholo elite. This high altitude town, with some 307,000 persons, was half the size of La Paz when it was created and is overwhelmingly bilingual and very closely associated with the surrounding Aymara rural communities. At the same time, the deterioration of the regional economies and the elimination of the old Spanish local hacendado elites in small towns as the result of the events of 1952 and afterward have created a more powerful cholo regional elite. It is from this elite and the upwardly mobile urban cholo population that a whole new generation of cholo university-trained professionals has emerged. While some cholos had obviously attended the university from the earliest times, they were a distinct minority and forced to abandon their language, culture, and origins and adapt to the norms of "white" culture. The new breed of educated cholos—far more numerous than ever before—now seems to have the option of retaining their ethnic ties, their traditional identities, and original Indian languages along with Spanish, which many of them choose to do.

Just as the social composition of Bolivian societies continues to evolve, so too are there important changes in the political sphere. Paz Estenssoro ruled for four years with a tight group of traditional advisers and with some new leaders emerging from the private sector. The most important of these younger leaders was the U.S.-educated Gonzalo Sánchez de Lozada, one of the richest of the new miners to emerge in the post-1952 period. Eventually rising to leadership of the Senate and then the position of Minister of Planning and head of the government's economic team, Sánchez Lozada proved a formidable opponent of the old Paz Estenssoro clique that included Guillermo Bedregal, who had been deeply involved in the bloody Natasch Busch regime of 1980-81.

At the same time, Paz Estenssoro worked closely with his former rival Hugo Banzer and his ADN in putting through his tough economic plan. With the two parties dominating the Congress, it was easy for the MNR government to control the legislation being passed as well as the army and other forces of the state which were relied upon to control worker protest. But the cost was high for his own party. Though Sánchez Lozada eventually took control of the historic MNR and ran as its presidential candidate in the May elections of 1989, he was now faced by a powerful opposition led by Hugo Banzer, and the growing power of the MIR—which had stood aside from the more excessive repression of the MNR regime.

The election of 1989 represented an important milestone in Bolivian political evolution. It officially marked the passage of an entire generation of political leaders who had dominated national life since the 1940s. The presidential candidates of all three parties were, for the first time, men who had come to political prominence after the Revolution of 1952. With Lechín out of the labor movement, Siles totally disgraced, and even Paz Estenssoro too old to govern, only Banzer remained from an earlier generation, and he only entered the political scene in the late 1960s. Moreover, in the hard-fought conflict which saw almost 1.6 million Bolivians voting, even Banzer was forced to concede defeat to open the way for new and younger leadership in his own party. Though Banzer had won the 1985 elections in terms of total votes, this time he came in second to Sánchez Lozada. The big winner in the 1989 elections was the MIR, which had taken only 8.9 percent of the votes in 1985, but now claimed 19.6 percent of the total cast. Given this strong showing of the MIR, the fact that the MNR actually garnered the most votes, and that his party was growing hungry for power, Banzer finally decided to concede the election and make a pact with the MIR to elect Jaime Paz Zamora as president of the republic. By this act Banzer both eliminated himself as a future contender for the presidency, preserved his right-wing party as a viable political force, and brought a member of the new post-revolutionary left to power for the first time.

The election also showed that a complex division of both parties and political preferences had been firmly established within the nation. The trends noted in the elections of 1980 and 1985 were present in 1989. That is, an electorate roughly voting along broad left-right divisions, and all parties from the populist and right-wing ADN to the MIR finding support in all regions and among all classes. The days of a single-party state, never complete even in the early days of the revolution, as well as the rote voting in mass among the rural populations, were a thing of the past. Though communities might vote as a block, they in turn split their votes among a multiple of parties, which meant that a return to the days of a peasant-military alliance seemed improbable in the current system.

The election of 1989 also showed the importance of a new series of essentially Indianist and cholo parties. Though the Katarista movement actually did poorly (garnering only some 23,000 votes), the media personality Carlos Palenque succeeded in capturing a large vote (173,000) with his ill-defined nationalist CONDEPA (Consciousness of the Fatherland) party. Though in many ways a classic populist, the primary appeal of Palenque was to the cholo and Aymara peasant populations in the La Paz region.

Equally impressive about the 1989 campaign was the fact that none of the three leading parties challenged the New Economic Plan and the dismantling of the state capitalist system. Even the MIR promised to respect the economic stability programs and refused to support the reconstruction of the old state enterprises. Rather, the effort was to stress the problem of growth and development. While there is no guaranteed stability for the three parties, it is clear that the ADN and MNR have established a clearly defined space in Bolivian politics. It is unclear if MIR will survive the current presidential period or be replaced by a more radical left movement willing to propose a more aggressive redistributional and socialist position. The capturing of the formal labor movement by the old Marxist parties with their anti-imperialist, nationalist, and state socialist ideas might lead to a new left coalition, though the weakened union structure suggests a less important political role for them in the future. More probable is the rise of some type of populist, left, and modern *indigenista* movement taking over the far left political scene, especially as the Indian and cholo masses are beginning to find more direct political expression at the national level.

Thus the decade of the 1990s began for Bolivia with both significant advances and serious problems. Long-term developmental growth is the single most important issue facing a nation which has had over a decade of declining growth rates. The softening of the international market for both its legal and illegal exports does not seem to promise a rapid change in the fortunes of the national economy. The political system, however, has survived and grown into a powerful and relatively stable force which, so far, has protected Bolivia from the political fragmentation and malaise that have affected Peru. The late 1970s and early 1980s experience of military anarchy and the effective civilian mobilization which brought these governments to an end have created a democratic consensus which has proved surprisingly strong.

Though neutralization of the military is never guaranteed, Bolivia has fought long, hard, and successfully to mobilize its people and political institutions in defense of the democratic process. With the cholo and Indian populations finding ever more possibilities for political expresson, in everything from the electoral system to the labor movement, the mass of the articulate working class is finding it worthwhile to commit itself to the democratic system. At the same time the wealth generated from mining and commercial and urban activities has found a comfortable representation in the ADN. The result appears to be that there exists no large civilian group willing, at this time, to use the army to protect or expand its interests. The continued economic crisis, of course, could lead to the collapse of these painfully constructed institutions and consensuses, but for the movement, the Bolivian political system seems to be functioning well.

Bolivia's social evolution also seems to be moving in original directions which may soon make of the country a truly bicultural society in which a white elite will not be able to dictate a dependent integration, but will be forced to find a compromise position. No left party now thinks to abandon the cholo masses and force their hispanization, and even the right seems willing to accept the choloization process which has been occurring. This is not to say that prejudice is not rampant in the dominant white elite, but that it has been more muted of late as the cholos have ascended in the social hierarchy and taken over more of the professional classes. What the demands of the newly emerging cholo elite will be, however, are difficult to predict at this early stage in the process. Acceptance may turn to outright hostility on the part of the whites if the demands are too extreme. But at this stage, Bolivia has reached an accommodation unusual even by the more open standards of the multi-racial and multi-ethnic societies of Latin America.

Political Chronology

2500 B.C.	Beginnings of Village Agriculture.
1800 B.C.	Beginnings of Ceramics.
800 B.C.	Chavin, first Pan-Andean civilization.
100 B.C.	Regional States: Early Tiahuanaco.
A.D. 600-	
A.D. 1100	Maturation of Tiahuanaco State (Middle Formative).
A.D. 1200-	
1500	Rise of Aymara kingdoms.
1460s	Inca Conquest of the Aymara kingdoms and creation of Kollasuyo.
1470	Aymara revolt against the Incas.
1532	Arrival of Spanish in Peru.
1537	Manco Inca rebellion.
1538	Beginning of Spanish settlement of Bolivian altiplano.
1545	Discovery of silver at Cerro Rico (Potosí).
1558	Creation of independent government for region as Audiencia de Charcas.
1560s	Final settlement of Bolivia's frontier regions.
1572-76	The *visita* of Viceroy Francisco Toledo to Upper Peru: beginnings of mita labor, mercury amalgamation of silver ores, and forced resettlement of Indian population.
1580s	Beginnings of the Shrine of Virgin of Copacabana on Lake Titicaca.

287

1584	Publication of the first Aymara grammar.
1624	Creation of a university at Chuquisaca.
1650s	Beginning of a century-long crisis in silver output at Potosí.
1695	Discovery of silver near Oruro.
1734	Tribute tax extended to *forasteros* and *yanaconas*.
1751	Creation of the Banco de San Carlos at Potosí to purchase minerals.
1776	Establishment of the Viceroyalty of the Rio de la Plata at Buenos Aires and the transference of the Audiencia de Charcas from Peru to the new viceroyalty.
1780-82	Túpac Amaru rebellion in both Perus. Túpac Catari, Tomas Catari, and Andres Amaru leaders in Upper Peru part of rebellion. Creole, cholo, and Indian revolt in Oruro only multi-ethnic movement in rebellion.
1784	Administrative reorganization of the Audiencia de Charcas with creation of intendants.
1789	French Revolution.
1796	Spain goes to war against England; beginnings of a major crisis in international trade which severely affects Upper Peru.
1808	French invasion of Spain and collapse of Royal Government.
1809	Elite rebellion in Chuquisaca (25 May). Popular rebellion for Independence in La Paz (16 July).
1809-25	Wars of Independence in Upper Peru.
1810	Independence of Viceroyalty of Rio de la Plata (25 May) and return of reconquered Audiencia de Charcas to Lima control and old Viceroyalty of Peru.
1824	Battle of Ayacucho. Sucre and his Colombian army defeat last royalist army in Lower Peru in December.
1825	Liberation of Upper Peru and Declaration of Bolivian independence (6 August).
1825-28	First Republican government under Antonio José de Sucre and nationalization of the Roman Catholic Church.
1829-39	Governments dominated by Andrés de Santa Cruz.
1836-39	Bolivia forms part of Peru-Bolivia Confederation government which is finally overthrown by invading Chilean troops.
1841	Battle of Ingavi brings to an end Peruvian and Bolivian involvement in each other's internal political affairs.
1841-47	Governments dominated by José Ballivian.
1847-55	Governments dominated by Manuel Isidoro Belzu.
1850s	Beginnings of modern silver mining industry.

1860s-70s Discovery of major mineral deposits of guano, silver, and nitrates in Bolivia's Atacama province by Chileans.

1864-70 Government of Mariano Melgarejo. Intense negotiations with foreign governments and foreign entrepreneurs.

1879 Chilean invasion of Bolivia's Pacific ports and beginnings of the War of the Pacific.

1880 Battle of Tacna (26 May) and end of Bolivian participation in War of Pacific with total defeat of Bolivian armies. Passage of a new Constitution which would become fundamental charter of new civilian era and last until 1938.

1880-99 Civilian Governments of Conservative Party control. Dominance of silver mine-owners in government and Congress.

1899 Federal Revolution of Liberal Party which overthrew Conservatives and Sucre Oligarchy. Capital city effectively becomes La Paz for all major governmental activities.

1899-1903 Separatist rebellions of rubber workers in Acre territory finally lead to cession of territory to Brazil.

1899-1920 Civilian Governments of Liberal Party control. Dominance of Liberal leader Ismael Montes.

1902 Tin passes silver as Bolivia's most valuable export and accounts for over 50 percent of the value of all exports.

1920-34 Civilian Governments of Republican Parties control. Period of peak of tin output in 1920s and of the Great Depression. Key leaders were Bautista Saavedra, Hernando Siles, and Daniel Salamanca.

1932-35 War with Paraguay over disputed Chaco territory. Most costly defeat in Bolivia's history.

1936-39 Military governments under David Toro and Germán Busch of left populist nature and known as "military socialism."

1937 Nationalization of Standard Oil of Bolivia and creation of YPFB, Bolivia's national oil company.

1939-43 Conservative civilian rule under Enrique Peñaranda.

1942 Foundation of the Movimiento Nacionalista Revolucionario (MNR) party.

1943-46 Radical military-MNR government under leadership of Gualberto Villarroel.

1944 Foundation of first successful national mine-workers' union: Federación Sindical de Trabajadores Mineros de Bolivia (FSTMB).

1945 Meeting of First National Congress of Peasants.

1946   "Thesis of Pulacayo"—radical declaration of FSTMB congress
            after Villarroel's overthrow.
1946-52   Civilian-military conservative regimes.
1952   National Revolution of MNR in April.
1952-64   Civilian governments under MNR leaders Víctor Paz Estens-
            sorro and Hernán Siles Zuazo. Nationalization of the mines
            and creation of COMIBOL; Land reform (1953), universal
            suffrage, and creation of national labor federation *Centro
            Obrero Boliciano* (COB).
1964-70   Populist military governments under René Barrientos and
            Alfredo Ovando.
1965-67   Che Guevara in Bolivia.
1970-71   Radical populist military government under Juan José Torres
            and establishment of "Popular Assembly" regime.
1971-78   Conservative military rule under Hugo Banzer.
1978-79   Transitional military regimes and political reorganization of
            civilian parties.
1979-80   National elections and the emergence of Siles Zuazo as leader
            of a left coalition of new and older parties. Temporary civilian
            governments under Walter Guevara Arze and Lydia Gueiler.
1980-82   Reactionary military rule with massive popular protest.
1982-85   Hernán Siles Zuazo made president in the return of civilian
            rule, but with problem of hyperinflation.
1985-89   Last administration of Víctor Paz Estenssoro and the imple-
            mentation of a radical "orthodox shock" on 29 August 1985.
1989-   Election of Jaime Paz Zamora of the MIR to the presidency
            with strong support from Banzer.

Bibliographical Essay

I. GENERAL SURVEYS

Bolivia has been well served by its traditional historians, with several general surveys providing a coherent organization of national development. The most important and influential of these histories are: Alcides Arguedas, *Historia general de Bolivia* (La Paz, 1922); and Enrique Finot, *Nueva historia de Bolivia* (Buenos Aires, 1946). A more recent work which has provided major insight into cultural history is Humberto Vazquez Machicado, José de Mesa, and Teresa Gisbert, *Manual de historia de Bolivia* (2nd ed. rev., La Paz, 1983); and a general survey of Bolivian developments in a comparative framework with Peru is undertaken by Magnus Mörner in *The Andean Past: Land, Societies and Conflicts* (New York, 1985). An alternative vision of national history is attempted in Xavier Albó and Josep M. Barnadas, *La cara campesina de nuestra historia* (La Paz, 1984). Some useful recent bibliographical surveys worth consulting are: Josep M. Barnadas, *Manual de bibliografía: introducción a los estudios bolivianos contemporáneos, 1960-1984* (Cuzco, 1987); and Brooke Larson, "Bolivia Revisited: New Directions in North American Research in History and Anthropology," *Latin American Research Review* 23:1 (1988). Finally, mention should be made of two important national historical journals: *Historia Boliviana*, edited by Josep Barnadas from 1981 to 1986; and the ongoing *Historia y Cultura* of La Paz (1973–).

In terms of more specialized works, Luis Peñaloza is rewriting his *Historia económica de Bolivia* (2 vols.; La Paz, 1953-54); and both this older work and his *Nueva historia económica de Bolivia* (La Paz, 1985-   ), a proposed 9-volume survey, give a reasonable though limited introduction to the field. More schematic, but with important retrospective statistical data, is Eduardo Arze Cuadros, *La economía de Bolivia . . . 1492-1979* (La Paz, 1979). A general survey of organized labor in Bolivian history is provided in Guillermo Lora, *History of the Bolivian Labour Movement, 1848-1971* (Cambridge, 1977). Intellectual thought is dealt with by Guillermo Francovich, *La filosofía en Bolivia* (Sucre, 1945); historians are well covered in Valentín Abecia Baldivieso, *Historiografía boliviana* (La Paz, 1965). Political thought is studied in Mario Rolan Anaya, *Política y Partidos en Bolivia* (rev. ed., La Paz, 1987), which also contains the most complete presentation of party programs and platforms. These in turn can usefully be supplemented with Guillermo Lora's, *Documentos políticos de Bolivia* (rev. ed., 2 vols.; La Pa, 1987). A recent survey of political parties is Raúl Rivadeneira Prada, *El laberinto político de Bolivia* (La Paz, 1984). The only serious, though now dated, analysis of the organizational structure of the republican government is N. Andrew N. Cleven, *The Political Organization of Bolivia* (Washington, D.C., 1940). All Bolivia's constitutions up to the 1950s are to be found in the compilation and analysis of Ciro Felix Trigo, *Las constituciones en Bolivia* (Madrid, 1958); while Bolivia's entire legislation on Indians and rural society is in two useful collections: José Flores Moncayo, *Legislación boliviana del indio, recopilación 1825-1953* (La Paz, 1953); and Abraham Maldonado, *Derecho agrario, historia-doctrina-legislación* (La Paz, 1956).

Among the numerous histories of Bolivia's complex international relations the best is that by Valentín Abecia Baldivieso, *Las relaciones internacionales en la historia de Bolivia* (2 vols; La Paz, 1979). Bolivia's close relationship with England is surveyed in Roberto Querejazu Calvo, *Bolivia y los ingleses, 1825-1948* (La Paz, 1971); while the analysis by León Enrique Bieber, *Las relaciones económicas de Bolivia con Alemania, 1880-1920* (Berlin, 1984), has provided a model study on the economic relations between Bolivia and a foreign nation. The controversial relations of Bolivia with Chile are seen from the Chilean viewpoint by Francisco Antonio Encina, *Las relaciones entre Chile y Bolivia, 1841-1963* (Santiago, 1963).

From different perspectives are two fine studies of national literature: Enrique Finot, *Historia de la literatura boliviana* (2nd ed.; La Paz, 1956); and Fernando Diez de Medina, *Literature boliviana* (Madrid, 1954). The more limited area of the novel is covered in excellent depth by Augusto Guzman in both his *La novela en Bolivia* (La Paz, 1955) and the work he did for the Pan American Union, *Diccionario de la literatura latinoameri-*

cana. Bolivia (Washington, D.C., 1955). There is as yet no single all-encompassing survey of the plastic arts, though as will be made clear in the following sections, the work of José de Mesa and Teresa Gisbert is fundamental for any appraisal of this area in the pre-conquest, colonial, and national periods. A good introduction to Bolivia's architecture is their survey, *Bolivia: Monumentos históricos y arqueologicos* (Mexico, 1970). Painting is treated in Pedro Querejazu, ed., *Pintura boliviana del siglo xx* (Milan, 1989); theater, in Mario Soria, *Teatro boliviano en el siglo xx* (La Paz, 1980); and films, in Afonso Gumucio, *Historia del cine en Bolivia* (La Paz, 1984).

While there are numerous histories of individual religious orders, along with several documentary collections and larger international surveys, the only general history of the Bolivian Church is the cursory survey done by Felipe Lopez Menendez, *Compendio de la historia eclesiastica de Bolivia* (La Paz, 1965). Another institution covered in some detail is the army, done by Julio Diaz A., *Historia del ejército de Bolivia, 1825-1932* (La Paz, 1940); James Dunkerley, *Orígenes del poder militar en Bolivia. Historia del ejército 1879-1935* (La Paz, 1987); and Gary Prado Salmon, *Poder y fuerzas armadas, 1949-1982* (La Paz, 1984). Medicine has been studied in Juan Manual Balcazar, *Historia de medicina en Bolivia* (La Paz, 1956). But the important profession of law has not been adequately treated. An original analysis of the evolution of the engineering profession is found in Manuel Contreras, "The Formation of a Technical Elite in Latin America: Mining Engineering and the Engineering Profession in Bolivia, 1900-1954" (Ph.D. diss., Columbia University, 1989).

Given the important role of mining and the extraordinary terrain of the country, Bolivia has been the subject of extensive research by national and foreign scholars in the geological and geographical fields. Much of the very extensive literature is summarized in Jorge Muñoz Reyes, *Geografía de Bolivia* (La Paz, 1977) and in Federico E. Ahlfeld, *Geología de Bolivia* (3rd ed.; La Paz, 1972). The latest and most comprehensive survey is Ismael Montes de Oca, *Geografía y recursos naturales de Bolivia* (2nd rev. ed., La Paz, 1989). An interesting attempt recently made to remap the soils and climate of Bolivia using more modern criteria was carried out by the Ministerio de Asuntos Campesinos y Agropecuarios, *Mapa ecologico de Bolivia* (La Paz, 1975). An English study provides a more traditional and quite important analysis of the soils of Bolivia, in Thomas T. Cochrane, *Potencial agricola del uso de la tierra de Bolivia* (La Paz, 1973); and a recent ecological analysis is C. E. Brockman, ed., *Perfil ambiental de Bolivia* (La Paz, 1986). Limited but nevertheless useful is the analysis of the distribution of commercial and subsistence plants in Gover Barja Berrios and Armando Cardozo Gonsalvez, *Geografía agrícola de Bolivia* (La Paz, 1971).

Still important because of their extensive statistical collections are the government's early twentieth-century surveys: Oficina Nacional de Inmigración Estadística y Propaganda Geografíca, *Sinopsis estadística y geográfica de la república de Bolivia* (2 vols.; La Paz, 1903); *Geografía de la república de Bolivia* (La Paz, 1905); and *Diccionario geográfico de la República de Bolivia* (4 vols.; La Paz, 1890-1904). An interesting political geography of Bolivia dealing with its famous frontier problems is by J. Valerie Fifer, *Bolivia. Land, Location and Politics Since 1825* (Cambridge, 1972). The urban geographic setting is explored in Wolfgang Schoop, *Ciudades bolivianas* (La Paz, 1981). Currently Bolivia also has extensive collections of aerial and satellite photo-mapping as well as modern demographic and geographic maps available from the Instituto Militar de Geografía and the Instituto Nacional de Estadística. The satellite maps are discussed and indexed in Lorrain E. Giddings, *Bolivia from Space* (Houston, 1977). The only serious, though still limited, attempt at providing historical maps is found in Ramiro Condarco Morales, *Atlas histórico de Bolivia* (La Paz, 1985). Finally, the large literature on exploration is described in Manuel Frontaura Argandona, *Descubridores y exploradores de Bolivia* (La Paz, 1971).

The nature of human physiological adaptation to high-altitude living has also been the subject of recent scholarly interest and has resulted in a major compilation in Paul T. Baker and M. A. Little, eds., *Man in the Andes: A Multidisciplinary Study of High-Altitude Quechua* (Stroudsburg, Pa., 1976). Some of the latest work on this subject has appeared in the *American Journal of Physical Anthropology*: see, for example, J. Arnaud, N. Gutierrez, and W. Tellez, "Haematology and Erythrocyte Metabolism in Man at High Altitudes: An Aymara-Quechua Comparison," Vol. 67 (1985).

II. PRE-COLONIAL AND COLONIAL WORLD

The most exciting recent developments in Bolivian historiography have concerned pre-Columbian themes and colonial social and economic history. Much of this work has been developed by historians and anthropologists who have interacted with each other to produce major new interpretations: Luis G. Lumbreras, *The Peoples and Cultures of Ancient Peru* (Washington, D.C., 1974), provides the best overview of the quickly changing field of Andean archaeology and revises the perspectives given in Dick Edgar Ibarra Grasso, *Prehistoria de Bolivia* (2nd ed.; La Paz, 1973); Arthur Posnansky, *Tiahuanacu* (2 vols.; New York, 1945) and the studies of Carlos Ponce Sanjines, *Descripción sumaria del templete semisubterraneo de Tiwanaku* (La Paz, 1964) and *Tiwanaku: espacio, tiempo y cultura* (La Paz,

1972). Full-scale excavations done by a foreign archaeologist occurred in the 1980s for the first time in decades. This was a study of agricultural raised fields and causeways on the shores of Lake Titicaca by Alan L. Kolata, "Tiwanaku: Portrait of an Andean Civilization," *Field Museum of Natural History Bulletin*, 53, no. 8 (Sept. 1982); "The Agricultural Foundations of the Tiwanaku State: View from the Heartland," *American Antiquity* 51, no. 4 (Oct. 1986); and *La tecnologia y organización de la producción agrícola en el estado de Tiwanaku* (La Paz, 1989). The best overall survey of extant knowledge of Tiwanaku is given in David L. Browman, "Toward the Development of the Tiahuanaco (Tiwanaku) State," in David L. Browman, *Advances in Andean Archeology* (The Hague, 1978). Given the enormous remains from the Tiwanaku civilization, this is a quite limited set of studies. Unfortunately, the closure of Bolivia to foreign archaeologists and the failure to develop a national group of scholars in this field have prevented a detailed analysis of the Bolivian materials since the 1930s. Thus the earlier works of Wendell C. Bennett, *Excavations at Tiahuanaco* (New York, 1934) and *Excavations in Bolivia* (New York, 1936) are still important; and the monopoly on research maintained for so long by the amateur Carlos Ponce Sanjines has forced contemporary scholars to continue to rely on only a few days of surface surveying for most of their results, as in the study by Jeffrey R. Parsons, "An Estimate of Size and Population of Middle Horizon Tiahuanaco, Bolivia," *American Antiquity* 33 (1968). The pre-conquest Aymara kingdoms also have been studied only from surface collections and then only on the Peruvian side of the border. The results of these studies are presented by John Hyslop in "El área Lupaca bajo el dominio incaico. Un reconocimiento arqueológico," *Histórica* (Lima) 3, no. 1 (1979), and "An Archeological Investigation of the Lupaca Kingdom and Its Origins" (Ph.D. diss., Columbia University, 1967); and by Catherine J. Julien, *Hatungolla: A View of Inca Rule from the Lake Titicaca Region* (Berkeley, 1983).

For interpreting the nature of Andean civilization at its most complete development prior to the Spanish conquest, the work of John Murra has been fundamental. Among his many studies the most important for the Bolivian perspective include *Formaciones políticos y económicos en el mundo andino* (Lima, 1975); "An Aymara Kingdom in 1576," *Ethnohistory* 15, no. 2 (1968), and his editing of the Garcí Diez de San Miguel, *Visita hecha a la provincia de Chuquito* (1576) (Lima, 1964). Work with the recent *visitas* on the Aymara kingdoms of the Lake Titicaca region has been the source for the studies of Franklin Pease, *Del Tawantinsuyu a la historia del Peru* (Lima, 1978). On the Inca period of Bolivian history, the works of John Murra, Alfred Metraux, J. H. Rowe, Sally Falk Moore, R. T. Zuidema, Maria Rostworowski de Diez Canseco, Waldemar Espinoza Soriano,

Franklin Pease, Nathan Wachtel and Craig Morris relating to Peruvian developments have also been helpful in understanding the Bolivian experience. For the special role of the Cochabamba region as a crucial granary in the Inca empire, see Nathan Wachtel, "The Mitimas of the Cochabamba Valley: The Colonization Policy of Hyana Capac," in George A. Collier, et al., *The Inca and Aztec States, 1400-1800* (New York, 1982); while the question of other ethnic groups under the Inca and Aymara rule has been examined by Thierry Saignes, *En Busca del Poblamiento Etnico de los Andes Bolivianos (siglos XV y XVI)* (La Paz, 1986).

The theme of the Spanish conquest has drawn a host of fine generalists to write about it, beginning in the English language with the nineteenth-century classic of William H. Prescott, *The History of the Conquest of Peru.* The best modern survey is by John Heming, *The Conquest of the Incas* (New York, 1970). Nathan Wachtel's *The Vision of the Vanquished* (New York, 1977) provides an extremely imaginative reconstruction of the Indian perspective of this event.

In the last three decades important studies have been undertaken on all aspects of the immediate pre-conquest and post-contact period in Bolivia. Much of this new work was summarized in a special "Andean ethnohistory" issue of the French journal *Annales, E.S.C.* (Paris) 33 (1978). This has just been translated into English and edited by John Murra, et al., *Anthropological History of Andean Polities* (Cambridge, 1986). This volume includes studies on the Uru by Nathan Wachtel and on the complex ethnic relations in the Larecaja Valley by Thierry Saignes, along with the study by Thérèse Bouysse-Cassagne on Aymara belief systems. These insights she developed more fully in her study *La identidad aymara. Aproximación histórica (siglo XV, siglo XVI)* (La Paz, 1987). Thérèse Bouysse-Cassagne also reconstructed sixteenth-century Amerindian languages in Bolivia which appeared as a chapter in Noble David Cook, ed., *Tasa de la visita general de Francisco de Toledo* (Lima, 1975). The most thorough reconstruction of the major highland Indian languages at the time of the Spanish conquest has recently been carried out by Alfredo Torero, "Lenguas y pueblos altiplanicos en torno al siglo XVI," *Revista Andina* 5, no. 2 (1987).

The eastern Amerindian frontier has been the subject of quite original works by Thierry Saignes, "Une Frontière fossile: la cordillère chiriguano au XVIe siècle" (2 vols.; 3rd Cycle doctorate, Université de Paris, 1974); *Los andes orientales: historia de un olvido* (La Paz, 1985); *Ava y Karai. Ensayos sobre la frontera chiriguano (siglos XVI-XX)* (La Paz, 1990); and William Denevan, *The Aboriginal Cultural Geography of the Llanos de Mojos of Bolivia* (Berkeley, 1966). These groups are dealt with in a comparative perspective in F. M. Renard Casevits, Thierry Saignes, and A. C. Taylor, *Al este de los Andes: relaciones entre las sociedades amazónicas y andines entre los siglos xv y xvii* (2 vols., Quito, 1988). The non-Aymara and non-quechua groups which have existed before and after the Spanish conquest on the altiplano are also being studied. This is the theme of Carmen Beatriz Loza, "Los Quirua de los valles paceños: una tentativa de identificación en la época prehispánica," *Revista Andina*, no. 2 (Dec. 1984). The extensive literature on the Uru was examined by Harriet E. Manelis Klein, "Los urus: el extraño pueblo del altiplano," *Estudios Andinos* 3, no. 1 (1973); and by Nathan Wachtel in a combined archival and ethnographic analysis in his state doctoral thesis, which was recently defended in Paris.

The early integration of the resident Amerindian peasant populations into the Spanish colonial system has been the subject of much new work. In the pages of the short-lived Bolivian review *Avances* (2 vols.; La Paz, 1978) appeared important articles on the transition from goods to money tribute by Tristan Platt, "Acerca del sistema tributario pre-toledano en el Alto Perú"; and two articles on the economic and social roles of the *kurakas*: Roberto Choque, "Pedro Chipana: cacique comerciante de Calamarca"; and Silvia Rivera, "El mallku y la sociedad colonial en el siglo xvii," all in Vol. I. This is also the theme in recent articles: John Murra, "Aymara Lords and Their European Agents at Potosí," *Nova Americana*, I (1978); Brooke Larson, "Caciques, Class Structure and the Colonial State in Bolivia," *Nova Americana* II (1979); and Roberto Choque, "Los caciques aymaras y el comercio en el Alto Perú," in Olivia Harris, et al., eds. *La participación indígena en los mercados surandinos* (La Paz, 1987). Thierry Saignes has also explored the same themes in *Cacques, Tribute and Migration in the Southern Andes* (University of London, Institute of Latin American Studies, Occasional Papers, no. 15, 1985); and early Indian rebellions and anti-Spanish movements in "'Algun día todo se andará': los movimientos étnicos en Charcas (siglo xvii)," *Estudios Andinos* 2, (1985). Finally the most important mission frontier in the Bolivian region has been the object of a series of studies by Alcides Parejas Moreno, *Historia del oriente boliviano: siglos xvi y xvii* (Santa Cruz, 1979) and *Historia de Moxos y Chuquitos a fines del siglo xviii* (La Paz, 1976).

Colonial Amerindian demographic history for Bolivia has been totally revised by the original study of Nicolás Sánchez-Albornoz, *Indios y tributos en el Alto Perú* (Lima, 1978), especially as it relates to the question of population growth and internal stratification. Others have used the Amerindian tribute lists to study population distribution and land tenure: Daniel Santamaría, "La propiedad de la tierra y la condición social del indio en el Alto Peru, 1780-1810," *Desarrollo Económico*, 66 (1977) and his *Haciendas y campesinos en el Alto Peru colonial* (Buenos Aires, 1988); Brooke Larson, "Hacendados y campesinos en Cochabamba en el siglo xviii," *Avances* 2 (1978); and two studies by Herbert S. Klein, "Hacienda and

Free Community in 18th-Century Alto Peru," *Journal of Latin American Studies* 75, no. 2 (1975), and "The Structure of the Hacendado Class in Late Eighteenth-Century Alto Peru," *Hispanic American Historical Review* 60, no. 2 (1980). Rural labor has also been the theme of the quite useful collection of notes and documents by Silvio Zavala, *El servicio personal de los indios en el Perú* (3 vols.; Mexico, 1978-80); a detailed analysis of rural estates is found in René Danilo Arze Aguirre, "Las haciendas jesuítas de La Paz (siglo xviii)," *Historia y Cultura* (La Paz) 1, (1973).

Spanish colonial society has been well studied through recent monographs as well as major collections of documents. Josep M. Barnadas in *Charcas, origines históricos de una sociedad colonial, 1535-1565* (La Paz, 1973) has examined the first decades of Audiencia rule. A reasonable survey of the published sources for the sixteenth century as a whole is provided in Eduardo Arze Quiroga, *Historia de Bolivia . . . siglo xvi* (La Paz, 1969). Alberto Crespo has produced an important series of studies on urban political history: *Historia de la ciudad de La Paz, siglo xvi* (Lima, 1961); *El corregimiento de la Paz, 1548-1600* (La Paz, 1972); *La guerra entre vicuñas y vascongados, Potosí, 1622-1625* (Lima, 1956). Together with several of his students, he published the only serious work on urban social and economic history in Alberto Crespo et al. *La vida cotidiana en La Paz durante la guerra de independencia, 1800-1825* (La Paz, 1975). An important recent addition to colonial urban history is the chronicle of urban life in seventeenth-century Chuquisaca by Lic. Pedro Ramirez del Aguila, *Noticias políticas de indias* [1639] (Sucre, 1978). The role of urban Indian women has also been studied by Luis Miguel Glave, "Mujer indígena, trabajo doméstico y cambio social en el virreinato peruano del siglo xvii: la ciudad de La Paz y el sur andino en 1684," *Bulletin de l'Institut Français d'Etudes Andines* 16, nos. 3-4 (1988); and Ann Zulawski, "Social Differentiation, Gender and Ethnicity: Urban Indian Women in Colonial Bolivia, 1640-1725," *Latin American Research Review* 25, no. 2 (1990).

Spanish colonial mining and Potosí itself were the subject of numerous chronicles in the colonial period, most of which have been printed only recently, several of them ably edited by Lewis Hanke. The most important are: Luis Capoche, *Relación general de la villa imperial de Potosí* (Madrid, 1959); Bartolomé Arzans de Orsua y Vela, *Historia de la villa imperial de Potosí* (3 vols.; Providence, R.I., 1965; eds. Lewis Hanke and Gunnar Mendoza); and Pedro Vicente Cañete y Dominguez, *Guía histórica geografica, física . . . de Potosí* (Potosí, 1952). In the Arzans reprint appear important articles by Gunnar Mendoza, Lewis Hanke, José de Mesa, and Teresa Gisbert on the history of the city. Hanke also surveyed the history of the city in *The Imperial City of Potosí* (The Hague, 1956). Gunnar Mendoza, Bolivia's national archivist, has also written several monographs on Potosí and its leading figures including *El Doctor don Pedro Vicente Cañete* (Sucre, 1954) and a document collection on *Guerra civil entre vicuñas y vascongados y otras naciones en Potosí, 1622-1645* (Potosí, 1945). A recent study of a seventeenth-century metallurgist and the colony's only distinguished scientist is Josep Barnadas, *Alvaro Alonso Barba (1569-1662)*, (La Paz, 1985).

Modern research on the colonial mining industry is dominated by the studies of Peter Bakewell. He has published two major monographs as well as numerous important technical essays. Among these works are: Peter Bakewell, *Miners of the Red Mountain: Indian Labour in Potosí, 1545-1650* (Albuquerque, 1984); *Silver and Entrepreneurship in Seventeenth Century Potosí* (Albuquerque, 1988); "Registered Silver Production in Potosí District, 1550-1735," *Jahrbuch für Geschichte von Staat, Wirtschaft und Gesellschaft lateinamerikas* 12 (1975); and "Technological Change in Potosí: The Silver Boom of the 1570s," *ibid.* 14 (1977); "Los determinantes de la producción minera en Charcas y en Nueva España durante el siglo XVII," 16 *HISLA* 8 (1986); David H. Brading and Harry E. Cross, "Colonial Silver Mining; Mexico and Peru," *Hispanic American Historical Review* 52, no. 2 (1972), provided an earlier comparative perspective. The mita labor system has been analyzed in Alberto Crespo, "La mita de Potosí," *Revista Histórica* (Lima) 22 (1955-56); Thierry Saignes, "Notes on the Regional Contribution to the Mita in Potosí in the Early Seventeenth Century," *Bulletin of Latin American Research* 4, no. 1 (1985); and Jeffrey Cole, *The Potosí Mita, 1573-1700: Compulsory Indian Labor in the Andes* (Stanford, 1985); and free wage labor in the mines of Oruro has been the theme of Ann Zulawski, "Labor and Migration in Seventeenth-Century Alto Peru" (Ph.D. diss., Columbia University, 1985). There are also two important new studies on the late colonial mining industry: Rose Marie Buechler, *The Mining Society of Potosí* (Ann Arbor, 1981); and Enrique Tandeter, "Forced and Free Labor in Late Colonial Potosí," *Past & Present* 93 (1981). Also see Buechler's article "Technical Aid to Upper Peru: The Nordenflict Expedition," *Journal of Latin American Studies* 5 (1973).

The eighteenth-century debate on the mita is examined in Rose Marie Buechler, "El Intendente Sainz y la 'mita neuva' de Potosí," *Historia y Cultura* (La Paz) 3 (1978), as well as in Tandeter's work. These debates are also reflected in the proposed eighteenth-century mining code of Pedro Cañete, *Codigo Carolina* (ed. E. Martire; 3 vols.; Buenos Aires, 1973-74). The regional economic impact of Alto Peruvian mining has been studied in a magisterial theoretical work by Carlos Sempat Assadourian, *El sistema de la economia colonial. Mercado interno, regiones y espacio economico* (Lima, 1982). Specific trades influenced by Potosí are examined in Carlos Sempat Assadourian, *El tráfico de esclavos en Cordoba de Angola a Potosí siglos xvi-xvii* (Cordoba, Arg., 1966); and Nicolás Sánchez-Albornoz, "La saca de mulas de Salta al Peru, 1778-1808," *Anuario del Instituto de Investigaciones Historicas* 8 (Rosario, 1965). The classic study on regional markets and conflicting elites involving Alto Peru was written by Guillermo Cespedes del Castillo, *Lima y Buenos Aires, repercusiones económicas y políticas de la creación del virreinato del Plata* (Sevilla, 1946); while inter-regional and international trade patterns are studied in Laura Escobari de Querejazu, *Producción y comercio en el espacio sur andino, siglo XVII, Cusco-Potosí 1650-1700* (La Paz, 1985); and Enrique Tandeter, et al., "El mercado de Potosí a fines del siglo xviii," in the anthology on markets edited by Olivia Harris, et al., cited below.

Recent studies on royal income and the fiscal structure of colonial Bolivia include those by Tibor Wittman, *Estudios históricos sobre Bolivia* (La Paz, 1975); Herbert S. Klein, "Structure and Profitability of Royal Finance in the Viceroyalty of the Rio de la Plata in 1790," *Hispanic American Historical Review* 53 no. 3 (1973); Clara Lopez, *Estructura económica de una sociedad colonial: Charcas en el siglo xvi* (La Paz, 1988); and John J. TePaske, "The Fiscal Structure of Upper Peru and the Financing of Empire," in Karen Spalding, ed., *Essays in the Political, Economic and Social History of Colonial Latin America* (Newark, Del., 1982). The treasury records themselves for the entire colonial period have been reproduced in "Upper Peru," volume 2 of John J. TePaske and Herbert S. Klein, *Royal Treasuries of the Spanish Empire in America* (3 vols.; Durham, N.C., 1982).

Work has finally begun on the non-mining economy. Among the studies of this sector are: Mary Money, *Los obrajes, el traje y el comercio de ropa en la Audiencia de Charcas* (La Paz, 1983); and that of a La Paz merchant fortune done by Herbert S. Klein, "Accumulation and Inheritance among the Landed Elite of Bolivia: The Case of Don Tadeo Diez de Medina," *Jahrbuch für Geschichte von Staat, Wirtschaft und Gesellschaft lateinamerikas* (Köln) 22 (1985). But there exist few, if any, studies on the construction industry so vital for the building of the urban centers and their monumental churches, on either unskilled or skilled labor, on local trade and credit, or on most aspects of economic urban life. Price history has finally become a serious concern with the first study being Enrique Tandeter and Nathan Wachtel, *Precios y producción agraria. Potosí y Charcas en el siglo xviii* (Buenos Aires, 1984).

Of major import in late colonial society was the massive peasant uprising of the early 1780s known as the Rebellion of Túpac Amaru. The most complete narrative of the political and military events that formed these revolts is still the book by Boleslao Lewin, *La rebelíon de Túpac Amaru* (Buenos Aires, 1957). More recent interpretations of the causes of this important movement have included Oscar Cornblit, "Society and Mass Rebellion in Eighteenth-Century Peru and Bolivia," St. Antony's Papers, no. 22 (1970); and those found in Alberto Flores Galindo, ed., Túpac Amaru II—1780, Antologia (Lima, 1976). An alternative explanation based on a detailed study of the institution of forced sales of imported goods is Jürgen Golte, Repartos y rebeliones, Túpac Amaru y las contradicciones de la economía colonial (Lima, 1980). The special nature of the combined mestizo-Indian sub-revolt in Oruro is being explored by Fernando Cajías, "Los objetivos de la revolucíon indígena de 1781: el caso de Oruro," Revista Andina 1, no. 2 (Diciembre, 1983), and María Eugenia del Valle de Siles has been working on the Indian seige of La Paz and its leader Tupac Katari, beginning with an edited edition of the 1781 report of Francisco Tadeo Diez de Medina, Diario del alzamiento de indios conjurados contra la ciudad de . . . La Paz, 1781 (La Paz, 1981); and most recently her Historia de la rebelión de Tupac Catari, 1781-1782 (La Paz, 1990).

The extraordinary artistic creativity of the colonial Bolivian society has been the domain of the distinguished pair of art historians, José de Mesa and Teresa Gisbert. Together and separately they have produced a major corpus on painters, sculptors, architects, and artists of all kinds and of all origins who worked in Upper Peru. Among the more important of their joint works are Holquín y la pintura altoperuana del virreinato (La Paz, 1956), Escultura virreinal en Bolivia (La Paz, 1972), El pintor Mateo Perez de Alesio (La Paz, 1972), Bitti: un pintor manerista en sudamérica (La Paz, 1974), and Arquitectura andina: historia y analisis (La Paz, 1983). Teresa Gisbert alone has recently written a monumental work on colonial Indian art: Iconogafía y mitas indígenas en el Arte (La Paz, 1980), as well as a survey of Literatura virreinal en Bolivia (La Paz, 1963). She has also studied the art of the native textiles in Teresa Gisbert, Silvia Arze and Marta Cajias, Arte textil y mundo andino (La Paz, 1987).

The study of Bolivian colonial history is also aided by more than a century of excellent documentary collections, among the most important of which are Pedro de Angelis, ed., Colección de obras y documentos relativos a la historia antigua y moderna de las provincias del Rio de la Plata (6 vols.; Buenos Aires, 1836-37); Marcos Jimenez de la Espada, ed., Relaciones geográficas de indias: Peru (4 vols.; Madrid, 1881-97); Victor M. Mauritua, ed., Juicio de limites entre el Perú y Bolivia (12 vols.; Barcelona, 1906-7); Roberto Levellier, ed., La Audiencia de Charcas. Correspondencia de Presidentes y Oidores (3 vols.; Madrid, 1918-22). Finally, most of the essays of the distinguished historian Humberto Vazquez Machicado gathered together in Obras completas (7 vols.; La Paz, 1988) deal with the colonial period.

III. INDEPENDENCE AND THE NINETEENTH CENTURY

The period of the wars of independence and the early years of the republic has also been the subject of major publications in the last few years which have considerably revised previous interpretations. The recent study by René Danilo Arze Aguirre, *Participación popular en la independencia de Bolivia* (La Paz, 1979), provides the crucial popular background to the elite study by Charles Arnade, *The Emergence of the Republic of Bolivia* (Gainesville, Fla., 1957). Equally, the important role of Sucre has been well illustrated by William Lee Lofstrom, *El Mariscal Sucre en Bolivia* (La Paz, 1983), and the complex role of Santa Cruz has been examined by Philip T. Parkerson, *Andrés de Santa Cruz y la Confederación Peru-Bolivia 1835-1839* (La Paz, 1984), complementing the popular biography of Alfonso Crespo, *Santa Cruz, el condor indio* (Mexico, 1944).

Several volumes of documents of this period have been published by Carlos Ponce S. and R. A. Garcia, eds., *Documentos para la historia de la Revolución de 1809* (4 vols.; La Paz, 1953-54); and Vicente Lecuna, ed., *Documentos referentes a la creación de Bolivia* (2 vols.; Caracas, 1975). Crucial information on this vital period is also provided in such contemporary travel accounts as Alcide D'Orbigny, *Voyage dans l'amérique meridionale* (9 vols.; Paris, 1844); John Barclay Pentland, *Report on Bolivia, 1827* (Royal Historical Society, 4th Camden Series, vol. 13; London, 1974)—a more complete edition in Spanish was published as *Informe Sobre Bolivia* (Potosí, 1975); and Edmond Temple, *Travels in Various Parts of Peru* (2 vols.; Philadelphia, 1833). Finally, much interesting documentation on nineteenth-century rural and urban life in Bolivia has been gathered together by various Peruvian scholars under the direction of Pablo Macera: *Fuentes de historia social americana [Bolivia]* (7 vols. to date, Lima, 1978).

For understanding the complex interaction of political and international history in this first century of independence, the older study by Jorge Basadre, *Peru, Chile y Bolivia independiente* (Barcelona, 1948), remains the classic work. This may be supplemented by the influential works of Alcides Arguedas, *Los caudillos letrados . . . (1828-48)* (Barcelona, 1923); *Le plebe en acción (1848-57)* (Barcelona, 1924); *La dictadura y la anarquía (1857-64)* (Barcelona, 1926); *Los caudillos barbaros . . . (1864-72)* (Barcelona, 1929). All these historical works of Arguedas have been reprinted several times including the Aguilar edition of his *Obras Completas* (2 vols., Mexico, 1957), vol. II. To this can be added studies of individual regimes and leaders, both by such nineteenth-century writers as Ramón Sotomayor Valdes, *Apuntes para la historia de Bolivia bajo la administración del general D. Augustin Morales* (La Paz, 1898), and José Maria Santivanez, *Vida del General José Ballivian* (New York, 1891); or the more recent Manuel Carrasco, *José Ballivian, 1805-52* (Buenos Aires, 1960). But for all their importance, such leading figures as Melgarejo and Belzu still lack serious biographies and few studies exist on the actual functioning of government in the nation. An important and vivid analysis of a major political event of this period does exist in the model study of Gabriel René Moreno, *Matanzas de Yañez* (2nd ed.; La Paz, 1976).

Far more original research has occurred in the economic and social history of the early nineteenth century than in the political area. To the major study of government finance by Casto Rojas, *Historia financiera de Bolivia* (La Paz, 1916), can be added the contemporaneous statistical study by José Maria Dalence, *Bosquejo estadístico de Bolivia* (Chuquisaca, 1851). The crucial role of Indian tribute in early republican finance is examined in Jorge Alejandro Ovando Sanz, *El tributo indígena en las finanzas bolivianas del siglo XIX* (La Paz, 1986), which should be supplemented with the works cited of Sánchez-Albornoz, Greishaber, Platt, and Klein. The crucial role of Bolivian coinage in the early republican regional economy of the other South American republics is explored in an original study by Antonio Mitre, *El monedero de los Andes: Región económica y moneda boliviana en el siglo xix* (La Paz, 1986); and Tristan Platt, *Estado tributario y libre cambio en Potosí (siglo xix)* (La Paz, 1986). Early attempts to revive the mining industry are analyzed in Enrique Tandeter, "Potosí y los ingleses a fines de 1826," *Historia y Cultura* 3 (1978); and William Lofstrom, *Damaso de Uriburu, a Mining Entrepreneur in Early 19th-Century Bolivia* (SUNY Buffalo, Special Studies, no. 35, 1973). A rather complete economic and social history of the early Bolivian development of the littoral is Fernando Cajias, *La provincia de Atacama, 1825-1842* (La Paz, 1975); while the Indian tribute lists have been explored for an original analysis of the native population of the city of La Paz in Rossana Barragán, *Espacio urbana y dinámica etnica, La Paz en el siglo xix* (La Paz, 1990).

IV. THE LATE NINETEENTH CENTURY

The second half of the nineteenth century has been subject to less attention than the earlier period until very recently. Most of the political literature of this period is cited in Herbert S. Klein, *Parties and Political Change in Bolivia, 1880-1952* (Cambridge, 1969), and in the works of Basadre and Arguedas. Mariano Baptista, the leading political theorist of the period, has had all his works published in *Obras Completas* (7 vols.; La Paz, 1932-34), and an interesting survey of the political upheavals of the period is catalogued in Nicanor Aranzaes, *Las revoluciones de Bolivia* (La Paz, 1918). A somewhat unsystematic but interesting survey of the society, economy, and political ideas in the last quarter of the nineteenth century is given by Danielle Demelas, *Nationalisme sans nation? La Bolivie aux xix-xx siècles* (Paris, 1980). But few serious studies of political life and even fewer biographies or administrative studies exist for this period. There is, however, a superb political novel which captures the era to an extraordinary degree and is one of the best of its genre in Latin America. This is Armando Chirveches, *La candidatura de Rojas* (La Paz, 1909).

An excellent analysis of the silver mining industry in the nineteenth century is provided in Antonio Mitre, *Los patriarcas de la plata. Estructura socio-económica de la minería boliviana en el siglo xix* (Lima, 1981). Several reasonable biographies exist on the leading miners of the period: Ernesto Rück, *Biografía de Don Avelino Aramayo* (Potosí, 1891); A. Costa du Rels, *Felix Avelino Aramayo y su época, 1846-1929* (Buenos Aires, 1942); Jaime Mendoza, *Gregorio Pacheco* (Santiago de Chile, 1924). But the concern is usually with the non-economic aspects of their lives. Moreover, most of the other sectors of the economy, such as the internal market, regional trade, and public finance are neglected. Nor is there any serious study of the revolution in transportation which occurred in this period or the modernization of the urban centers. That the primary literature exists is evident, for example, in the interesting listing given in Edgar A. Valdes, *Catálogo de folletería de ferrocarriles del repositario nacional* (La Paz, 1980).

In contrast to this relative neglect in economic studies there has been a major renaissance in the social history of this period. This began with an innovative study challenging all the traditional assumptions about the political isolation of the Indian carried out by Ramiro Condarco Morales, *Zarate "El Temible" Wilke. Historia de la rebelíon indígena de 1899* (2nd rev. ed.; La Paz, 1982); and further elaborated on by Marie-Danielle Demelas, "Jacqueries indiennes, politique créole, la guerre civile de 1899," *Caravelle* 44 (1985). This was followed by a critique of the ideas that rural Bolivia was dominated by haciendas in the nineteenth century and was defined by its isolation from the market economy. These assumptions were challenged in two important works: Silvia Rivera, "La expansion del latifundio en el altiplano boliviano: elementos para la caracterizacion de una oligarquía regional," *Avances* 2 (1978); and Erwin P. Greishaber, "Survival of Indian Communities in Nineteenth-Century Bolivia: A Regional Comparison," *Journal of Latin American Studies* 12, no. 2 (1980). A major literature has now developed detailing the complex evolution of rural society in the major regions of the country. Among these works are Brooke Larson, *Colonialism and Agrarian Transformation in Bolivia, Cochabamba, 1550-1900* (Princeton, 1988); Erick D. Langer, *Economic Change and Rural Resistance in Southern Bolivia, 1880-1930* (Stanford, 1989); and Tristan Platt, *Estado boliviano y ayllu andino: Tierra y tributo en el Norte de Potosí* (La Paz, 1982). An alternative model of nineteenth century growth stressing the role of the forasteros inside the ayllus is given in Herbert S. Klein, *Haciendas and Ayllus: Rural Society in the Bolivian Andes in the 18th and 19th Centuries* (Stanford, 1992). Finally a challenge to the post-1880 model of complete destruction of peasant communities is presented in a short and provocative essay by Gustavo Rodriguez, *¿Expansión del latifundio o supervivencia de las comunidades indígenas? Cambios en la estructura agraria boliviana del siglo XIX* (IESE, Universidad Mayor de San Simon, Cochabamba, 1983).

V. THE EARLY TWENTIETH CENTURY

With the twentieth century, the pace of research in all areas increased greatly. The first decades of the twentieth century were ones of intellectual ferment. From the initial stirrings of a critique of racist society in the novels and "sociology" of Alcides Arguedas, to the more systematic development of an *indigenista* viewpoint in Franz Tamayo, *La creación de una pedagogía nacional* (La Paz, 1910), writers began to challenge the assumptions of their society. A good survey of this activity is found in Guillermo Francovich, *El pensamiento boliviano en el siglo xx* (Mexico, 1956), and in the literature studies by Díez de Medina and Finot previously cited.

There has been a general neglect of the Liberal era, with the exception of the study of Juan Albarracin Millán, *El poder minero en la administración liberal* (La Paz, 1972). On the other hand, Bolivian intellectuals have been attracted to the political leaders of the 1920s and 1930s, producing the very best such biographies yet written. There exist two outstanding biographies for this period, one by Benigno Carrasco, *Hernando Siles* (La Paz, 1961), and the other by David Alvestegui, *Salamanca, su gravitación sobre el destino de Bolivia* (3 vols.; La Paz, 1957-62). An overall assessment of this period is provided in Klein, *Parties and Political Change*, and in two outstanding surveys: the first volume of the two-volume history of modern Bolivian political history by Augusto Cépedes, *El dictador suicida, 40 años de historia de Bolivia* (Santiago de Chile, 1956); and in the first three volumes of the five-volume series by Porfirio Díaz Machicado, *Historia de Bolivia. Saavedra, 1920-25* (La Paz, 1954), *Historia de Bolivia, Guzman, Siles, Blanco Galindo, 1925-31* (La Paz, 1954), and *Historia de Bolivia. Salamanca, La guerra del Chaco, Tejada Sorzano* (La Paz, 1955). The major Indian rebellion of the period has been examined by Roberto Choque *Las masacre de Jesús de Machaca* (La Paz, 1986).

The economic history of this period has also been more fully developed than in previous eras. The tin mining industry has finally received an overall economic analysis of some sophistication in the study by Walter Gomez, *La minería en el desarrollo económico de Bolivia, 1900-1970* (La Paz,

1978). Complementing this macro-analysis are detailed studies of the early industry by Pedro Aniceto Blanco, *Monografía de la industria minera en Bolivia* (La Paz, 1910); Herbert S. Klein, "The Creation of the Patiño Tin Empire," *Inter-American Economic Affairs* 19, no. 2 (1965), which was updated and published in Spanish in *Historia Boliviana* 3, no. 2 (1983); and Donaciano Ibañez C., *Historia mineral de Bolivia* (Antofagasta, 1943). There are several biographies of the leading miners, among which are Charles F. Geddes, *Patiño: The Tin King* (London, 1972); and Alfonso Crespo, *Los Aramayo de Chichas: Tres generaciones de mineros bolivianos* (Barcelona, 1981). The economics of labor in the early tin industry is studied by Manuel E. Contreras, "Mano de obra en la minería estañifera de principios de siglo, 1900-1925," *Historia y Cultura* (La Paz) 8 (1985), who has also surveyed "La minería estañifera boliviana en la Primera Guerra Mundial," in Raul España-Smith, et al., *Minería y economia en Bolivia* (La Paz, 1984). The early growth of the industry is also studied by John Hillman, "The Emergence of the Tin Industry in Bolivia," *Journal of Latin American Studies* 16 (1984). The political role of the miners is assessed in the previously cited work of Albarracin and William Lofstrom, *Attitudes of an Industrial Pressure Group in Latin America, the "Associación de Industriales Mineros de Bolivia,"* 1925-1935 (Ithaca, 1968).

Good general assessments of the national economy at this time are found in W. L. Schurz, *Bolivia, A Commercial and Industrial Handbook* (Washington, D.C., 1921), and Paul Walle, *Bolivia, Its People and Resources* (New York, 1914). Specific aspects of the economy or national economic policy are reviewed in Charles A. McQueen, *Bolivian Public Finance* (Washington, D.C., 1925), and the excellent study by Margaret A. Marsh, *Bankers in Bolivia. A Study in American Foreign Investment* (New York, 1928). Among the many surveys on banking history, that by Julio Benavides, *Historia bancaria de Bolivia* (La Paz, 1955), is of some utility. The short-lived Acre rubber boom is examined in Valerie Fifer, "The Empire Builders: A History of the Bolivian Rubber Boom and the Rise of the House of Suarez," *Journal of Latin American Studies* 2, no. 1 (1970).

While the social changes affecting the society with the growth of the tin industry, the modernization of the cities, and the completion of the hacienda expansion have not been seriously analyzed by scholars, there does exist a wealth of data with which to study this problem. Thus in 1900 came the first and one of the best national censuses: Oficina Nacional de Inmigración, Estadística y Propaganda Geográfica, *Censo nacional de la población de la república de Bolivia, 1° septiembre de 1900* (2 vols.; La Paz, 1902-4). This government office also published numerous geographical studies which have been cited above; and from approximately the late 1880s onward, with increasing tempo under the very efficient Liberals, almost all the government ministries were publishing annual statistics on the national society and economy.

VI. THE 1930S TO THE PRESENT

The Chaco War has produced an enormous literature, from novels to memoirs of individual battles and war experiences. Much of this literature is summarized in Roberto Querejazu Calvo, *Masamaclay. Historia, política, diplomática y militar de la guerra del Chaco* (3rd ed.; La Paz, 1975). For the English reader a good history of the war itself and of the diplomatic disputes behind it is found in David H. Zook, Jr., *The Conduct of the Chaco War* (New York, 1960). The politics of the war and the radical military regimes that followed are treated in detail in the previously cited works of Céspedes, Díaz Machicado, and Klein, as well as in the second volume of Augusto Céspedes's modern history, *El presidente colgado* (La Paz, 1971), and the last two volumes of the history of Porfirio Diaz Machicado, *Historia de Bolivia, Toro, Busch Quintanilla, 1936-1940* (La Paz, 1957) and *Historia de Bolivia Peñaranda, 1940-1943* (La Paz 1958). The best study of the internal impact of the war, which also contains an innovative oral history of Chaco veterans, is René Danilo Arze Aguirre, *Guerra y conflictos sociales. El caso rural boliviano durante la campaña del Chaco* (La Paz, 1987).

The Chaco War, the rise of the so-called Chaco generation, and the profound political changes in society since the 1930s have been examined by a number of national and foreign scholars. From very different perspectives have appeared: Sergio Almaraz, *El poder y la caida. El estaño en la historia de Bolivia* (2d ed.; La Paz, 1969); two major studies of René Zavaleta Mercado, *El poder dual en América Latina. Estudio de los casos de Bolivia y Chile* (Mexico, 1974) and *La nacional—popular en Bolivia* (Mexico, 1986). Foreign scholars examining these developments have included Robert J. Alexander, *The Bolivian National Revolution* (New Brunswick, N.J., 1958); James Malloy, *Bolivia, the Uncompleted Revolution* (Pittsburgh, 1970); and Christopher Mitchell, *The Legacy of Populism in Bolivia, from the MNR to Military Rule* (New York, 1977). The most recent political surveys are those by James Dunkerley, *Rebellion in the Veins: Political Struggle in Bolivia, 1952-1982* (London, 1984); and James Malloy and Eduardo Gamarra, *Revolution and Reaction: Bolivia, 1964-1985* (New Brunswick, N.J., 1988).

Also of importance in understanding twentieth-century political beliefs are several unique works which have helped define new modes of thought. Of these, the three most important are the previously cited *indigenista* declaration of Franz Tamayo in 1910, Tristan Marof's *La tragedia del altiplano* (Buenos Aires, 1934), and Carlos Montenegro, *Nacionalismo y coloniaje* (3rd ed.; La Paz, 1953).

Detailed studies of parties and persons are also available for the modern period. The best party history is by Luis Peñaloza, *Historia del Movimiento Nacionalista Revolucionario, 1941-1952* (La Paz, 1963). Useful for an analysis of the origins of the Trotskyite party is Guillermo Lora, *José Aguirre Gainsborg, fundador del POR* (La Paz, 1960). No full-scale studies exist on the other Marxist parties, and while numerous campaign biographies exist of all the leading figures in the post-1952 period, few serious works of scholarship have yet to be published. Useful for particular periods or incidents are the study by Philippe Labrevuex, *Bolivia bajo el Che* (Buenos Aires, 1968), and the collection of Che Guevara's writings of this period in Juan Maestre Alfonso, ed., *Bolivia: victoria o muerte* (Madrid, 1975). The Minister of the Interior under Torres has written a full account of this remarkable period in Jorge Gallardo Lozada, *De Torres a Banzar, diez meses de emergencia en Bolivia* (Buenos Aires, 1972). The background and ideology of the army leadership in this period are analyzed in Jean-Pierre Lavaud, "L'art du coup d'état. Les militaires dans la société bolivienne (1952-1982),' *Revue française de Sociologie* 30, no. 1 (1989).

In contrast to the dearth of good works on leaders, the newly politicized movements of workers and peasants have received considerable attention. Aside from the previously cited history of the organized labor movement by Guillermo Lora, there is an original history recently completed by Zulema Lehm and Silvia Riveira, *Los artesanos libertarios y la ética del trabajo* (La Paz, 1988), on the anarchists in the first half of the twentieth century. The central labor federation has recently been treated in Jorge Lazarte Rojas, *Movimento obrero y procesos politicos en Bolivia: historia de la C.O.B., 1952-1987* (La Paz, 1989), and there also exists a survey by John H. Magill, *Labor Unions and Political Socialization. A Case Study of Bolivian Workers* (New York, 1974). The evolution of a professional mining proletariat and its process of unionization and radicalization are considered in Gustavo Rodríguez, "Los mineros: su proceso de formación (1825-1927)," *History y Cultura* 15 (1989); Rene Zavaleta M., "Forma clase y forma multitud en el proletariado minero en Bolivia," in Rene Zavaleta M, ed. *Bolivia, hoy* (Mexico, 1983); Lawrence Whitehead, "Sobre el radicalismo de los trabajadores mineros en Bolivia," *Revista Mexicana de Sociología* 42, no. 4 (1980) and his "Miners as Voters: The Electoral Process in Bolivia's Mining Camps," *Journal of Latin American Studies* 13 (1981). The mine workers have also been the subject of an extraordinary biography by the wife of a miner, Domitila Barrios de Chungara, *Let Me Speak!* (New York, 1978), and an unusual anthropological study by June Nash, *We Eat the Mines and the Mines Eat Us* (New York, 1979). The recent crisis of organized labor is debated in FLACSO, *Crisis del sindicalismo en Bolivia* (La Paz, 1987).

Studies on the peasants have been even more numerous than those on the workers. An original survey is provided by Silvia Rivera, *Oprimidos pero no vencidos: luchas del campesinado aymara y qhechwa de Bolovia, 1900-1980* (La Paz, 1986). The two key centers of peasant syndicalization in the Cochabamba Valley and on the altiplano have been studied by Jorge Dandler, *El sindicalismo campesino en Bolivia: los cambios estructurales en Ucureña* (Mexico, 1969), and Xavier Albó, *Achacachi: medio siglo de lucha campesina* (La Paz, 1979)—two very fine historical as well as contemporary studies by anthropologists. On contemporary political and ideological developments among the peasant unions see Xavier Albó, "De MNRistas a Kataristas: Campesinado, estado y partidos, 1953-1983," *Historia Boliviana* 5, nos. 1-2 (1985); Javier Hurtado, *El Katarismo* (La Paz, 1986) and the anthology edited by Calderon and Dandler cited below. Also many of the works cited in the section on social conditions below deal with peasant syndicalization and political activities.

Bolivia's strained and complex relations with the United States, the most influential power affecting its development in the twentieth century, is partially surveyed in Bryce Wood, *The Making of the Good Neighbor Policy* (New York, 1961), and Cole Blaiser, *The Hovering Giant: U.S. Responses to Revolutionary Change in Latin America* (Pittsburgh, 1976). An assessment of United States aid was carried out by James W. Wilkie, *The Bolivian Revolution and United States Aid Since 1952* (Los Angeles, 1969), and for the latest view on U.S. relations with the MNR, see Carlos Navia Ribera, *Los Estados Unidos y la Revolución Nacional* (Cochabamba, 1984).

The Bolivian economy since the 1920s has also been the subject of modern studies of exceptional quality. The best general history of the economy from the 1920s to the late 1950s was done by the United Nations Economic Commission for Latin America, CEPAL, *El desarrollo económico de Bolivia* (Mexico, 1957). To this can be added the work by Cornelius H. Zondag, *The Bolivian Economy, 1952-1965* (New York, 1966). Although there is no general synthesis of the modern period, there exist numerous specialized studies on given economic developments. A detailed study by one of the participants in the stabilization program implemented in the late 1950s is that of George Jackson Eder, *Inflation and Development in Latin America. A Case History of Inflation and Stabilization in Bolivia* (Ann Arbor, 1968). The debt crisis as it affects Bolivia has been studied by Oscar Ugarteche, *El estado deudor. Economía política de la deuda: Perú y Bolivia, 1968-1984* (Lima, 1986) and Robert Devlin and Michael Mortimore, *Los bancos transnacionales, el estado y el endeudamiento externo de Bolivia* (Santiago de Chile, 1983). The recent "orthodox" shock of the 1980s is studied in Juan Antonio Morales and Jeffrey D. Sachs, "Bolivia's Economic Crisis," in Jeffrey D. Sachs, ed., *Developing Country Debt and the World Economy*

(Chicago, 1989); Jeffrey Sachs, "The Bolivian Hyperinflation and Stabilization," *American Economic Association, Papers and Proceedings* 77, no. 2 (May 1987); and Oscar R. Antezana Malpartida, *Analisis de la Nueva Política Económica* (La Paz, 1988). Estimating the size and shape of the important informal economy is carried out by Samuel Doria Medina, *La economia informal en Bolivia* (La Paz, 1986) and in volume 14 of economic essay series *Foro Economico* (La Paz, 1986). Good surveys of health and nutritional conditions are given in two UNICEF-sponsored volumes by Rolando Morales Anaya, *Desarrollo y pobreza en Bolivia: Analysis de la situacion del niño y la mujer* (La Paz, 1984) and *La crisis economica en Bolivia y su impacto en las condiciones de vida de los niños* (La Paz, 1985).

For mining, the already cited work of Walter Gomez is the standard source of the pre-1970 period, which can be supplemented for the more recent era by Mahmood Ali Ayub and Hideo Hashimoto, *The Economics of Tin Mining in Bolivia* (Washington, 1985). The rise of new medium-sized private mining companies in the modern period is treated in Manuel E. Contreras and Mario Napoléon Pacheco, *Medio siglo de minería mediana en Bolivia, 1939-1989* (La Paz, 1989). Debates over COMIBOL and worker co-government of the mines in the 1950s were provided by Amado Canelos O., *Mito y realidad de COMIBOL* (La Paz, 1966), and Sinforosa Canelas R., *La burocracia estrángula a la COMIBOL* (La Paz, 1960). A detailed survey of the mining tax structure is provided in Malcolm Gillis, ed., *Taxation and Mining. Nonfuel Minerals in Bolivia and Other Countries* (Cambridge, Mass., 1978). There is an excellent analysis of the international tin schemes in which Bolivia was a major participant in K. E. Knoor, *Tin Under Control* (Stanford, 1945); with new materials treated in John Hillman, "Bolivia and the International Tin Cartel, 1931-1941," *Journal of Latin American Studies* 20 (1988). Sergio Almaraz, *El petroleo en Bolivia* (La Paz, 1958), provides a dated but useful introduction to this theme.

Detailed studies of the state fiscal structure were carried out in a multi-authored project led by Richard Musgrave, ed., *Fiscal Reform for Bolivia* (Cambridge, Mass., Harvard Law School, 1981). Interesting surveys of the several key issues in early post-1952 economic policy appear in Melvin Burke, *Estudios criticos sobre la economía boliviana* (La Paz, 1973), and Carter Goodrich, *The Economic Transformation of Bolivia* (Ithaca, 1955). The agricultural sector has finally received a full-scale modern treatment of some sophistication in E. Boyd Wennergren and Morris D. Whitaker, *The Status of Bolivian Agriculture* (New York, 1975). This work primarily deals with agricultural production since 1952. Analysis of pre-reform structures and production on the haciendas was done by Edmundo Flores, "Taraco: monografía de un latifundio del altiplano boliviano," *El Trimestre Económico* 22, no. 2 (1955); and Paul Robert Turovsky, "Bolivian Haciendas Before and After the Revolution" (Ph.D. diss, University of California at Los Angeles, 1980). On the profound changes in the economic and social situation produced by the Agrarian Reform of 1953, there now exist numerous studies covering most of the major regions in Bolivia. A good introduction to the problem is found in William J. McEwen, *Changing Rural Society. A Study of Communities in Bolivia* (New York, 1975). More detailed assessments on individual regions can be found in William E. Carter, *Aymara Communities and the Bolivian Agrarian Reform* (Gainesville, Florida, 1964); Roger A. Simmons, *Palca & Pucara. A Study of . . . Two Bolivian Haciendas* (Berkeley, 1974); Daniel Heyduk, *Huayrapampa: Bolivian Highland Peasants and the New Social Order* (Ithaca, 1971); Kevin Healy, *Caciques y patrones: una experiencia de desarrollo rural en el sud de Bolivia* (Cochabamba, 1983); Barbara Leons, "Land Reform in the Bolivian Yungas," *America Indígena* (Mexico) 27, no. 4, (1967); Melvin Burke, "Land Reform and Its Effect Upon Production and Productivity in the Lake Titicaca Region," *Economic Development and Cultural Change* 18 (1970); Dwight B. Heath et al., *Land Reform and Social Revolution in Bolivia* (New York, 1969); Dwight B. Heath, "New Patterns for Old: Changing Patron-Client Relations in the Bolivian Yungas," *Ethnology* 12 (1973); the Bolivian section in Andrew Pearse, *Latin American Peasant* (London, 1975); Daniel Heyduk, "The Hacienda System and Agrarian Reform in Highland Bolivia: A Re-evaluation," *Ethnology* 13 no. 1 (1974); and Ricardo Godoy, "Ecological Degradation and Agricultural Intensification in the Andean Highlands," *Human Ecology* 12, no. 4 (1984).

The migration of rural Quechua and Aymara peasants to the eastern lowlands has been a major development within rural Bolivian society in the last three decades, though it is barely keeping up with population growth in the altiplano and highland valleys. As yet there has been no single study encompassing all the features of this complex movement; however, there have been some important dissertations written on this phenomenon. The more interesting of these studies are those by Ray Henkel, "The Chapare of Bolivia: A Study of Tropical Agriculture in Transition" (Ph.D. diss., University of Wisconsin, 1971); Hernan Zeballos, "From the Uplands to the Lowlands: An Economic Analysis of Bolivian Urban-Rural Migration" (Ph.D. diss., University of Wisconsin, 1975); and Connie Weil, "The Adaptiveness of Tropical Settlement in the Chapare of Bolivia" (Ph.D. diss., Columbia University, 1979). The most recent work on migrations to the Santa Cruz region are by Leslie Gill, *Peasants, Entrepreneurs, and Social Change: Frontier Development in Lowland Bolivia* (Boulder, Colo., 1987); Allyn Maclean Stearman, *Camba and Kolla: Migration and Development in Santa Cruz, Bolivia* (Gainesville, Fla., 1985); and Michael Redclift, "Sustainability and the Market: Survival Strategies on the Bolivian

Frontier," *Journal of Development Studies* 23 (1986). Highland and valley groups have also been the subject of numerous community studies by social scientists and community development people. Unquestionably, the most scholarly of such studies are those carried out in the last three decades by two Jesuit-run research organizations, CIPCA of La Paz and ACLO of Sucre. Urban migration has been the basis of a major CIPCA-sponsored statistical survey carried out for La Paz by Xavier Albó, Tomas Greaves, and Godofredo Sandoval, *Chukiyawu, la cara Aymara de La Paz* (4 vols.; La Paz, 1981-87). The city of El Alto and its cholo population were studied by Godofredo Sandoval and M. Fernanda Sostres, *La ciudad prometida: pobladores y organizaciones sociales en El Alto* (La Paz, 1989).

Bolivia in the last half-century has also been the subject of detailed anthropological investigations on all aspects of Amerindian culture. On the contemporary Aymara populations, for example, the earlier studies of Weston La Barre, *The Aymara Indians of the Lake Titicaca Plateau, Bolivia* (Washington, D.C., 1948); Harry Tschopik, "The Aymara," in the *Handbook of South American Indians* (5 vols.; Washington, D.C., 1946), vol. II; and Hans and Judy Buechler, *The Bolivian Aymara* (New York, 1971), have been supplemented by a host of new studies on all aspects of contemporary Aymara peasant life. The best single introduction to the new materials is found in Xavier Albó, ed., *Raices de America: el mundo Aymara* (Madrid, 1988). Specific aspects of Aymara culture include older studies on religious belief by William Carter, "Secular Reenforcement in Aymara Death Ritual," *American Anthropologist* 70, no. 2 (1968); Jacques Monast, *L'Universe religieux des aymaras de Bolivie* (Cuernavaca, 1966), and the studies cited in the anthologies cited earlier edited by Murra. Kinship has been studied by Xavier Albó, *Esposas, suegros y padrinos entre los aymaras* (2nd ed.; La Paz, 1976); while a full-scale community study was done by William Carter and Mauricio Mamani, *Irpa Chico, individuo y comunidad en la cultura Aymara* (La Paz, 1982). The mixture of medical belief systems in the small towns on the altiplano is analyzed in an interesting essay by Libbet Crandon, "Medical Dialogue and the Political Economy of Medical Pluralism: A Case from Rural Highland Bolivia," *American Ethnologist* 13 (1986), while the Aymara in a rural town setting was examined by J. R. Barstow, "An Aymara Class Structure: Town and Community in Carabuco" (Ph.D. diss., University of Chicago, 1979). Olivia Harris has studied the symbolism of an Aymara group in the unusual multi-lingual northern Potosí region in a series of essays. One on "symbolic transformations" of the Laymi group appeared in the Murra edited volume cited above, and essays on their economic organization in her book *Economia etnica* (La Paz, 1987). The unusual organization of peasant society in this Northern Potosí region of mixed Quechua and Aymara speakers in terms of part-time mining and agriculture is studied in Ricardo Godoy, *Mining and Agriculture in High-land Bolivia* (Tucson, Ariz., 1990). A summary of recent work in Aymara linguistics, which has become a major area of scientific study, is found in Lucy Briggs, "A Critical Survey of the Literature on the Aymara Language," *Latin American Research Review* 14 no. 3 (1979); Juan de Dios Yapita and Lucy Briggs, "Aymara Linguistics in the Past 22 Years," *Latin American Indian Literatures Journal* 4, no. 2 (Fall 1988); and Harriet E. Manelis Klein and Louisa Stark, eds., *South American Indian Languages: Retrospect and Prospect* (Austin, 1985). Major academic studies on Aymara linguistics can be found in the collection edited by Martha J. Hardman, *The Aymara Language in Its Social and Cultural Context* (Gainesville, 1981).

The Quechua population of Bolivia is also now being studied intensively, though still less than their Peruvian counterpart. A fine socio-linguistic study was carried out by Xavier Albó, *Los mil rostros del quechua: sociolin-güística de Cochabamba* (Lima, 1974). Also, the above-cited work of Dand-ler and Simmons deals with Quechua-speaking communities in the Cocha-bamba Valley, along with the study by John F. Goins, *Huayculi. Los indios quechua del Valle de Cochabamba* (Mexico, 1967). Tristan Platt has analyzed Quechua symbolism in *Espejos de maiz* (La Paz, 1976) and in an essay in the Murra volume as well as surveyed the historical evolution of these groups in northern Potosí in the works cited above. Another Potosí Quechua group was recently analyzed by Roger Neil Rasnake, *Domination and Cultural Resistance: Authority and Power among an Andean People* (Durham, N.C., 1988); and the unusual medical practices of the Calla-huaya Indians located in the altiplano region—a subject of numerous earlier studies—have recently been analyzed in two works by Joseph W. Bastien, *Mountain on the Condor, Metaphor and Ritual in an Andean Ayllu* (St. Paul, Minn., 1978); and *Healers of the Andes: Kallawaya Herbalists and Their Medical Plants* (Salt Lake City, 1987); and by Louis Girault, *Kalla-waya, curanderos itinerantes de los andes* (La Paz, 1987).

The lowland Indians of the eastern frontier have attracted ethnographers for a long time. The classic studies of this region were done at the beginning of the century by Erland Nordenskiold, *The Ethnography of South America Seen from Mojos in Bolivia* (2nd ed.; New York, 1979). There also exists the classic work by A. Holmberg, *Nomads of the Long Bow. The Siriono of Eastern Bolivia* (Washington, D.C., 1950). Also on this unusual lowland group is the work by Harold Schefer and Floyd Lounsbury, *A Study in Structural Semantics. The Siriono Kinship System* (Englewood Cliffs, N.J., 1971). Jürgen Riester has recently studied many of these lowland peoples in *En busca de la Loma Santa* (La Paz, 1976), and *Los Guarasug'we. Crónica de sus últimos días* (La Paz, 1977). A recent survey of the demography and languages of these numerous groups is found in Pedro Plaza Martinez and

Juan Carvajal Carvajal, *Etnias y languas de Bolivia* (La Paz, 1985).

Bolivian folklore has also received considerable attention from such authors as M. Rigoberto Paredes, *Mitos, supersticiones y supervivencias popu-
lares de Bolivia* (La Paz, 1920); Jesus Lara, *Leyendas quechuas* (La Paz,
1960); Enrique Oblitas Poblete, *Magica, hechiceria y medicina popular
boliviana* (La Paz, 1971); and Gustavo Adolfo Otero, *La piedra magica,
vida y costumbres de los indios callahuayas de Bolivia* (Mexico, 1951), to
mention only a few of the more prolific writers. For the English reader there
is the study by Weston La Barre, "Aymara Folktales," *International Journal
of American Linguistics* 16 (1950).

General surveys of the social situation of the contemporary Bolivian population are still lacking, but some major areas or specific problems have received considerable attention. The use of coca among the peasant populations has been surveyed recently by William Carter et al., *Coca en Bolivia*
(La Paz, 1980); and in a collection of articles on Bolivia and Peru in an
entire issue devoted to coca in *American Indígena* (Mexico) 38, no. 4
(1978). The problem of cocaine has spawned a large literature, most of it
highly polemical. Among the more thoughtful studies are the essays in
Deborah Pacine and Christine Franquemont, eds., *Coca and Cocaines
Effects on People and Policy in Latin America* (Boston, 1986); Mario de
Franco and Ricardo Godoy, "The Economic Consequence of Cocaine Production in Bolivia," unpublished mss, 1990; and Gonzalo Flores and José
Blanes, *Dónde va el Chapare?* (Cochabamba, 1984). There have also been
large surveys of contemporary education, health, and demographic statistics
in the works of N. Thomas Chirikos et al., *Human Resources in Bolivia*
(Columbus, Ohio, 1971); USAID Mission to Bolivia, *Bolivia Health Sector Assessment* (La Paz, 1975); and the numerous UN-CELADE studies
on changes in mortality and fertility patterns. Contemporary social mobility
in rural society is studied in Jonathan Kelley and Herbert S. Klein, *Revolution and the Rebirth of Inequality: A Theory Applied to the Bolivian National Revolution* (Berkeley, 1981). The social structure and labor market
of urban populations have finally been the subject of recent concern not only
in the above-cited works of Albó on La Paz and Sandoval on El Alto, but also
CEDLA-sponsored work by Roberto Casanovas Sainz and Antonio Rojas
Rosales, *Santa Cruz de la Sierra. Crecimiento urbano y situación ocupacional*
(La Paz, 1988); and Silvia Escobar de Pabón and Carmen Ledo Garcia,
Urbanización, migraciones y empleo en la ciudad de Cochabamba (La Paz,
1988).

Important anthologies of essays should also be mentioned. Several cover
political, economic, and social developments in Bolivia since 1952. These
include James M. Malloy and Richard S. Thorn, eds., *Beyond the Revolution: Bolivia Since 1952* (Pittsburgh, 1971); J. Lademan, ed., *Modern Day*

Bolivia: Legacy of the Revolution and Prospects for the Future (Tempe: Center for Latin American Studies, Arizona State University, 1982); and a special issue of *Problèmes d'Amerique Latine* (Paris), no. 62 (1981). Others contain primarily historical and or ethnographic studies and include: J. P. Deler and Y Saint-Geours, eds., *Estados y naciones en los Andes* (2 vols.; Lima, 1986); Olivia Harris et al., eds., *La participación indígena de los mercados surandinos. Estrategias y reproducción social siglos xvi a xx* (La Paz, 1987); and special Bolivian issues of the French journals *Caravelle* (Toulouse) 44 (1985); and *Cahiers des Ameriques Latines* (Paris), Nouvelle Série, vol. 6 (1987). Finally a major collection of essays on peasant syndicalization and on peasant movements in general is contained in Fernando Calderon and Jorge Dandler, eds., *Bolivia: La fuerza histórica del campesinado* (Cochabamba, 1984).

From the survey above it is evident that both national and foreign scholars have been fascinated by the Bolivian experience and have attempted to understand the complex forces that have created this society. Since my primary aim has been to provide the reader with an introduction to basic issues without listing all studies produced in any given subject, I have omitted many works. The books and articles cited, however, will provide the interested reader with further sources for an in-depth investigation. Finally, it is hoped that my comments will have provided interested scholars with some guidelines on what has been done and the exciting possibilities that remain in Bolivian studies.

Tables

TABLE I. POPULATION OF BOLIVIA FOR THE PRINCIPAL DEPARTMENTS AND CAPITAL CITIES ACCORDING TO THE NATIONAL CENSUS, 1846-1988

Dept.	Capital	1846	1900	1950	1976	1988**	Sq. Miles
LA PAZ	La Paz*	412,867	426,930	948,446	1,484,151	1,926,200	51,731
		42,849	52,697	321,073	654,713	976,800	
COCHABAMBA	Coch	279,048	326,163	490,475	730,358	982,000	21,479
		30,396	21,881	80,795	205,002	403,600	
ORURO	Oruro	95,324	86,081	210,260	311,245	388,300	20,690
		5,687	13,575	62,975	124,121	176,700	
POTOSI	Potosí	243,269	325,615	534,399	658,713	667,800	45,643
		16,711	20,910	45,758	77,334	110,700	
CHUQUISACA	Sucre	156,041	196,434	282,980	357,244	442,600	19,893
		19,235	20,907	40,128	62,207	105,800	
STA CRUZ	St. Cruz	78,581	171,592	286,145	715,072	1,110,100	143,096
		6,005	15,874	42,746	256,946	529,200	
TARIJA	Tarija	63,800	67,887	126,752	188,655	246,600	14,526
		5,129	6,980	16,869	39,087	66,900	
BENI	Trinidad	48,406	25,680	119,770	167,969	215,400	82,457
		3,194	2,556	10,759	27,583	50,200	
Sub-total		1,377,336	1,626,382	3,019,031	4,647,816	5,979,000	399,515
Total Country		1,378,896	1,633,610	2,999,227	4,613,497	6,405,100	424,162

NOTES:

* The figures for the city of La Paz include that for the newly established municipality of El Alto, which only recently was separated from La Paz.

** 1988 is a sampled census rather than a full count.

Sources

1846: José M. Dalence, *Bosquejo estadístico de Bolivia* (Chuquisaca, 1851).

1900: República de Bolivia, Oficina Nacional de Inmigración, Estadística y Propagando Geográfica, *Censo general de población, I° de setiembre de 1900* (2 vols.; La Paz, 1902-4).

1950: República de Bolivia, Dirección General de Estadística y Censos, *Censo demografico, 1950* (La Paz, 1955). (This census also contains the land surface figures.)

1976: República de Bolivia, Ministerio de Planeamiento y Coordinación, Instituto Nacional de Estadística, *Censo de 1976. Resultados provisionales. Total del País* (La Paz, Setiembre, (1977)).

1988: Instituto Nacional de Estadística, Bolivia, *encuestra nacional de población y vivienda. Resultados finales* (La Paz, 1989).

TABLE 2. SILVER PRODUCTION IN BOLIVIA, 1550-1909
(Output per decade in marks of silver)

Decade	Average Annual Production	Maximum Year Output	Minimum Year Output
1550-59	278,055	379,244	207,776
1560-69	241,348	284,443	216,516
1570-79	278,093	613,344	114,878
1580-89	750,073	865,185	668,517
1590-99	803,272	887,448	723,591
1600-1609	762,391	844,153	624,666
1610-19	666,082	746,947	620,477
1620-29	590,900	646,543	536,473
1630-39	598,287	793,596	530,674
1640-49	520,859	619,543	463,799
1650-59	461,437	523,604	424,745
1660-69	362,425	398,459	321,889
1670-79	343,478	380,434	289,216
1680-89	370,646	409,338	326,904
1690-99	290,526	375,459	236,935
1700-1709	198,404	226,186	178,087
1710-19	152,696	198,682	114,310
1720-29	145,555	200,693	119,576
1730-39	140,186 e*	169,707	82,811
1740-49	92,119 e	111,947	81,081
1750-59	123,864 e	126,957	115,373
1760-69	142,114	158,883	117,323
1770-79	170,381	242,067	150,746
1780-89	378,170	416,676	335,848
1790-99	385,283	404,025	369,371
1800-1809	297,472	371,416	194,535
1810-19	208,032	338,034	67,347
1820-29	156,110	177,727	132,433
1830-39	188,319	228,154	169,035
1840-49	191,923	256,064	142,029
1850-59	201,482	224,313	189,573
1860-69	344,435 e	391,304	312,174
1870-79	955,629 e	1,150,770	391,304
1880-89	1,111,568 e	1,660,804	597,686
1890-99	1,655,762	2,630,907	1,202,927
1900-1909	799,791	1,288,452	385,522

Sources: Peter J. Bakewell, "Registered Silver Production in Potosí, 1550-1735,"
Jahrbuch für geschicte von staat, wirtschaft und gesellschaft Lateinamerikas, 12
(1975), Table 1, 92-97; Ernesto Rück, Guía general de Bolivia, Primer Año

TABLE 3: TIN PRODUCTION IN BOLIVIA, 1900-1979
(output in metric tons)

Decade	Average Annual Production	Maximum Year Output	Minimum Year Output
1900-1909	14,909	21,342	9,739
1910-19	24,710	29,100	21,324
1920-29	33,216	47,191 (1929)	19,086
1930-39	25,864	38,723	14,957 (1933)
1940-49	38,827	43,168	33,800
1950-59	28,861	35,384	18,013
1960-69	24,705	29,961	19,718
1970-79	29,731	32,626	25,568
1980-88	19,001	29,801	7,231 (1988)

Sources: Walter Gomez, La minería en el desarrollo económico de Bolivia (La Paz, 1978), pp. 218-20 for 1900-1970; James W. Wilkie and Peter Reich, eds., Statistical Abstract of Latin America (Los Angeles, 1980), vol. xx, p. 225 for 1971-76; U.S. Department of the Interior, Minerals Yearbook 1978-79 (Washington, D.C., 1980), vol. I, p. 926 for 1977-79; and Banco Central Boletín Estadístico, Sector Externo, 1980-1988 (La Paz, 1989), p. 43 for 1980-88.

(Sucre, 1865), pp. 170-71 for 1755-1859; [Lamberto de Sierra], "Manifiesto" de la plata extraida del cerro de Potosí, 1556-1800 (Buenos Aires, 1971), pp. 35-37 for the years 1735-54; Adolf Soetbeer, Edelmetall-production und werthverhaltniss zwischen gold und silber (Gotha, 1879), pp. 78-79 for 1860-75; The Mining Industry, Its Statistics, Technology and Trade, vol. I (1892), p. 207 for 1876-1891; ibid., vol. II (1893), p. 333 for 1892-1893; ibid., vol. VII (1898), p. 203 for 1894; República de Bolivia, Oficina Nacional de Inmigración, Estadística y Propaganda Geográfica, Geografía de la república de Bolivia (La Paz, 1905), pp. 354-55 for 1895-1904; and Walter Gomez, La minería en el desarrollo económico de Bolivia (La Paz, 1978), pp. 218-20 for 1905-9.

Notes:
* The letter "e" signifies estimated production figures. All production figures after 1859 have been converted from kilograms to marks at the conversion rate of 230 grams = 1 mark. With production data currently unavailable for the years 1734-55, I used the tax figures given in Sierra. A multiplier of .52 was used to convert the pesos corrientes to marks of silver. This figure came from the ratio found between Sierra's tax figures and Rück's production figures in the period 1756-60. The number .52 was the highest in a range that began at .43.

TABLE 4. BOLIVIA'S LEGAL FOREIGN TRADE IN 1988
(in millions of dollars)

A) Export of Goods		
	Minerals	270.5
	Natural & Liquid Gas	214.9
	Agriculture and Industry	111.1
	Total	600.5
B) Imports of Goods		
	Capital Goods	240.4
	Primary Materials & Intermediary Products	203.2
	Consumer Goods	130.0
	Others	5.0
	Total	578.6
C) Major Trading Partners, Exports		
	South America	307.4
	Western Europe	154.1
	United States	111.9
	Asia	11.1
D) Major Trading Partners, Imports		
	United States	120.8
	Brazil	117.7
	Argentina	80.7
	Japan	57.6

Source: Banco Central de Bolivia, *Boletín Estadistico, Sector Externo, 1980-1988* (La Paz 1989), pp. 23, 25, 38, 40.

TABLE 5. INDICATORS OF SOCIAL AND ECONOMIC CONDITIONS IN CONTEMPORARY
BOLIVIA AND BOLIVIA'S RELATIVE RANK WITHIN LATIN AMERICA

Indicators		Rank Among 20 Latin American Countries
1. Population Growth Rate (1976-88)	2.2%	10th
2. Population Density		
(persons per square mile)	5.1	20th
3. Urban Concentration		
(% over 20,000)	34%	14th
4. Population 14 years & under	42.5%	8th
5. Average Life Expectancy:		
Males	48.6	20th
Females	53.0	20th
6. Infant Mortality Rate		
(deaths per 1000 live births)	102.0	1st
7. Hospital Beds per 1000 Population (1976)	1.8	15th
8. Population with Electricity	59%	14th
9. Population with Drinking Water:		
Urban	89%	13th
Rural	31%	18th
10. Illiteracy Rate		
(15 years of age and older)	25.8%	3rd
11. Students Age 6-11 as Share of Total		
Population 6-11 years (1980)	76.6%	13th
12. Military Expenditures as % of GDP (1984)	2.2%	11th
13. % of Economically Active Population in		
Agriculture (1986)	43.4%	5th
Mining (1976)	4.0%	4th
Manufacturing (1976)	9.7%	19th
14. Share of GDP by Economic Activity (1980-87)		
Agriculture	20.9%	12th
Mining	10.5%	2nd
Manufacturing	11.9%	19th
15. Per Capita GDP in 1987		
(in 1986 dollars)	721	19th
16. External Public Debt Service as a		
% of Value of Exports (1985)	29.1%	6th
17. Value of Foreign Trade (in dollars)		
Exports (1985)	713 million	14th
Imports (1985)	765 million	17th

Source: James W. Wilkie and Enrique Ochoa, eds., *Statistical Abstract of Latin America* (Los Angeles, 1989), Vol. 27, passim.

Index